Peachtree COMPLETE® ACCOUNTING

to accompany

ACCOUNTING PRINCIPLES

7th Edition

MEL COE, JR. M.B.A.
DeVry University
Atlanta, Georgia

REX A SCHILDHOUSE M.B.A., C.M.A.
San Diego Community College District – Miramar Campus
San Diego, California

JERRY J. WEYGANDT Ph.D., C.P.A.
Arthur Andersen Alumni Professor of Accounting
University of Wisconsin - Madison
Madison, Wisconsin

DONALD E. KIESO Ph.D., C.P.A.
KPMG Peat Marwick Emeritus Professor of Accountancy
Northern Illinois University
DeKalb, Illinois

PAUL D. KIMMEL Ph.D., C.P.A.
Associate Professor of Accounting
University of Wisconsin - Milwaukee
Milwaukee, Wisconsin

WILEY
JOHN WILEY & SONS, INC.

COVER PHOTO © Pete Turner/The Image Bank/Getty Images.

To order books or for customer service call 1-800-CALL-WILEY (225-5945).

ISBN 0-471-47735-4

Printed in the United States of America

10 9 8 7 6 5 4 3

Printed and bound by Malloy, Inc.

NOTE TO INSTRUCTORS:

If you need to install a network version of Peachtree and you are an
instructor, you can now obtain a license for a free network version of
Peachtree by visiting the following URL:

http://www.peachtree.com/training/html/educational_partnerships.cfm

Table of Contents

Peachtree Complete Accounting 2004

Educational Version

PEACHTREE INSTALLATION, SETUP, AND GENERAL HOUSEKEEPING

REQUIRED COMPUTER EQUIPMENT

To install Peachtree Complete Accounting 2004, (Educational) from the CD-ROM included with this workbook, Peachtree Software, Inc. recommends you have the following hardware and software available on your system:

- IBM PC compatible with a Pentium processor, 150 MHz or higher
- 32 MB (megabytes) of RAM (Random Access Memory; 64 MB or higher is highly recommended
- Microsoft Windows 95, Windows 98, Windows 2000, or Windows NT 4 (with Service Pack 3 or higher already installed)
- Hard Disk with the following free space requirements:

The Educational version of Peachtree Complete Accounting	48 MB
The uncompressed (unzipped) Data Files that go along with the workbook	52 MB

Note: The recommended Peachtree Complete Accounting memory requirements are in addition to the memory required by your system software and memory used when working with company data.

- MPC compatible CD-ROM drive
- SVGA monitor that can display at least 256 colors and a minimum resolution of 640x480; 64K colors and 800x600 resolution (or higher) are highly recommended

Use small fonts in your Windows Control Panel Display settings; DO NOT USE LARGE FONTS – Peachtree will not display properly.

- Printers supported by Microsoft Windows 95, Windows 98, Windows 2000 or Windows NT 4
- Mouse or compatible pointing device
- If multiple users will access company data, Peachtree Complete Accounting can operate on any peer-to-peer network that supports Microsoft Windows 95, Windows 98, Windows 2000 or Windows NT 4 (with Service Pack 3 or higher applied). Peachtree can also operate on client/server networks such as Windows NT Server and Novell NetWare 4.x (or higher). For

more information on networking Peachtree Complete Accounting and obtaining a site license contact Best Software, Inc.

INSTALLING PEACHTREE COMPLETE ACCOUNTING

Peachtree Complete Accounting and the student data set is supplied on the accompanying CD-ROM disk. This disk should "self start" to the initial screen, shown here, when it is placed into a CD-ROM.

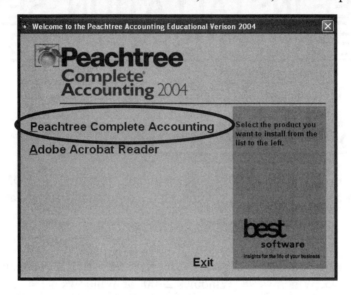

If your system does not have "AutoRun" enabled, you may start the installation process by locating the "Autorun.exe" file on the CD-ROM with Windows Explorer and double clicking on that file.

This will initiate the installation of Peachtree Complete Accounting. Peachtree Complete Accounting is commonly referred to as "Peachtree" in the profession and through most of this text.

From the first installation screen, click or double click on "Peachtree Complete Accounting". This

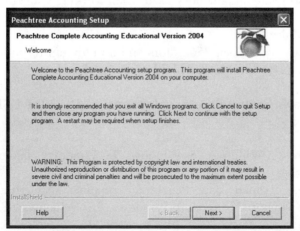

welcome and advisory screen is presented. You should read and heed the advice to provide the highest probability of successful installation. Once the screen is read, click on the "Next" button.

The next screen presented is the Peachtree Software License Agreement. This agreement should be read as it states the conditions for which you have the use of the software. Once it is read, you must select "I accept the terms in the License Agreement" or "I do not accept the License Agreement (Exit Setup)" at the bottom left corner of the screen. You can do this by mouse clicking your choice.

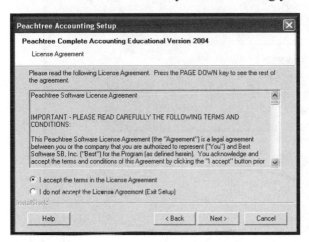

Once you choose an option from this screen, you can click on "Next" and continue the installation process. The next screen presented is the "Setup Options" screen, shown here. The option to select is "Standard Setup". This will provide a common, well documented, installation of Peachtree. Select you option with a mouse click and then click "Next".

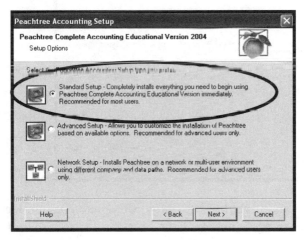

Once the "Next" button is clicked on the "Setup Options" screen, Peachtree Complete Accounting will begin the install. This screen should appear and the "Progress Monitor" will begin to indicate the progress through the installation.

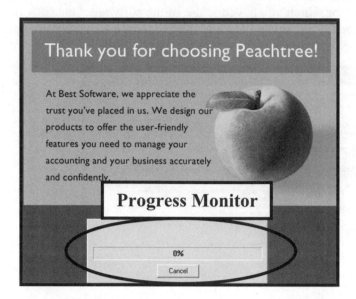

When the installation process is almost complete Peachtree will provide the following screen:

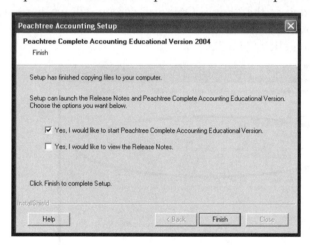

You can make your selections of starting Peachtree Complete Accounting Educational Version or reading the Release Notes by clicking or removing the checkmarks from the selection boxes. When your choices have been made, mouse click the "Finish" button.

Assuming you left the selections in the previous screen and clicked "Next", Peachtree Complete Accounting will start and present you with this "Dialog" box or screen.

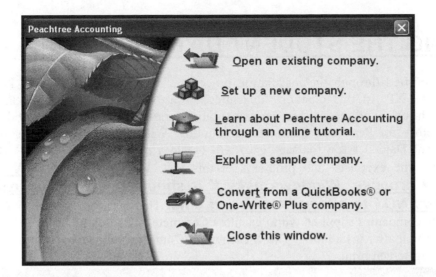

This is a very common screen within Peachtree as you will see it upon each startup and occasionally as you maneuver within the program. You can click or double click your choice of options. The "Open an existing company." will take you to a dialog box which will allow you to select or locate your choice. Selecting "Set up a new company." will start the creation process of a new company. This process is covered in the text and is fairly simple.

Assuming that you select "Open an existing company." you will be presented with a dialog box similar to this screen once your Student Data Set is installed:

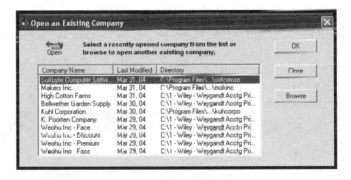

Within this screen Peachtree will present you with the name of company, the date that company was last opened or modified, and the location of that file. The name of the company for the Student Data Sets is the same as the textbook provides unless this text states otherwise. There are many sample company files created for this text and two sample companies created by and provided by Peachtree. If there are too many companies in the database, Peachtree will provide you with scroll bars on the right side to move through the options. Under the "Directory" column Peachtree states where this file is at. This information can be used with Microsoft Windows Explorer to locate this file and move it to the common directory.

6

INSTALLING THE STUDENT DATA SET

Peachtree, unless modified through the installation procedure, should install into the "Program Files" directory of Windows XP. In this position "Peachtree" is a "subdirectory" of the "Program Files" directory. The "Peachtree" subdirectory has its own subdirectories. The "Company" subdirectory is the "Default" data directory for Peachtree Complete Accounting. Within the "Peachtree" subdirectory the self-extracting Student Data Set file (datasets.exe) will create a new directory called "datasets". This subdirectory contains the exercises and problems of this text. ***VERY IMPORTANT NOTE: If, during the copy process, Windows asks if it should overwrite an existing file, instruct Windows NOT to overwrite existing data.*** This question is most likely because of the Peachtree sample companies supplied with Peachtree Complete Accounting. These sample companies should not be overwritten after installation. The "Peachtree" "Company" and "datasets" subdirectories are shown in the following screen print.

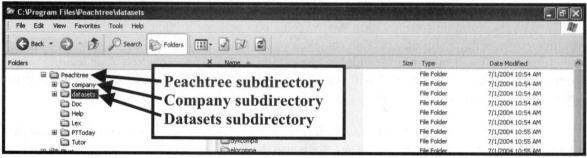

To "Unzip" the Student Data Set, contained on your data disk, to your hard drive:
1) Close the Peachtree Complete Accounting application to ensure that its directories are not in use during the "unzipping" process,
2) Click on the My Computer icon. If the My Computer icon is not visible, you can access it through the Microsoft Windows Explorer,
3) Right click on the Peachtree accounting icon (CD drive),
4) Select "Explore",
5) Go to "Student Data Set" folder,
6) Click on datasets.exe
7) Confirm that the following path is provided:
    "C:\Program Files\
        Peachtree\datasets"

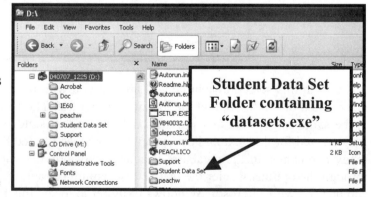

8) Click Unzip,
9) Click "OK" then close WinZip,
10) Open Peachtree accounting software
11) Select "Open a company"
12) Click on "Browse",
13) You will find company data sets in the following folder: C:\Program Files\Peachtree\datasets,
14) Select the appropriate company.

Here are graphics and a walk through to open companies in "datasets". Now open the Peachtree Complete Accounting application. At the opening screen, select "Open an Existing Company". Click on the "Browse" button, shown in this screen print.

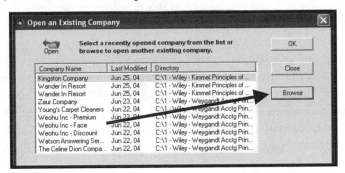

Peachtree will provide you with a new "Open Company" dialog box. From within this dialog box ensure you are in the path of "C:\Program Files\Peachtree\datasets" You should be presented a listing of all the data sets necessary to complete the challenges of the Kimmel Principles of Accounting Peachtree exercises and problems.

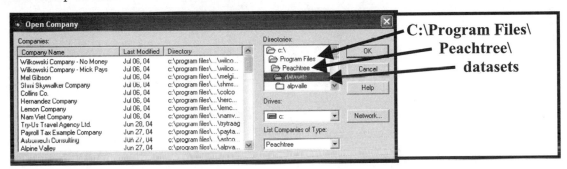

When you examine the subdirectory of the "datasets" with Microsoft Windows Explorer, you may see a resemblance to the example, sample, and problem data sets. Peachtree creates a subdirectory for each company within its "books". For example, the "falcompa" subdirectory may be the subdirectory that contains the Falcetto Company data for the Student Data Set while "fropark" is most likely Frontier Park. However, the "!_PDG" subdirectory most likely contains the Pavilion Design Group and "BCS" may contain the Bellwether Garden Supply Company, both Peachtree furnished sample companies, so subdirectory naming may not be consistent. If you tell Peachtree to "Browse" because you do not see your desired company in the "history" windows, Peachtree will look first into the "Company" subdirectory. Peachtree will not show you the subdirectory names, it will "look through" the subdirectories and show you the actual name of the company within the subdirectory. If there are too many companies to show in one window presentation, you will have a scroll bar to the right so you can scroll down through the choices. However, armed with the knowledge of how Peachtree creates and names subdirectories, if you "lose" a company, you can use Windows Explorer to locate possible subdirectories and then use the "Browse" capability of the "Open an existing company" to select the directory and subdirectory. Since Peachtree does not have a large area to present information, it is more functional to utilize Windows Explorer to locate possible subdirectories and use "Browse" to confirm the location. Double clicking on the desired company or single clicking it and then clicking on the "OK" button.

As part of the installation process, Peachtree will normally install an icon on the desktop for easy access to Peachtree Complete Accounting. This icon is the trademarked "Peach", shown here. The actually text may vary but the capability is the same – double click the icon and Peachtree Complete Accounting should open to the default screen asking you if you would like to open an existing company, create a new company, select a sample company or the other options listed on the screen.

If Peachtree Complete Accounting does not create this icon on your desktop, you can ask Windows Help how to build a desktop icon and build it yourself. If the Peachtree Complete Accounting installation was through default, the application should be in the "Program Files" directory within a subdirectory such as "Peachtree" or "Peach".

Peachtree data is backed up not as a "global" process but as a company process. That is, when you are working with the sample company "Bellwether Garden Supply Company" and you decide to backup your data to safeguard it, you are only backing up and safeguarding Bellwether. Any other company within the application's capability is not backed up. The Peachtree backup process is controlled or initiated through the "File > Back up" path. Peachtree will ask you where you would like to save the backup data and then advise you of how much room it will take. This process is normally only 30~60 seconds in length so you can backup data without excessive delay.

If you utilize the capabilities of Microsoft Windows to "Uninstall" Peachtree Complete Accounting, Windows will normally leave the data files behind. However, do not rely on this. You should copy the company files into a "safe" directory, one not associated with the Peachtree subdirectory, before the uninstall process in initiated.

CHAPTER 1

Accounting in Action

OBJECTIVES

- Be able to understand the basic accounting equation and relate it to entries made in Peachtree Complete Accounting
- Be able to launch the Peachtree Complete Accounting application
- Be able to open a previously set up business
- Be able to enter transactions into Peachtree's general journal system

- Be able to understand how to generate and read the four basic financial statements in Peachtree Complete Accounting
- Be able to check for errors in entries made into the general journal
- Be able to edit a general journal entry

BASIC ACCOUNTING

Before you start entering data into the Peachtree software, there are several simple basic principles of accounting you must learn first. Specifically, you must be aware that there are two groupings in which fiscal events are classified: 1) what a business owns and 2) what a business owes. Assets are what a company owns. They are the resources owned by a business. The second group, liabilities and owner's equity, are the rights or claims against these resources. The claims by creditors are called liabilities. Claims by the owners are called owner's equity. You use these groupings whether you're using a computerized or a manual accounting system.

The relationship between the assets and the liabilities and owner's equity is referred to as the basic accounting equation. The total assets of a firm must be equal to the sum of liabilities and owner's equity. The accounting equation applies to all economic and business entities regardless of size, nature of the business, or how the organization is formed and operated.

Let's look in detail at the categories that make up the basic accounting equation.

- **Assets** - Assets are all of the resources owned by a business that are used in carrying out the firm's activities such as production, consumption of goods, and exchange.
- **Liabilities** - Liabilities are the company's existing debts and obligations. They are the claims against the assets by creditors. For example, businesses usually borrow money from banks and purchase merchandise on credit. These transactions result in the business *owing* money and are recorded in the books as liabilities.

- **Owner's Equity** - The ownership claim on total assets is known as owner's equity. It is equal to total assets minus total liabilities. Here's why: The assets of a business are supplied or claimed by either creditors or owner. To find out what belongs to owners, you subtract the creditors' claims, the liabilities, from the assets. The remainder is the owner's claim on the assets, the owner's equity. Because the claims of creditors must be paid before ownership claims, the owner's equity is sometimes referred to as residual equity. In a proprietorship, the owner's investments and revenues increase owner's equity.

    Investments by the Owner - Investments by the owner are the assets that the owner puts into the business. These investments increase owner's equity. The investments may be cash or material items.

    Drawings - An owner may take cash or other assets from the business, a withdrawal, for personal use. Drawings decrease owner's equity.

    Revenues - Revenues are the gross increase in owner's equity resulting from business activities that have been entered into for the purpose of earning income. Generally, revenues result from the sale of merchandise (a retail establishment) or the performance of services (a service related company). A business may also earn money by other means including the rental of property or the lending of money to another company.

    Expenses - Expenses decrease owner's equity. A business incurs expenses that result from the actual operation of the business. The cost of assets purchased and consumed or services that are used in the process of earning revenue are considered expenses. Expenses are the actual or expected cash outflows (payments) of doing business.

THE TRANSACTION PROCESS

A transaction is often referred to as an external or internal economic event of an enterprise. Transactions are recorded. An external transaction involves economic events between the company and some outside enterprise. For example, the purchase of equipment from a supplier or the payments of rent to a landlord are external transactions. Sales and purchases are also external transactions.

An internal transaction is an economic event that occurs entirely within a company; for example, when office supplies are used up.

A company may also carry on activities that do not in themselves represent business transactions. Hiring employees, answering the phone, and taking a sales order are examples. Some of those activities will eventually lead to a business transaction. You will soon have to pay wages to workers you hired and merchandise must be delivered to customers

Before you enter any transaction, you must install (if needed) and launch Peachtree, then open the company in which you wish to work. Only then can any data can be entered.

LAUNCHING PEACHTREE COMPLETE ACCOUNTING 2004 SOFTWARE

Step 1: Follow the instructions given to you by your instructor or lab administrator in opening the Peachtree software package.

Step 2: Once Peachtree is open, you will see the Peachtree splash screen.

Step 3: This screen will change to Peachtree's main menu screen as shown in Figure 1.1.

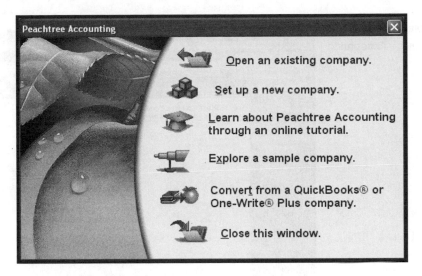

Figure 1. 1 Opening Peachtree menu screen.

Step 4: Click on the first icon. Open an existing company, to get the screen shown in Figure 1.2. Depending on your system, your screen may or may not have the exact same companies listed.

Step 5: Click on "Softbyte Computer Software" which should appear if the Student Data Sets were correctly loaded from the CD-ROM. (Reload the Student Data Sets if "Softbyte Computer Software does not appear.)

Step 6: Check to make sure "Softbyte Computer Software" appears in the Title bar above the main window of Peachtree. The full screen is illustrated in Figure 1.3.

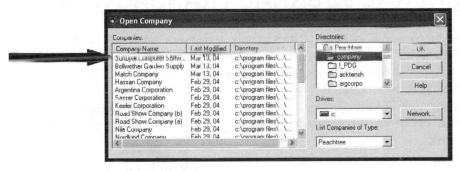

Figure 1. 2 Open company menu screen.

Even though your text does not cover General Journal entries in the first chapter, you can get a little ahead by working in Peachtree and start to understand how the accounting process works.

With that in mind, now you may enter transactions into Peachtree Complete Accounting by following the step-by-step instructions that follow. You will be working with a make believe company called Softbyte Computer Software which can be found within your Student Data Set and in the first chapter of your text. You will build on this file for the next several chapters. So, be sure to back up your data on a regular basis. Good luck and have fun.

Figure 1. 3 Main Window of Peachtree Complete Accounting 2004.

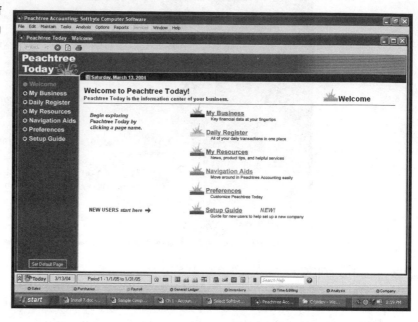

ENTERING GENERAL JOURNAL TRANSACTIONS

Transaction (1) Investment by Owner. Ray Neal decides to open a computer programming service. On January 1, 2005, he invests $15,000 cash in the business, which he names Softbyte Computer Software. This transaction results in an equal increase in assets and owner's equity. The asset cash increases by $15,000 and the owner's equity, R. Neal, Capital, capital increases by the same amount. Using Peachtree Complete Accounting, step through this initial entry.

    Step 1: Using the menu bar from the main Peachtree window, click on Tasks.

    Step 2: On the pull down menu, as shown in Figure 1.4, click on General Journal Entries.

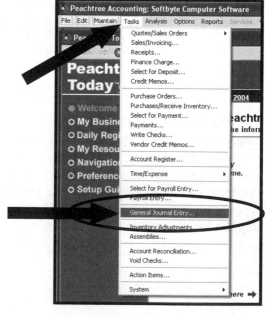

Figure 1. 4 Pull down menu from "Tasks" on menu bar.

Make sure that your window looks like that shown in Figure 1.5.

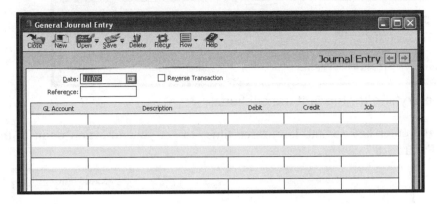

Figure 1. 5 Blank screen for General Journal entry.

Note: The actual color scheme of your presentation may vary from that presented here. The color scheme is selectable by the system and is controlled through Options > Global > General.

Step 4: As a reference, type in "Trans# 1" in the blank "Reference" window, just under the date which is preset for January 1, 2005.

Step 5: Click on the magnifying glass that appears next to the Account No. column to get a pull down menu that lists the available accounts for Softbyte, the Chart of Accounts, as shown in Figure 1.6.

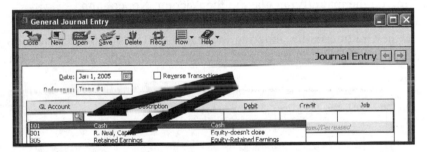

Figure 1. 6   Journal
Entry with Chart of Accounts Drop Down shown.

Step 6: Double click on Account Number 101 (Cash). In the description column type in "Owner's investment in business" And, in the Debit column, type in "1-5-0-0-0-decimal point-0-0." (Don't type in the minus signs – they represent the *separation* of each numeral.)

> Be careful in Peachtree Complete Accounting how you enter numbers. The "system" may *automatically* insert a decimal point two places within the entered number. For example, if you entered "1-5-0-0-0," Peachtree may recognize it as $150.00 not $15,000.00. Make sure your screen looks like Figure 1.7.

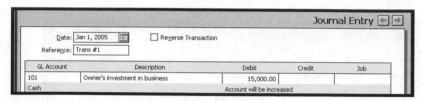

Figure 1. 7 First entry line for the first transaction.

Step 7: Press the enter key (or tab key) three times to get your insertion point to the next line, as shown in Figure 1.8.

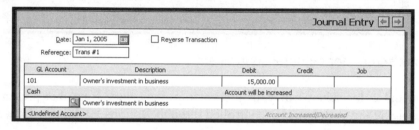

Figure 1. 8 Beginning the second entry line for Transaction 1.

Using the illustrated examples above, enter the amount for owner's equity by:

Step 8: Clicking on the magnifying glass in the Account No. column.
Step 9: Double clicking the account number 301
Step 10: In the Credit column, entering the amount, $15,000.00 – the dollar sign is not necessary, but the decimal point should be entered manually. Your entry should look like Figure 1.9.

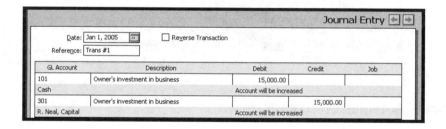

Figure 1. 9 Entry for owner's investment of cash in the business.

BEFORE YOU CONTINUE

Look at the window in Figure 1.10. Notice the amounts at the bottom of the window, in the gray area outside the entry area. They indicate whether or not your entry is in balance. In Figure 1.10, $15,000 appears under the Debit column and under the Credit column. The figure next to "Out of Balance" is zero. Therefore, your entry is in balance. (Note: This screen has been reduced in size by eliminating unneeded rows, your presentation will show more rows.)

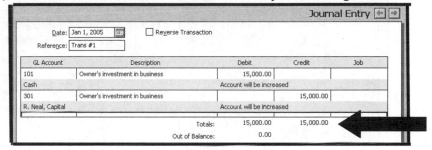

Figure 1. 10 In balance journal entries.

If you had mistakenly entered both amounts in the Debit column as shown in Figure 1.11 (or even both amounts in the credit column), you would be "Out of Balance."

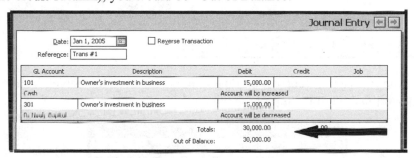

Figure 1. 11 Entry error as shown by out of balance tally.

Always double-check your entries before continuing. Just because the system indicates you are "In Balance" does not necessarily mean your transaction is correct. It just means what you have entered is "In Balance." However, as shown in Figure 1.12, the system will not let you continue if you are "Out of Balance" and will return an error message.

Figure 1. 12 The system will not let you continue if you are "Out of Balance" on your entry.

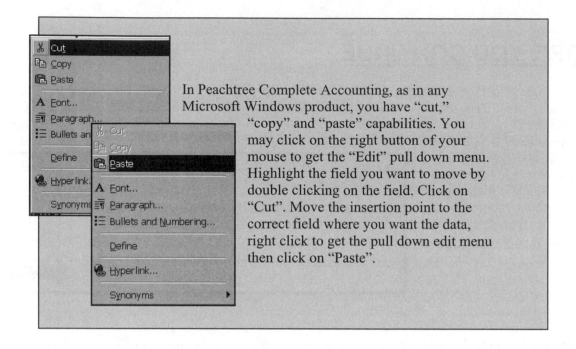

In Peachtree Complete Accounting, as in any Microsoft Windows product, you have "cut," "copy" and "paste" capabilities. You may click on the right button of your mouse to get the "Edit" pull down menu. Highlight the field you want to move by double clicking on the field. Click on "Cut". Move the insertion point to the correct field where you want the data, right click to get the pull down edit menu then click on "Paste".

POSTING THE TRANSACTION

Step 1: To post the transaction (enter it into the system) click on the "Save" icon (see Figure 1.13) in the tool bar section toward the top of the window.

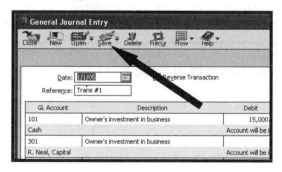

Figure 1. 13 Click on the "Save" icon to enter your transaction.

Step 2: The General Journal window clears all that has been previously entered and is now ready for the second transaction. Notice that the General Journal window's Reference window has now automatically advanced to "Trans #2".

You are now ready for the next transaction.

Transaction (2). Purchase of Equipment for Cash. On January 1, 2005, Softbyte purchases computer equipment for $7,000 cash. This transaction will result in an equal increase and decrease in total assets. Cash is decreased by $7,000 whereas the asset Equipment is increased by $7,000.

Using the process you learned in Transaction 1 make this General Journal entry.

Step 1: Type in "Transaction 2" in the reference box, if it is different. Leave the date as it is, January 1, 2005.

Step 2: Click on the magnifying glass to get the pull down menu of the Chart of Accounts. Highlight "Equipment" and double click (you may also press the <ENTER> key).

Step 3: Press the <TAB> key to move your insertion point over to the Description column and type in "Paid cash for equipment."

Step 4: Press the <TAB> key to move your insertion point to the next column, the Debit column and enter, in error the amount $8,000.00. This amount is in error because in the second part of this exercise you will learn how to edit a General Journal entry, after it has been posted. Remember you do not have to enter the "$," but you should enter the decimal point.

Step 5: Press the <ENTER> key three times so that your insertion point is in the Account No. column of the next line. Click on the magnifying glass to get the pull down menu of the Chart of Accounts. Highlight "Cash" and double click (you may also press the <ENTER> key).

Step 6: Press the <TAB> key to move your insertion point over to the Description column and type in "Paid cash for equipment." (The system may have already generated this for you.)

Step 7: Press the <TAB> key twice to move your insertion point to the credit column and enter the amount, *purposely in error* $8,000.00. You enter this amount in error for your books to balance. This will be edited in the next part of this exercise. Again, remember you do not have to enter the "$," but you should enter the decimal point.

Step 8: Make sure your screen looks like Figure 1.14 before continuing. If there are no errors (besides the intentional ones you typed in) go ahead and post your transaction. Notice that even though you know there is an error, the system will let you post because technically your books are in balance.

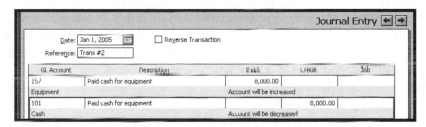

Figure 1. 14 General Journal entry shown with amount in error.

EDITING A GENERAL JOURNAL ENTRY

Editing a General Journal entry is just as simple as making the original entry.

Step 1: Make sure you have a blank General Journal screen. If not, create one by clicking on Tasks, then General Journal Entry.

Step 2: On the Toolbar menu, illustrated in Figure 1.15, click on the OPEN icon.

Figure 1. 15 General Journal tool bar.

Step 3: You will be presented with a Select General Journal Entry menu listing all of the General Journal entries you have entered in this accounting period. Do not worry about accounting periods at this time. Figure 1.16 below shows only two entries for demonstration purposes. The first transaction, for $15,000 is the first entry you made and the second one, for $8,000 is the one with the error, which you are going to correct. Click on the second entry.

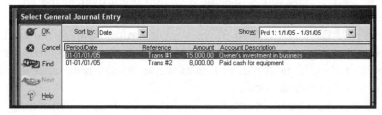

Figure 1. 16 Select General Journal entry menu.

Step 4: You will be returned to the General Journal entry screen like the one you had when you made the earlier entry. Your screen should look like Figure 1.14, shown earlier.

Step 5: Any field on the screen can be changed and reposted. However, you are only interested in changing the amounts, $8,000 to $7,000. Place the insertion point in the first amount field, highlight the $8,000, and change it to $7,000.

Step 6: Do the same with the second amount. Your screen should match the one shown in Figure 1.17.

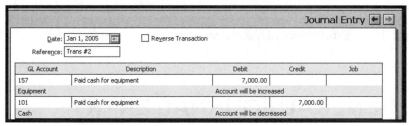

Figure 1. 17 Corrected General Journal Entry for Transaction 2.

SOME ADDITIONAL POINTS

Notice that written below the amount you entered in the "Debit" column in Figure 1.17, the system has told you that the account is going to be increased by the amount you entered. A "Debit" entry will always increase an Asset account.

Also, notice that written below the amount you entered in the "Credit" column in Figure 1.17, the system has told you that the account is going to be decreased by the amount you entered. A "Credit" entry will always decrease an asset account.

Now click on "SAVE" on the General Journal Entry toolbar to save the corrected journal entry.

Transaction (3). Purchase of Supplies on Credit. On January 1, 2005, Softbyte purchases computer paper and other supplies expected to last several months for $1,600.00 from Acme Supply Company. Acme will allow Softbyte to pay this bill next month. This transaction is referred to as a purchase on account or a credit purchase. Assets will be increased (a debit – remember a debit entry will increase an asset account) because the expected future benefits of using the paper and supplies. Liabilities will also be increased (a credit – a credit entry will increase a liability account) by the amount due to Acme Company. With an equal debit and credit entry, your accounting equation will remain in balance.

Using the process you learned in Transaction 1 make this General Journal entry on your own.

> **Step 1:** Type in "Trans #3" in the reference window if required. Leave the date as it is, January 1, 2005.
>
> **Step 2:** Click on the magnifying glass to get the pull down menu of the Chart of Accounts. Highlight "Supplies" and double click (you may also press the <ENTER> key).
>
> **Step 3:** Press the <TAB> key to move your insertion point over to the Description column and type in "Purchased supplies on account."
>
> **Step 4:** Press the <TAB> key to move your insertion point to the next column, the Debit column and enter $1,600.
>
> **Step 5:** Press the <ENTER> key three times so that your insertion point is in the Account No. column of the next line. Click on the magnifying glass to get the pull-down menu of the Chart of Accounts. Highlight "Accounts Payable" and double click (you may also press the <ENTER> key).
>
> **Step 6:** Press the <TAB> key to move your insertion point over to the Description column "Purchased supplies on account" should have automatically been generated for you; if not go ahead and enter it
>
> **Step 7:** Press the <TAB> key twice to move your insertion point to the credit column and enter the amount $1,600.
>
> **Step 8:** Make sure your screen looks like Figure 1.22 and correct any errors before continuing.

Before you post your entry, double-check what you have entered. Make sure your entries match Figure 1.18.

Figure 1.18 Journal entry for a credit (on account) purchase.

Before you "Save" Transaction 3, notice that both accounts, Supplies and Accounts Payable, are going to be increased by this operation. You have added $1,600 worth of supplies to the company (an asset) and you have also incurred $1,600 worth of liabilities (money they owe).

Looking at the "big picture," total assets are now $16,600. This total is matched by a $1,600 creditor's claim (the supplies just purchased on account)) and a $15,000 ownership claim (the initial cash the owner put into the business).

Now click on the "Post" icon on the toolbar to post your transaction into the General Journal.

Transaction (4). Services Rendered for Cash. On January 1, 2005, Softbyte receives $1,200 cash from customers for programming services it has provided. This transaction represents the company's principal revenue producing activity. Remember that revenue will increase owner's equity. However, revenue does have its own account of "Service Revenue, an income account.

Make the General Journal entry:

Step 1: The account no. 101, Cash, should be increased by $1,200 (a debit entry).

Step 2: The account no. 401, Service Revenue, should be increased by $1,200 (a credit entry). Remember that an asset is increased by a debit entry and that revenue is increased by a credit entry.

Step 3: Before posting, make sure your entry matches the one below in Figure 1.19.

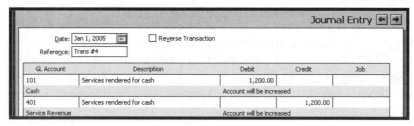

Figure 1. 19 General Journal entry for Service Revenue.

Step 4: If there are no errors, "Post" the entry.

Transaction (5). Purchase of Advertising on Credit. On January 2, 2005, Softbyte receives a bill for $250 from the *Daily News* for advertising. Softbyte decides to postpone payment of the bill until a later date. This transaction results in an increase in liabilities and an increase in expenses (or a decrease in equity).

Step 1: The expense Account No. 610, Advertising Expense, is increased (debited) by $250.

Step 2: The Accounts Payable Account No. 201, is also increased (credited) by $250.

As a rule of thumb, it is rare that any expense account would be credited. So it is relatively safe to say that all expense accounts will only be debited. The entry is shown in Figure 1.20 below.

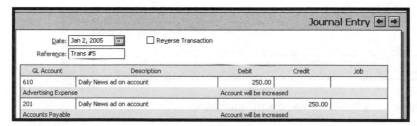

Figure 1. 20 Advertising Expense to be paid later.

Step 3: If your entries are correct, go ahead and post the General Journal entry.

The two sides of the equation still balance at $17,800. Owner's Equity will be decreased when the expense (Advertising Expense) is incurred and is noted. Expenses do not have to be paid in cash at the time they are incurred. When payment is made at a later date, the liability Accounts Payable will be decreased and the asset Cash will be decreased. You will see how that works in Transaction 8. The cost of advertising is considered an expense.

Transaction (6). Services Rendered for Cash and Credit. On January 7, 2005, Softbyte provides $3,500 of programming services for customers. Cash, $1,500 is received from customers and the balance of $2,000 is billed on account. This transaction results in an equal increase in assets and owner's equity.

Three specific accounts are affected:

- Cash is increased by $1,500
- Accounts Receivable is increased by $2,000
- The sales revenue account is increased by $3,500.

Cash and Accounts Receivable, both assets, will be increased (debited). Cash increases by $1,500, Accounts Receivable increases by $2,000, and revenues increase by $3,500.

Step 1: Change the date from January 1 to January 7. You may enter the date directly in the date box or by clicking on the calendar icon, you will be able to click the appropriate date for entry directly from a pull-down calendar as shown in Figure 1.21.

Figure 1. 21 Pull down calendar.

Step 2: Change the Transaction number under the date to "Transaction 6".

Step 3: Using the magnifying glass, find the account number (#101) for Cash and press <ENTER>. In the Description column type in "Received cash from customers for services rendered" and enter the amount, $1,500 in the Debit column.

Step 4: Using the magnifying glass, find the account number (#112) for Accounts Receivable and press <ENTER>. In the Description column type in "Services On Account" and enter the amount, $2,000, in the Debit column.

Step 5: And again, using the magnifying glass, find the account number (#401) for Service Revenue and press <ENTER>. In the Description column type in "Service revenue." Tab over to the Credit column and enter the amount, $3,500.

Step 6: Notice that all three entries will increase the appropriate accounts and that glancing at the bottom of the window, you should be in balance at $3,500.

Step 7: Your entry should match Figure 1.22. Make any necessary changes before posting your entry.

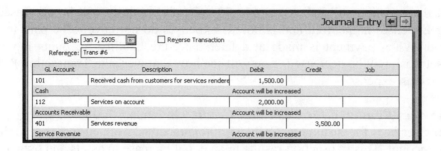

Figure 1. 22 General Journal Entry showing date change and account entries.

Transaction (7). Payment of Expenses. Expenses paid in cash on January 15 include the Store Rent $600; Salaries of employees $900; and Utilities $200. These payments will result in an equal decrease in assets (cash) and owner's equity (the individual expense items).

Step 1: Change the date to January 15, 2005.

Step 2: Change the transaction number to "Transaction 7".

Step 3: Identify the Store Rent Expense account, #729, highlight it and press <ENTER> (or click) to place it the account number column. Type in "Paid store rent" in the description column and $600 in the debit column.

Step 4: On the next line, identify the salaries expense account number, #726 making sure it appears in the account number column on the second line. Type in "Paid Employee's salaries" on the description line and type in $900 in the debit column. (You'll worry about payroll tax in a later chapter.)

Step 5: On the third line, identify and place account #732, the utilities expense account number in the appropriate column. In the description column, type in "Paid utilities". And, in the debit column, type in $200.

Step 6: Cash will be decreased by the total amount of the above expenses, $1,700. By now you should know that the account number for Cash is 101. You may type that in directly or search for it using the magnifying glass. Type in a description of each of the expenses paid in the description column along with the corresponding debit amount – the amount paid on the expense. The total credit amount (you're decreasing an asset) is $1,700 which is credited to cash.

Step 7: Check to see that your entries are in balance before posting. Your entry should match the one in Figure 1.23.

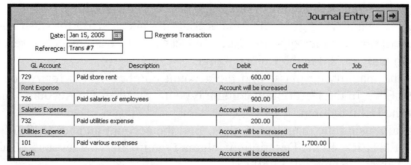

Figure 1.23 Paid cash for monthly expenses.

Transaction (8). Payment of Accounts Payable. Softbyte pays its *Daily News* advertising bill of $250 in cash. The bill had been previously recorded in Transaction (5) as an increase in Accounts Payable and an increase in expenses (a decrease in owner's equity). This payment "on account" will decrease the asset cash (a credit) and will also decrease the liability accounts payable (a debit) – both by $250.

Step 1: Keep the date, January 15, 2005 as is, but change the transaction number to "Transaction 8".

Step 2: Entering the debit amount first, the account number is 201 for Accounts Payable.

Step 3: Type in "Paid Daily News for ads on account" in the description column. And, type in $250 in the debit column to complete the first line.

Step 4: Account number 101 is the number for the cash account which goes in the first column of the second line.

Step 5: "Paid *Daily News* for ads on account." This should have been automatically generated by the system. If so, press the <TAB> key twice to move to the credit column and enter $250.

Step 6: Check to make sure your entry is in balance and matches Figure 1.24.

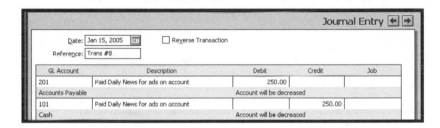

Figure 1.24 Paid Daily News account due.

Transaction (9). Receipt of Cash on Account. The sum of $600 in cash is received from those customers who have previously been billed for services in Transaction 6. This transaction does not change any of the totals in assets, but it will change the composition of those accounts. Cash is increased by $600 and Accounts Receivable is decreased by $600.

Step 1: If you went directly to Transaction 9 from Transaction 8, you will notice that the reference has automatically changed to "Transaction 9." If that change did not occur, enter "Transaction 9" in the reference box. Leave the date at January 15.

Step 2: Enter account number 101 for the Cash account. And, in the Description column type in "Received Cash from customers." In the Debit column, enter $600.

Step 3: On the second line, enter account number 112 for the Accounts receivable account. "Received Cash from customers" should have been automatically entered by the system. However, you need to enter $600 in the Credit column so that your entry will balance.

Step 4: Check your entry with the one in Figure 1.25 before posting. Make any necessary changes.

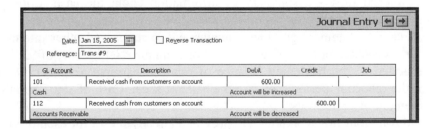

Figure 1.25 Received cash from customers on account.

Transaction (10). Withdrawal of Cash By Owner. On January 31, Ray Neal withdraws $1,300 in cash from the business for his personal use. This transaction results in an equal decrease in assets (Cash) and Owner's Equity (Drawing).

Step 1: Change the date to January 31. Also, make sure that Transaction 10 is in the reference window.

Step 2: Account number 302 is the Drawing account that will be debited. Enter 305 as the account number. In the Description column, type in "Ray Neal, Drawing" and in the Debit column (a decrease to capital), enter $1,300.

Step 3: Because Neal wants cash for his withdrawal, the asset cash must be decreased (a credit). Enter account number 101 for the Cash account. "Ray Neal, Drawing" will most likely have been defaulted in the Description column; if not, make the appropriate entry. And, in the Credit column, enter $1,300.

Step 4: Check your entry with Figure 1.26 and make any corrections before posting your entry.

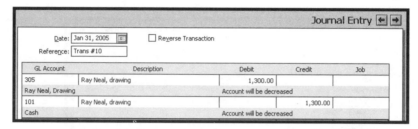

Figure 1. 26 Owner withdraws cash from the business for personal use.

FINANCIAL STATEMENTS

After transactions have been identified, analyzed, and entered into the computer, four financial statements can be prepared from your data. In fact, when you made your first entry each of the statements was updated, and kept up to date as you went along.

Those statements are:

- An income statement - presents the revenues and expenses and resulting net income or net loss for a specific period of time.
- A statement of retained earnings (very similar to statement of owner's equity) - summarizes the changes in owner's equity for a specific period of time due to earnings and withdrawals.
- A balance sheet - a company's report of the assets, liabilities, and owner's equity at a specific date.
- A statement of cash flow - a summary of information about the cash inflows (receipts) and outflows (payments) for a specific period of time.

Each Peachtree financial statement provides management, owners, and other interested parties with relevant financial data. The statements are interrelated. For example, Net income of $2,750 shown on the income statement is added to the beginning balance of retained earnings (equity). Owner's capital of $16,450 at the end of the reporting period shown in the balance sheet. Cash of $8,050 on the balance sheet is reported on the statement of cash flows.

The reports used throughout this workbook are provided already preset for each of your assignments. The assignments in Peachtree appear in the 7th edition of Accounting Principles by Weygandt, Kieso, and Kimmel and are noted by the Peachtree logo - a peach, in the margin.

In addition to the four statements mentioned previously, several other reports also deserve attention. They are included, under the General Ledger heading:

-   The Chart of Accounts
-   The General Journal
-   The General Ledger

GENERATING THE INCOME STATEMENT

Step 1: On the main menu bar click on "Reports" to get the drop down menu shown in Figure 1.27.

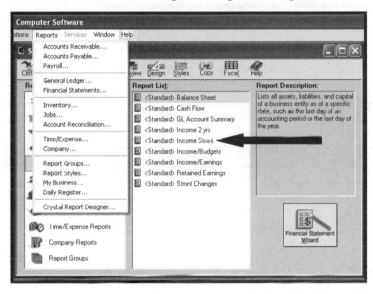

Figure 1. 27 Main Menu Bar and Reports List

Step 2: Click on Financial Statements to get the "Select A Report" menu of shown in Figure 1-27.

Step 3: Double click on <Standard> Income Stmnt (Statement) toward the middle of the list.

Step 4: The Dialog Box, shown in Figure 1.28, gives several option choices including the choice of financial periods, the margins for the report, whether or not you want to show accounts that have a zero balance, whether or not you want page numbers, and so on. If you wish to print the Income Statement, make sure the printer at the bottom of the dialog box matches the printer you are using on your computer system.

26

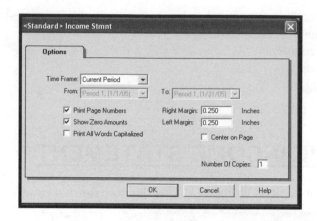

Figure 1.28 Dialog box to prepare Income Statement for display

Step 5: Click OK to show the income statement, Figure 1.29, on your computer screen.

The <Standard> Income Statement is a complete income statement already set up by the Peachtree system during the original company set up.

<Standard> Income Stmnt					
Close Save Options	Print Setup	Preview Design Excel	Help		

Softbyte Computer Software
Income Statement
For the One Month Ending January 31, 2005

	Current Month		Year to Date	
Revenues				
Service Revenue	$ 4,700.00	100.00	$ 4,700.00	100.00
Total Revenues	4,700.00	100.00	4,700.00	100.00
Cost of Sales				
Total Cost of Sales	0.00	0.00	0.00	0.00
Gross Profit	4,700.00	100.00	4,700.00	100.00
Expenses				
Advertising Expense	250.00	5.32	250.00	5.32
Salaries Expense	900.00	19.15	900.00	19.15
Rent Expense	600.00	12.77	600.00	12.77
Utilities Expense	200.00	4.26	200.00	4.26
Total Expenses	1,950.00	41.49	1,950.00	41.49
Net Income	$ 2,750.00	58.51	$ 2,750.00	58.51

Figure 1.29 Full Screen display of the Income Statement for Softbyte.

The revenues and expenses are reported for a specific period of time, the month ending on January 31, 2005. The statement was generated from all of the data you entered since the beginning of the chapter. Make sure your data matches what is shown in Figure 1.29. Go back and edit changes if your figures do not match.

On the income statement the revenues are listed first, followed by expenses. Finally net income (or net loss) is determined. Although practice sometimes varies in the "real world," the expenses in the example have been generated based on account number. In some cases, expenses appear in order of financial magnitude. Investment and withdrawal transactions between the owner and the business are not included in the measurement of net income.

GENERATING THE STATEMENT OF RETAINED EARNINGS

Peachtree Complete Accounting utilizes a "Statement of Retained Earnings" to record the changes in owner's equity. This statement is very similar to a Statement of Owner's Equity. It shows the period changes caused by revenues and expenses summarized as "Net income" and withdrawals by the owner. Changes in owner's equity are also shown in the "Statement of Changes in Financial Position".

Note: When learning accounting principles, Retained Earnings, is usually covered as a part of corporate accounting and not while learning about sole proprietorships. You will look at Retained Earnings more in depth in the section on corporate accounting. However, the Peachtree Complete Accounting system, when setting up the original company, requires the creation of a Retained Earnings account in the set up procedure.

By definition, retained earnings are the net income retained in a corporation. Net income is recorded and added to Retained Earnings1 by a closing entry in which Income Summary is debited and Retained Earnings is credited just as you credited the capital account. Closing entries will also be covered later. R. Neal's Capital account would contain all of the paid-in contributions by the sole proprietor (R. Neal).

To generate the Statement of Retained Earnings:
Step 1: On the main menu bar, click on "Reports" to get the pull down menu.
Step 2: Click on Financial Statements to get the "Select A Report" menu of shown in Figure 1.30.

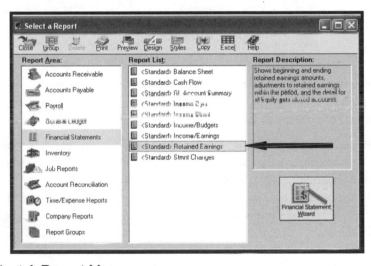

Figure 1.30 Select A Report Menu

Step 3: Double click on <Standard> Retained Earnings toward the bottom of the list.
Step 4: Again, the Dialog Box, as shown in Figure 1.31, gives us several choices including the choice of financial periods, the margins for the report, whether or not you want to show accounts that have a zero balance, whether or not you want page numbers, etc. If you wish to print the Statement of Retained Earnings, make sure the printer at the bottom of the dialog box matches the printer you are using on your computer system.

---

[1] Peachtree Complete Accounting, 2004 is a professional software package. The Retained Earnings account is a required account within the Peachtree system and cannot be changed. Net Income will be reflected in the Peachtree Retained Earnings account as a Balance Sheet item. This is not discussed in the Weygandt text.

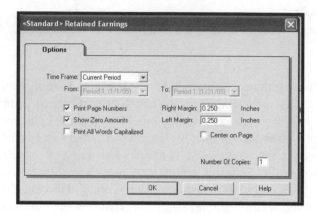

Figure 1.31   Dialog box to prepare Statement of Retained Earnings for display

Step 5: Click OK to show the Statement of Retained Earnings, Figure 1.32, on your computer screen.

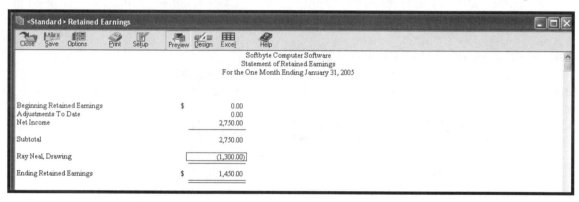

Figure 1. 32   The Statement of Retained Earnings.

The beginning Retained Earnings is shown on the first line of the statement. The balance is zero since this is a start up company with no previous earned income. Next month, the amount should equal (for the beginning balance) the ending balance, $1,450 as of January 31, 2005.

The next line shows the amount of net income of $2,700. This figure was acquired by subtracting all of this period's expenses from all of the period's revenue. The results: Net Income, which will eventually be "rolled into" Retained Earnings.

The amount Neal took out or withdrew from the company is shown next as a subtraction from equity. And, the final figure is the ending balance, Ending Retained Earnings of $1,450 which will be the beginning balance for the next accounting period.

The statement of changes in financial condition is obtained in a similar manner and not covered here.

THE BALANCE SHEET

The balance sheet also is prepared from all of the data you previously entered. The assets will appear at the top of the balance sheet, followed by liabilities, then owner's equity. Recall from the beginning of the chapter that assets must equal the total of the liabilities plus (in addition to) the owner's equity. Peachtree Complete Accounting will make sure this balances for you. The system will let you know if it does not balance.

The balance sheet is obtained in the same way the Income Statement and Statement of Retained Earnings were obtained.

Step 1: On the main menu bar click on Reports to get the pull-down menu.

Step 2: Click on Financial Statements to get the "Select A Report" menu.

Step 3: Double click on <Standard> Balance Sheet.

Step 4: Again, the Dialog Box gives us several choices including the choice of financial periods, the margins for the printer, whether or not you want to show accounts that have a zero balance, whether or not you want page numbers, and so on. If you wish to print reports, make sure the printer at the bottom of the Dialog Box matches the printer you are using on your computer system.

Step 5: Click OK to show the Softbyte Balance Sheet, Figure 1.33, on your computer screen. It is shown in figure 1-33.

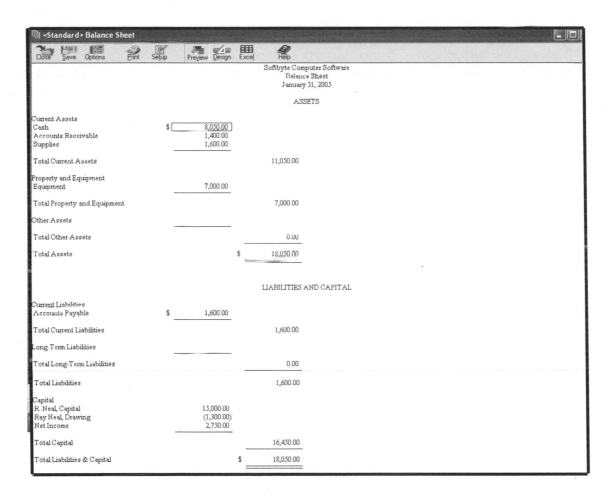

Figure 1. 33 Full screen balance sheet for Softbyte.

GENERATING THE STATEMENT OF CASH FLOW

The statement of cash flows reports:
1. The cash effects of a company's operations during a period
2. Its investing transactions
3. Its financing transactions
4. The net increase or decrease in cash during the period
5. The cash amount at the end of the period

Reporting the sources, uses, and net increase or decrease in cash is useful because investors, creditors, and others want to know what is happening to a company's most liquid resource. Thus the statement of cash flows provides answers to the following simple but important questions:

Where did the cash come from during the period?
1. What was the cash used for during the period?
2. What was the change in the cash balance during the period?

The statement of cash flows for Softbyte is shown in Figure 1.36. Cash increased by $8,050 during the period (January). Net Cash flow provided from operating activities increased cash $1,350. Cash flow from investing transactions decreased cash $7,000 and cash flow from financing transactions increased cash $13,700. Do not be concerned at this point with how these amounts were determined, but, be aware that they are based on your earlier entries.

Step 1: On the main menu bar click on "Reports" to get the pull down menu. Click on Financial Statements to get the "Select A Report" menu.

Step 2: Double click on <Predefined> Cash Flow.

Step 3: Again, the Dialog Box gives us several choices including the choice of financial periods, the margins for the printer, whether or not you want to show accounts that have a zero balance, whether or not you want page numbers, etc. If you wish to print the Statement of Retained Earnings, make sure the printer at the bottom of the dialog box matches the printer you are using on your computer system.

Step 4: Click OK to show the Cash Flows statement for Softbyte, Figure 1.34, on your computer screen. It is shown full screen below.

```
                                    Softbyte Computer Software
                                      Statement of Cash Flow
                                 For the one Month Ended January 31, 2005

                                 Current Month              Year to Date

Cash Flows from operating activities
  Net Income                    $     2,750.00    $           2,750.00
  Adjustments to reconcile net
  income to net cash provided
  by operating activities
  Accounts Receivable                (1,400.00)              (1,400.00)
  Supplies                           (1,600.00)              (1,600.00)
  Accounts Payable                    1,600.00               1,600.00

  Total Adjustments                  (1,400.00)              (1,400.00)

  Net Cash provided by Operations     1,350.00               1,350.00


Cash Flows from investing activities
  Used For
  Equipment                          (7,000.00)              (7,000.00)

  Net cash used in investing         (7,000.00)              (7,000.00)


Cash Flows from financing activities
  Proceeds From
  R. Neal, Capital                   15,000.00               15,000.00
  Ray Neal, Drawing                       0.00                    0.00
  Used For
  R. Neal, Capital                        0.00                    0.00
  Ray Neal, Drawing                  (1,300.00)              (1,300.00)

  Net cash used in financing         13,700.00               13,700.00

Net increase <decrease> in cash  $    8,050.00    $          8,050.00
```

Figure 1.34 Statement of Cash Flows

Demonstration Problem, Joan Robinson, Attorney at Law, Directory "joarobat"

Joan Robinson opens her own law office on July 1, 2005. During the first month of operations, the following transactions occurred: (Note: Dates have been added as required for journalizing order.)
1. July 1, 2005, Joan invested $10,000 in cash to open her law practice.
2. July 15, 2005, paid $800 for July rent on her office space.
3. Purchased office equipment on July 18, 2005, on account, $3,000
4. July 20, 2005, rendered legal services to clients for cash, $1,500
5. Borrowed $700 cash, on July 22, 2005 from a bank on a note payable.
6. Billed legal services on July 23, 2005 to a client (on account) for $2,000.
7. On July 31, 2005, she paid additional monthly expenses: salaries $500; utilities $300 and telephone $100.

Instructions:
a. Open the company "Joan Robinson, Attorney at Law" found within your Student Data Set.
b. Enter and post the above transactions in Peachtree Complete Accounting.
c. Print out Joan Robinson's <Standard> Income Statement, Statement of Retained Earnings, and <Standard> Balance Sheet.

Solution to Demonstration Problem

General Journal Entries (Provided for reference.)

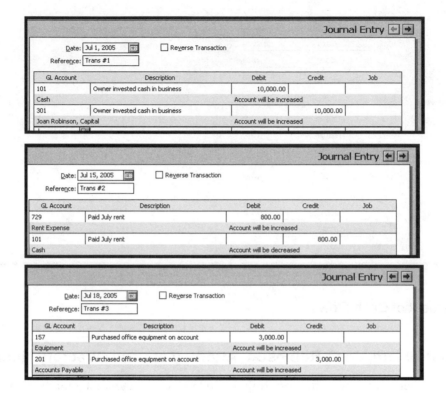

Journal Entry ⬅ ➡

Date: Jul 20, 2005   ☐ Reverse Transaction
Reference: Trans #4

GL Account	Description	Debit	Credit	Job
101	Earned service revenue in cash	1,500.00		
Cash		Account will be increased		
401	Earned service revenue in cash		1,500.00	
Service Revenue		Account will be increased		

Journal Entry ⬅ ➡

Date: Jul 22, 2005   ☐ Reverse Transaction
Reference: Trans #5

GL Account	Description	Debit	Credit	Job
101	Borrowed cash from bank on N/P	700.00		
Cash		Account will be increased		
200	Borrowed cash from bank on N/P		700.00	
Notes Payable		Account will be increased		

Journal Entry ⬅ ➡

Date: Jul 23, 2005   ☐ Reverse Transaction
Reference: Trans #6

GL Account	Description	Debit	Credit	Job
112	Performed services on account	2,000.00		
Accounts Receivable		Account will be increased		
401	Performed services on account		2,000.00	
Service Revenue		Account will be increased		

Journal Entry ⬅ ➡

Date: Jul 31, 2005   ☐ Reverse Transaction
Reference: Trans #7

GL Account	Description	Debit	Credit	Job
726	Paid salaries	500.00		
Salaries Expense		Account will be increased		
732	Paid utilities	300.00		
Utilities Expense		Account will be increased		
733	Paid telephone	100.00		
Telephone Expense		Account will be increased		
101	Paid various expenses in cash		900.00	
Cash		Account will be decreased		

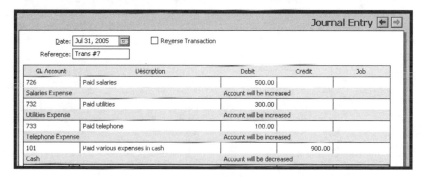

34

General Journal (Provided for reference.)

Joan Robinson, Attorney at Law
General Journal
For the Period From Jul 1, 2005 to Jul 31, 2005

Filter Criteria includes: Report order is by Date. Report is printed with Accounts having Zero Amounts and with Truncated Transaction Descriptions and in Detail Format.

Date	Account ID	Reference	Trans Description	Debit Amt	Credit Amt
7/1/05	101	Trans #1	Owner invested cash in business	10,000.00	
	301		Owner invested cash in business		10,000.00
7/15/05	729	Trans #2	Paid July rent	800.00	
	101		Paid July rent		800.00
7/18/05	157	Trans #3	Purchased office equipment on acc	3,000.00	
	201		Purchased office equipment on acc		3,000.00
7/20/05	101	Trans #4	Earned service revenue in cash	1,500.00	
	401		Earned service revenue in cash		1,500.00
7/22/05	101	Trans #5	Borrowed cash from bank on N/P	700.00	
	200		Borrowed cash from bank on N/P		700.00
7/23/05	112	Trans #6	Performed services on account	2,000.00	
	401		Performed services on account		2,000.00
7/31/05	726	Trans #7	Paid salaries	500.00	
	732		Paid utilities	300.00	
	733		Paid telephone	100.00	
	101		Paid various expenses in cash		900.00
		Total		18,900.00	18,900.00

Income Statement

Joan Robinson, Attorney at Law
Income Statement
For the Seven Months Ending July 31, 2005

	Current Month		Year to Date	
Revenues				
Service Revenue	$ 3,500.00	100.00	$ 3,500.00	100.00
Total Revenues	3,500.00	100.00	3,500.00	100.00
Cost of Sales				
Total Cost of Sales	0.00	0.00	0.00	0.00
Gross Profit	3,500.00	100.00	3,500.00	100.00
Expenses				
Salaries Expense	500.00	14.29	500.00	14.29
Rent Expense	800.00	22.86	800.00	22.86
Utilities Expense	300.00	8.57	300.00	8.57
Telephone Expense	100.00	2.86	100.00	2.86
Total Expenses	1,700.00	48.57	1,700.00	48.57
Net Income	$ 1,800.00	51.43	$ 1,800.00	51.43

Statement of Retained Earnings

Joan Robinson, Attorney at Law
Statement of Retained Earnings
For the Seven Months Ending July 31, 2005

Beginning Retained Earnings	$ 0.00
Adjustments To Date	0.00
Net Income	1,800.00
Subtotal	1,800.00
Joan Robinson, Drawing	0.00
Ending Retained Earnings	$ 1,800.00

Balance Sheet

Joan Robinson, Attorney at Law
Balance Sheet
July 31, 2005

ASSETS

Current Assets		
Cash	$ 10,500.00	
Accounts Receivable	2,000.00	
Total Current Assets		12,500.00
Property and Equipment		
Equipment	3,000.00	
Total Property and Equipment		3,000.00
Other Assets		
Total Other Assets		0.00
Total Assets		$ 15,500.00

LIABILITIES AND CAPITAL

Current Liabilities		
Notes Payable	$ 700.00	
Accounts Payable	3,000.00	
Total Current Liabilities		3,700.00
Long-Term Liabilities		
Total Long-Term Liabilities		0.00
Total Liabilities		3,700.00
Capital		
Joan Robinson, Capital	10,000.00	
Net Income	1,800.00	
Total Capital		11,800.00
Total Liabilities & Capital		$ 15,500.00

CHAPTER 2

The Recording Process

OBJECTIVES

- Explain what an account is, how it is created in Peachtree.
- Define debits and credits and explain how they are used to record business transactions.

- Generate the Trial Balance provided in Peachtree Complete Accounting.
- Explain the General Journal and General Ledger in Peachtree Complete Accounting

THE ACCOUNT

An account is an individual accounting record of the increases and decreases in a specific asset, liability, or owner's equity item. For example, Softbyte has separate accounts for Cash, Accounts Receivable, Accounts Payable, Service Revenue, Salaries Expense, and so on.

In its simplest form, an account has three parts:

1. The title
2. The left side or debit side
3. A right side or credit side

The accounting term debit refers to the left side of a column and credit refers to the right. Therefore, entering an amount on the left side is called debiting the account; the right side is called crediting the account. That is an accounting rule which is comparable the custom of driving on the right hand side of the road in the United States or stopping for a stoplight. The common abbreviations are Dr. for debit and Cr. for credit.

To "balance" your account, add up the debit amounts entered, then add up the credit amounts entered. Subtract the smaller total from the larger total. The difference is called the balance. Peachtree will balance your accounts for you.

In the first chapter, as you made General Journal entries for each of the Softbyte transactions, you learned how a transaction affects the basic accounting equation. Each transaction must affect two or more accounts, and for each transaction debits must equal credits. That keeps the accounting equation in balance. This is the basis for the double entry accounting system, which is the heart of Peachtree Complete Accounting.

THE GENERAL JOURNAL

In manual accounting, transactions are recorded in sequential order, as they happen, in a journal, before being transferred to the actual accounts. This journal is referred to as the Book of Original Entry. For each transaction the journal shows the debit and credit effects on the individual accounts. Companies use various kinds of journals but every company uses the most basic form of journal - a General Journal.

Peachtree's automated version of the General Journal was used when you made your entries for Softbyte Computer Software in Chapter 1. As you recall, the general journal has spaces for dates, account titles and explanations/references (descriptions) and money columns.

In Peachtree Complete Accounting, you use the General Journal to enter those types of transactions that are not readily categorized in the Tasks menu. Typical General Journal entries include chart of account beginning balances, depreciation, and account transfers. Unlike other screens in Peachtree, you provide all the accounting distributions in the General Journal. At other times, Peachtree automatically distributes certain amounts, based on guidelines you set in Maintain menus.

Look at Softbyte's General Journal. Open Softbyte Computer Software found within your Student Data Set. This will be the same file you used during the exercises in Chapter 1.

Step 1: On the Menu bar click on Reports.

Step 2: On the pull down menu, click on General Ledger.

Step 3: Select General Journal from the Report Select menu.

Part of the General Journal is shown in Figure 2.1. It shows the initial entry for Cash and Capital from the first transactions in the previous chapter. Notice the debit entry (increasing) cash and the credit entry (increasing) capital, each for $15,000. Some of the other entries made in January also appear in this

Softbyte Computer Software
General Journal
For the Period From Jan 1, 2005 to Jan 31, 2005
Filter Criteria includes: Report order is by Date. Report is printed with Accounts having Zero Amounts and with Truncated Transaction Descriptions and in Detail Format.

Date	Account ID	Reference	Trans Description	Debit Amt	Credit Amt
1/1/05	101	Trans #1	Owner's investment in business	15,000.00	
	301		Owner's investment in business		15,000.00
1/1/05	157	Trans #2	Paid cash for equipment	7,000.00	
	101		Paid cash for equipment		7,000.00
1/1/05	126	Trans #3	Purchased supplies on account	1,600.00	
	201		Purchased supplies on account		1,600.00
1/1/05	101	Trans #4	Services rendered for cash	1,200.00	
	401		Services rendered for cash		1,200.00
1/2/05	610	Trans #5	Daily News ad on account	250.00	
	201		Daily News ad on account		250.00
1/7/05	101	Trans #6	Received cash from customers for s	1,500.00	
	112		Services on account	2,000.00	
	401		Services revenue		3,500.00

General Journal example.

Figure 2. 1 General Journal entries for Softbyte

It is not shown in Figure 2.1, however during the operation of the Peachtree application, when you click on the General Journal report (as with each of the other reports) your cursor turns into a small magnifying glass with a "Z" in the middle. If you click on a specific transaction on the report with the magnifying glass Peachtree will go directly to the form or journal where that transaction was entered. In the case of the General Journal report, you will be taken directly to that specific General Journal entry.

One more point, when "Save" is clicked on the menu bar, after making General Journal entries, the entry made in the General Journal was then automatically posted to the appropriate journals and ledgers, one in particular: *The General Ledger*.

THE GENERAL LEDGER

The entire group of accounts maintained by a company is called the General Ledger. The ledger as it is commonly referred to, keeps in one place all of the information about any changes in individual account balances. Each transaction is entered in the ledger, which was the "posting" process performed in the previous chapter.

Every company has some type of general ledger that contains all of the assets, liabilities, and owner's equity accounts, their related transactions and balances.

The ledger provides management with the balances in various accounts. For example, the Cash account shows the amount of cash that is available to meet current obligations. Amounts due from customers can be found by examining Accounts Receivable and amounts owed to creditors can found by looking at Accounts Payable.

Let's look at the General Ledger for Softbyte. Open Softbyte Computer Software file from within your Student Data Set. This will be the same file you used in Chapter 1.

Step 1: On the Menu bar click on Reports.

Step 2: On the pull down menu, click on General Ledger.

Step 3: Select General Ledger from the Report Selection menu as shown in Figure 2.2.

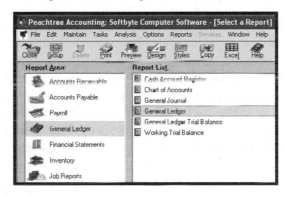

Figure 2. 2 Report Selection Menu

Peachtree then presents a complete General Ledger report, a portion of which is shown Figure 2.3. The entire report would list each active account, the ones without a zero balance, and the associated transactions. However, you have an option to list the accounts with zero balances if you wish, which would make for an even longer report.

Softbyte Computer Software
General Ledger
For the Period From Jan 1, 2005 to Jan 31, 2005

Filter Criteria includes: Report order is by ID. Report is printed with Truncated Transaction Descriptions and in Detail Format.

Account ID Account Description	Date	Reference	Jrnl	Trans Description	Debit Amt	Credit Amt	Balance
101	1/1/05			Beginning Balanc			
Cash	1/1/05	Trans #1	GEN	Owner's investme	15,000.00		
	1/1/05	Trans #2	GEN	Paid cash for equi		7,000.00	
	1/1/05	Trans #4	GEN	Services rendered	1,200.00		
	1/7/05	Trans #6	GEN	Received cash fro	1,500.00		
	1/15/05	Trans #7	GEN	Paid various expe		1,700.00	
	1/15/05	Trans #8	GEN	Paid Daily News f		250.00	
	1/15/05	Trans #9	GEN	Received cash fro	600.00		
	1/31/05	Trans #10	GEN	Ray Neal, drawing		1,300.00	
				Current Period Ch	18,300.00	10,250.00	8,050.00
	1/31/05			**Ending Balance**			**8,050.00**
112	1/1/05			Beginning Balanc			
Accounts Receivable	1/7/05	Trans #6	GEN	Services on accou	2,000.00		
	1/15/05	Trans #9	GEN	Received cash fro		600.00	
				Current Period Ch	2,000.00	600.00	1,400.00
	1/31/05			**Ending Balance**			**1,400.00**
126	1/1/05			Beginning Balanc			
Supplies	1/1/05	Trans #3	GEN	Purchased suppli	1,600.00		
				Current Period Ch	1,600.00		1,600.00
	1/31/05			**Ending Balance**			**1,600.00**
157	1/1/05			Beginning Balanc			
Equipment	1/1/05	Trans #2	GEN	Paid cash for equi	7,000.00		
				Current Period Ch	7,000.00		7,000.00
	1/31/05			**Ending Balance**			**7,000.00**

Figure 2. 3 Portion of General Ledger Report

ASSETS AND LIABILITIES

In the Softbyte exercise in Chapter 1, you were shown that increases in cash (an asset) were entered on the left side (debit side) of the journal amount column and decreases in cash were entered on the right side (credit side) of the journal amount column. You also know that both sides of the basic accounting equation (Assets = Liabilities + Owner's Equity) must be equal. It makes sense that increases and decreases in liabilities will be recorded opposite from each other, therefore, increases in liabilities must be entered on the right (credit side), and decreases in liabilities must be entered on the left (debit side).

Knowing the normal balance in an account may help you trace errors. For example, a credit balance in an asset account such as Land or a debit balance in a liability account such as Wages Payable would indicate an error. Occasionally, however, an abnormal balance may be correct. For example, the Cash account could have a credit balance when a company has overdrawn its bank balance.

OWNER'S EQUITY

Owner's equity is increased either by additional investments by the owner or by revenue earned in the business. Investments by the owner are credited to the owner's capital account. For example, when cash is invested in the business, cash is debited (increased) and owner's capital is credited (also increased). It is decreased by owner's drawings. An owner may withdraw cash or other assets from the business for personal use. Withdrawals could be debited directly to owner's capital to indicate a decrease in owner's equity. However, it is preferable to establish a separate account, the Owner's Drawing account. Expenses also decrease the owner's equity.

REVENUES AND EXPENSES

When revenues are earned, owner's equity is increased. That means simply that the effect of debits and credits on revenue accounts is the same as their effect on owner's capital. Revenue accounts are increased by credits (sales) and decreased by debits (expenses).

THE CHART OF ACCOUNTS

The number and type of accounts used are likely to differ for each enterprise depending on the amount of detail required by management. Although Softbyte is able to manage and report its activities with just a few accounts, a large corporation such as Robinson-Humphrey, a stock brokerage firm in Atlanta, requires thousands of accounts to keep track of its activities.

Companies have a chart of accounts, a master listing of the accounts and the account numbers, which identify their location in the ledger. The numbering system used to identify the accounts usually starts with the balance sheet accounts and ends with the expenses on the income statement.

Examine the Chart of Accounts for Softbyte.

Step 1: On the Menu bar, click on Reports.

Step 2: On the pull down menu, click on General Ledger.

Step 3: Then, select Chart of Accounts from the Select Report menu as shown in Figure 2.4.

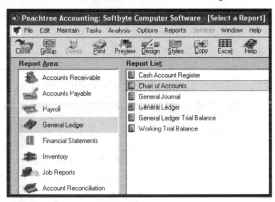

Figure 2. 4 Select Report menu for Chart of Accounts

The complete Chart of Accounts for Softbyte is shown in Figure 2.5. You may print the Chart of Accounts by clicking on the Print icon.

Figure 2. 5 Chart of Accounts report for Softbyte.

Softbyte Computer Software
Chart of Accounts
As of Jan 31, 2005

Filter Criteria includes: Report order is by ID. Report is printed with Accounts having Zero Amounts and in Detail Format.

Account ID	Account Description	Active?	Account Type
101	Cash	Yes	Cash
112	Accounts Receivable	Yes	Accounts Receivable
126	Supplies	Yes	Other Current Assets
157	Equipment	Yes	Fixed Assets
201	Accounts Payable	Yes	Accounts Payable
301	R. Neal, Capital	Yes	Equity-doesn't close
305	Ray Neal, Drawing	Yes	Equity-gets closed
310	Retained Earnings	Yes	Equity-Retained Earnings
401	Service Revenue	Yes	Income
610	Advertising Expense	Yes	Expenses
726	Salaries Expense	Yes	Expenses
729	Rent Expense	Yes	Expenses
732	Utilities Expense	Yes	Expenses

HOW ACCOUNTS ARE ASSIGNED NUMBERS

The numbering system used to identify accounts can be quite sophisticated or as in Softbyte's case, fairly simple. For example, one major company uses an 18-digit account numbering system. The first three digits identify the division or plant; the second set of three digit numbers contain the plant location, and so on. Softbyte uses a three-digit classification.

Softbyte Computer Software
Account Number Classification

100 – 199	Assets
200 – 299	Liabilities
300 – 399	Equity/Capital
400 – 499	Revenue
500 – 799	Expenses

When setting up a new business, you will discover that Peachtree contains many sample companies and their related charts of accounts. You will be given a choice of setting up your own chart of accounts (which you'll do later in this chapter) or you may select one of the sample company's Chart of Account.

To see the sample companies and their Charts of Accounts open up either of the two sample companies, Bellwether Garden Supply and Pavilion Design Group. Both of these companies are part of the standard installation of Peachtree Complete Accounting.

You can also access the Help screens of Peachtree through:

Step 1: On the menu bar, click on Help.

Step 2: Select Contents and Index on the pull down menu, as illustrated in Figure 2.6.

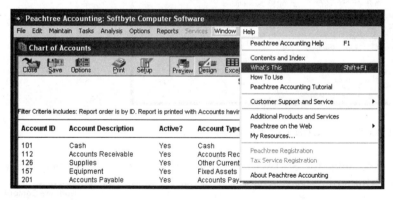

Figure 2. 6 Pull down window for help

Step 3: Then select either "Index" or "Contents". The Index table and Contents table both provide many options on numerous subjects. If one does not provide the answer, try the other or the "Search" option. The Index and Help dialog boxes are shown in Figure 2.7.

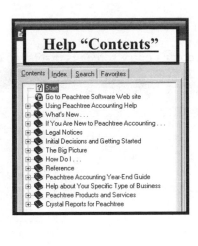

Figure 2. 7 Index and Contents dialog boxes.

SETTING UP A NEW ACCOUNT

If you choose to use a company that has accounts already set up, you still may create new accounts, as needed, at any time. For example, let's say the owner of Softbyte would like to set up an account for Telephone Expense. Originally Ray Neal classified the phone bill as part of the Utilities Expenses. But now he wants the Utilities Expense account to reflect only the Gas and Power bills and would like a separate account, the Telephone Expense account, to reflect payments for regular phone service.

Setting up the new account:

Step 1: Click on "Maintain" from the main menu bar.

Step 2: From the pull down menu (Figure 2.8) click on Chart of Accounts.

Figure 2. 8 Maintain pull Down Menu - click on Chart of Accounts

Step 3: The Chart of Accounts entry screen is displayed on your screen as shown in Figure 2.9.

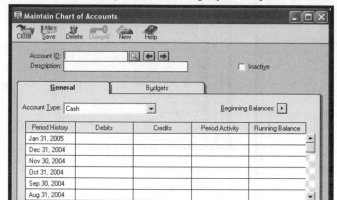

Figure 2. 9 Account entry form.

Step 3: In the Account No. window, enter "733" as the new Account Number.
Step 4: The name of the account or description is "Telephone Expense."
Step 5: The account must have a type that is assigned by Peachtree. (Account Types are discussed in the next section.) Next to Account Type found under the "General" tab, click on the pull down menu and scroll down until "Expenses" is shown in the window. (See Figure 2.10.)

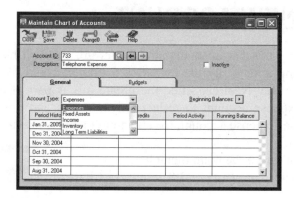

Figure 2. 10 New account entry, assigning Account Type.

Step 6: Double click on "Expenses" to classify the account as an expense account within the Peachtree system. You will not enter a beginning balance nor any budget items at this time.
Step 7: Click Save on the toolbar to save the new account.
Step 8: To make sure your new account has been entered and saved properly, run a Chart of Accounts report (Figure 2.11.)

```
                              Softbyte Computer Software
                                   Chart of Accounts
                                   As of Jan 31, 2005
Filter Criteria includes: Report order is by ID. Report is printed with Accounts having Zero Amounts and in Detail Format.

Account ID    Account Description    Active?    Account Type

101           Cash                   Yes        Cash
112           Accounts Receivable    Yes        Accounts Receivable
126           Supplies               Yes        Other Current Assets
157           Equipment              Yes        Fixed Assets
201           Accounts Payable       Yes        Accounts Payable
301           R. Neal, Capital       Yes        Equity-doesn't close
305           Ray Neal, Drawing      Yes        Equity-gets closed
310           Retained Earnings      Yes        Equity-Retained Earnings
401           Service Revenue        Yes        Income
610           Advertising Expense    Yes        Expenses
726           Salaries Expense       Yes        Expenses
729           Rent Expense           Yes        Expenses
732           Utilities Expense      Yes        Expenses
733           Telephone Expense      Yes        Expenses
```

Figure 2. 11 New Chart of Accounts Report reflecting the Telephone Expense Account

ACCOUNT TYPES

When creating new accounts in Peachtree, account types will define how the account will be grouped in reports and financial statements. (Figure 2.12) They also control what happens during fiscal year-end.

Accounts Payable	Equity – Gets closed	Long-Term Liabilities
Accounts Receivable	Equity – Retained Earnings	Other Assets
Accumulated Depreciation	Expenses	Other Current Assets
Cash	Fixed Assets	Other Current Liabilities
Cost of Sales	Income	
Equity – Doesn't close	Inventory	

Figure 2. 12 Menu of account types in creating new accounts

Accounts Payable - Account balances owed to vendors for goods, supplies, and services purchased on an open account that are generally due in 30 or 60 days, and do not bear interest. Select this account type if you are setting up open vendor accounts or credit card (purchase) accounts.

Accounts Receivable - Account balances owed by customers for items or services sold to them when cash is not received at the time of sale.

Accumulated Depreciation - This is a contra asset account to depreciable (fixed) assets such as buildings, machinery, and equipment. Recording depreciation is a way to indicate that assets have declined in service potential. Accumulated depreciation represents total depreciation taken to date on the assets.

Cash - This represents deposits in banks available for current operations, plus cash on hand consisting of currency, undeposited checks, drafts, and money orders. Select this account type if you are setting up bank checking accounts, petty cash accounts, money market accounts, and certificates of deposit (CDs).

Cost of Sales - This represents the known cost to your business for items or services when sold to customers. Cost of sales is also known as cost of goods sold for inventory items and computed based on inventory costing method FIFO, LIFO or Average. Select this account type if you are setting up cost-of-goods-sold accounts to be used when selling inventory items.

Equity - Doesn't Close - This represents the paid in equity or capital that is carried forward from period to period. It is also used for common stock.

Equity - Gets Closed - This represents equity that is closed or zeroed out at the end of the fiscal year, with their amounts moved to the capital or retained earnings account.

Equity - Retained Earnings - This represents the earned capital or equity of the enterprise. Its balance is the cumulative, lifetime earnings of the company that have not been distributed to owners. Peachtree Complete Accounting requires you to have a Retained Earnings accounting.

Expenses - These represent the costs incurred to produce revenues. The assets surrendered or consumed when serving customers are the company's expenses. If revenue exceeds expenses, net income results. If expenses exceed income, the business is operating at a net loss.

Fixed Assets - These represent property, plant, or equipment assets that are acquired for use in a business rather than for resale. They are called fixed assets because they are to be used for long periods of time. Select this account type if you are setting up any of the following fixed assets:
- **Land** - property.
- **Buildings** - structures in which the business is carried out.
- **Machinery** - heavy equipment used to carry out business operations.

For example, you may want to set up any of the following: store equipment or fixtures, factory equipment of fixtures, office equipment or fixtures (including computers and furniture), and delivery equipment (including autos, trucks, and vans used primarily in making deliveries to customers).

Income - Revenue is the inflow of assets resulting from the sale of products and services to customers. If revenue exceeds expenses, net income results. If expenses exceed revenues, the business is operating at a net loss. Select this account type if you are setting up sales and service revenue accounts. It is common practice to create different revenue accounts for each category of revenue that you want to track (for example, retail revenue, service revenue, interest revenue, and so on).

Inventory - This represents the value of goods on hand and available for sale at any given time. Inventory is considered to be an asset that is purchased, manufactured (or assembled), and sold to customers for revenue. Select this account type if you are setting up assets that are intended for resale. It is common practice to create different accounts for each category of inventory that you want to track. For example, retail inventory, raw materials inventory, work in progress inventory, finished goods inventory, and so on can be tracked through the inventory account.

Long Term Liabilities - This represents debts that are not due for a relatively long period of time, usually more than one year. Portions of long-term loans due and notes payable with maturity dates at least one year or more beyond the current balance sheet date are considered to be long-term liabilities.

Other Assets - This represents assets that are considered nonworking capital and are not due for a relatively long period of time, usually more than one year. Notes receivable with maturity dates at least one year or more beyond the current balance sheet date are considered to be "noncurrent" assets. Select this account type if you are setting up assets such as deposits, amortization values, noncurrent notes receivable, and so on.

Other Current Assets - This represents those assets that are considered nonworking capital and are due within a short period of time, usually less than a year. Prepaid expenses, employee advances, and notes receivable with maturity dates of less than one year of the current balance sheet date are considered to be "current" assets. Select this account type if you are setting up assets such as prepaid expenses, employee advances, current notes receivable, and so on.

Other Current Liabilities - This represents debts that are due within a short period of time, usually less than a year. The payment of these debts usually requires the use of current assets. Select this account type if you are setting up accrued expenses from a vendor, extended lines of credit, short-term loans, sales tax payables, payroll tax payables, client escrow accounts, suspense (clearing) accounts, and so on.

THE TRIAL BALANCE AND THE WORKING TRIAL BALANCE

A trial balance is a list of accounts and their balances at a given time. Using a manual accounting system, a trial balance usually would be prepared at the end of an accounting period. However, Peachtree keeps a continual trial balance available for you. In a manual system, the primary purpose of a trial balance is to prove that the debits equal the credits after posting. Because Peachtree will not let you continue an entry unless it is in balance, the trial balance Peachtree generates will always be "in balance." As mentioned earlier, however, that does not mean your system is error free, that all transactions have been recorded, or that the ledger entries are correct.

The Working Trial Balance in Peachtree has a somewhat different purpose than in manual accounting. In Peachtree, the Working Trial Balance report prints the accounts and their balances, together with spaces to fill in information so you can have a "worksheet" to help make adjustments to account balances.

To see the Working Trial Balance in Peachtree:

Step 1: On the menu bar, click on Reports, and then click General Ledger.

Step 2: On the pull down menu, click on "Working Trial Balance"

A portion of the Working Trial Balance for Softbyte is shown in Figure 2.13.

\multicolumn{9}{c}{Softbyte Computer Software}

Softbyte Computer Software
Working Trial Balance
As of Jan 31, 2005

Filter Criteria includes: Report order is by ID. Report is printed with Accounts having Zero Amounts and in Detail Format.

Account ID Account Description	Last FYE Bal	Current Bal	Debit Adj	Credit Adj	End Bal	Reference
101 Cash	0.00	8,050.00	_____	_____	_____	_____
112 Accounts Receivable	0.00	1,400.00	_____	_____	_____	_____
126 Supplies	0.00	1,600.00	_____	_____	_____	_____
157 Equipment	0.00	7,000.00	_____	_____	_____	_____
201 Accounts Payable	0.00	-1,600.00	_____	_____	_____	_____
301	0.00	15,000.00				

Figure 2. 13 Working Trial Balance

Notice that under the Current Balance column, the Debit balances are positive amounts while the Credit balances have a negative sign or a negative balance.

Demonstration Problem, Campus Laundromat, Directory "camlaund"

Bob Sample opened the Campus Laundromat on September 1, 2005. During the first month of operations the following transactions occurred.

Sept 1 Invested $20,000 cash in the business.
2 Paid $1,000 cash for store rent for the month of September.
3 Purchased washers and dryers for $25,000, paying $10,000 in cash and signing a $15,000, 6-month, 12% note payable.
4 Paid $1,200 for one-year accident insurance policy.
10 Received bill from the *Daily News* for advertising the opening of the Laundromat $200.
20 Withdrew $700 cash for personal use.
30 Determined that cash receipts for laundry services for the month were $6,200.

Load Campus Laundromat from the Student Data Set.

Instructions:
a. Verify the Campus Laundromat's chart of accounts and beginning balances.
b. Journalize in Peachtree's General Journal the September transactions. Use "Trans #1", "Trans #2", etc. as the reference number.
c. Print a copy of the General Journal, General Ledger and the General Ledger Trial Balance.

Solution to Demonstration Problem

General Journal

Campus Laundromat					
General Journal					
For the Period From Sep 1, 2005 to Sep 30, 2005					
Filter Criteria includes: Report order is by Date. Report is printed with Accounts having Zero Amounts and with Truncated Transaction Descriptions and in Detail Format.					

Date	Account ID	Reference	Trans Description	Debit Amt	Credit Amt
9/1/05	101	Trans #1	Owner's investment of cash in busin	20,000.00	
	301		Owner's investment of cash in busin		20,000.00
9/2/05	729	Trans #2	Paid September rent	1,000.00	
	101		Paid September rent		1,000.00
9/3/05	154	Trans #3	Purchased washers and dryers	25,000.00	
	101		Purchased washers and dryers, pai		10,000.00
	200		Purchased washers and dryers, bal		15,000.00
9/4/05	130	Trans #4	Paid one-year insurance policy	1,200.00	
	101		Paid one-year insurance policy		1,200.00
9/10/05	610	Trans #5	Received bill from Daily News for ad	200.00	
	201		Received bill from Daily News for ad		200.00
9/20/05	306	Trans #6	Withdrew cash for personal use	700.00	
	101		Withdrew cash for personal use		700.00
9/30/05	101	Trans #7	Received cash for services provided	6,200.00	
	400		Received cash for services provided		6,200.00
		Total		54,300.00	54,300.00

50

General Ledger

Campus Laundromat
General Ledger
For the Period From Sep 1, 2005 to Sep 30, 2005
Filter Criteria includes: Report order is by ID. Report is printed with Truncated Transaction Descriptions and in Detail Format.

Account ID Account Description	Date	Reference	Jrnl	Trans Description	Debit Amt	Credit Amt	Balance
101	9/1/05			Beginning Balanc			
Cash	9/1/05	Trans #1	GEN	Owner's investme	20,000.00		
	9/2/05	Trans #2	GEN	Paid September r		1,000.00	
	9/3/05	Trans #3	GEN	Purchased washe		10,000.00	
	9/4/05	Trans #4	GEN	Paid one-year ins		1,200.00	
	9/20/05	Trans #6	GEN	Withdrew cash for		700.00	
	9/30/05	Trans #7	GEN	Received cash for	6,200.00		
				Current Period Ch	26,200.00	12,900.00	13,300.00
	9/30/05			Ending Balance			13,300.00
130	9/1/05			Beginning Balanc			
Prepaid Insurance	9/4/05	Trans #4	GEN	Paid one-year ins	1,200.00		
				Current Period Ch	1,200.00		1,200.00
	9/30/05			Ending Balance			1,200.00
154	9/1/05			Beginning Balanc			
Laundry Equipment	9/3/05	Trans #3	GEN	Purchased washe	25,000.00		
				Current Period Ch	25,000.00		25,000.00
	9/30/05			Ending Balance			25,000.00
200	9/1/05			Beginning Balanc			
Notes Payable	9/3/05	Trans #3	GEN	Purchased washe		15,000.00	
				Current Period Ch		15,000.00	-15,000.00
	9/30/05			Ending Balance			-15,000.00
201	9/1/05			Beginning Balanc			
Accounts Payable	9/10/05	Trans #5	GEN	Received bill from		200.00	
				Current Period Ch		200.00	-200.00
	9/30/05			Ending Balance			-200.00
301	9/1/05			Beginning Balanc			
Bob Sample, Capital	9/1/05	Trans #1	GEN	Owner's investme		20,000.00	
				Current Period Ch		20,000.00	-20,000.00
	9/30/05			Ending Balance			-20,000.00
306	9/1/05			Beginning Balanc			
Bob Sample, Drawin	9/20/05	Trans #6	GEN	Withdrew cash for	700.00		
				Current Period Ch	700.00		700.00
	9/30/05			Ending Balance			700.00
400	9/1/05			Beginning Balanc			
Service Revenue	9/30/05	Trans #7	GEN	Received cash for		6,200.00	
				Current Period Ch		6,200.00	-6,200.00
	9/30/05			Ending Balance			-6,200.00
610	9/1/05			Beginning Balanc			
Advertising Expense	9/10/05	Trans #5	GEN	Received bill from	200.00		
				Current Period Ch	200.00		200.00
	9/30/05			Ending Balance			200.00
729	9/1/05			Beginning Balanc			
Rent Expense	9/2/05	Trans #2	GEN	Paid September r	1,000.00		
				Current Period Ch	1,000.00		1,000.00
	9/30/05			Ending Balance			1,000.00

General Ledger Trial Balance

Campus Laundromat
General Ledger Trial Balance
As of Sep 30, 2005
Filter Criteria includes: Report order is by ID. Report is printed in Detail Format.

Account ID	Account Description	Debit Amt	Credit Amt
101	Cash	13,300.00	
130	Prepaid Insurance	1,200.00	
154	Laundry Equipment	25,000.00	
200	Notes Payable		15,000.00
201	Accounts Payable		200.00
301	Bob Sample, Capital		20,000.00
306	Bob Sample, Drawing	700.00	
400	Service Revenue		6,200.00
610	Advertising Expense	200.00	
729	Rent Expense	1,000.00	
	Total:	**41,400.00**	**41,400.00**

P2-1B, Frontier Park, Directory "fropark"

Frontier Park was started on April 1, 2005, by C. J. Amaro. The following selected events and transactions occurred during April 2005:

April	1	Amaro invested $50,000 cash in the business.
	4	Purchased land costing $30,000 for cash.
	8	Incurred advertising expense of $1,800 on account.
	11	Paid salaries to employees $1,500
	12	Hired park manager at a salary of $4,000 per month, effective May 1.
	13	Paid $1,500 cash for a one-year insurance policy.
	17	Withdrew $600 cash for personal use.
	20	Received $5,700 in cash for admission fees.
	25	Sold 100 coupon books for $25 each. Each book contains 10 coupons entitling the holder to one admission to the park.
	30	Received $8,900 in cash admission fees.
	30	Paid $900 on account for advertising incurred on April 8.

Instructions:
   a. Load "Frontier Park" into Peachtree from your Student Data Disk.
   b. Verify the chart of accounts and the beginning balances.
   c. Journalize the transactions in the General Journal using Peachtree Complete Accounting.
   d. Check your work by viewing and printing a General Ledger Trial Balance.

P2-5B, Lake Theater, Directory "laktheat"

The Lake Theater is owned by Alvin Wasicko. All facilities were completed on March 31, 2005. At that time, the ledger, in Peachtree Complete Accounting showed: No. 101 Cash $6,000; No. 140 Land $10,000; No. 145 Building (concession stand, projection room, ticket booth and screen) $8,000; No. 157 Equipment $6,000; No. 201 Accounts Payable $2,000; No. 275 Mortgage Payable $8,000 and No. 301 Alvin Wasicko, Capital $20,000. Lake Theater, with the accounts and balances, can be loaded from your Student Data Disk. During April 2005, the following events and transactions occurred.

April	2	Paid film rental of $800 on first movie.
	3	Ordered two additional films at $1,000 each.
	9	Received $1,800 cash from admissions.
	10	Made $2,000 payment on mortgage and $1,000 on Accounts Payable.
	11	Lake Theater contracted with R. Zarle Company to operate the concession stand. Zarle is to pay 17% of gross concession receipts (payable monthly) for the right to operate the concession stand.
	12	Paid advertising expenses $300.
	20	Received one of the films ordered on April 3 and was billed $1,000. The film will be shown in April.
	25	Received $5,200 cash from admissions.
	29	Paid salaries $1,600.
	30	Received statement from R. Zarle showing gross concession receipts of $1,000 and the balance due to The Lake Theater of $170 (17% of $1,000) for April. Zarle only paid half the balance due and will remit the remainder on May 5th.
	30	Prepaid rental on special film to be run in May, $900.

In addition to the accounts identified above, the following accounts are in the Chart of Accounts: No. 112 Accounts Receivable; No. 136 Prepaid Rentals; No. 405 Admission Revenue; No. 406 Concession Revenue; No. 610 Advertising Expense, No. 632 Film Rental Expense; and No. 726 Salaries Expense.

Instructions:

a. Verify the chart of accounts and beginning balances.
b. In Peachtree, utilizing the General Journal, Journalize and post the April transactions. Transaction numbers may be used for the reference number such as Trans #1.
c. Prepare an Income Statement, a Retained Earnings Statement and a Balance Sheet for the Lake Theater.

CHAPTER 3

Adjusting the Accounts

OBJECTIVES
- Explain why adjusting entries are needed.
- Prepare adjusting entries for prepaid and accrued accounts..

- Identify the major types of adjusting entries.
- Generate an adjusted trial balance.

SELECTING AN ACCOUNTING TIME PERIOD

In the previous chapter you worked with the General Journal recording process and how Peachtree keeps a running record of the trial balance and balance sheet. Before you can prepare the final set of financial statements there are some additional steps that must be taken.

What portion of your assets' costs, if any, should be recognized as an expense for the current accounting period? Those relevant account balances must be adjusted before you continue.

Because management usually wants monthly financial statements, and the Internal Revenue Service requires all businesses to file annual tax returns, accountants divide the economic life of a business into artificial time periods. This convenient assumption is referred to as the time period assumption.

Many business transactions affect more than one of these arbitrary time periods. For example a milking machine purchased by a farmer a couple years ago probably is still being used in active production today. Airplanes purchased by Delta Airlines two years ago most likely are still in use today. You must determine the relevance of each business transaction to specific accounting periods.

FISCAL AND CALENDAR YEARS

All companies prepare financial statements periodically in order to assess their financial condition and results of operations. Accounting time periods are generally a month, a quarter, or a year. Monthly and quarterly time periods are called interim periods. Many large companies are required to prepare both quarterly and annual financial statements.

An accounting time period that is a year in length is referred to as a fiscal year. A fiscal year usually begins with the first day of a month and ends 12 months later on the last day of a month. However, the accounting period used by most businesses coincides with the calendar year, January 1 to December 31. Some companies have a fiscal year that differs from the calendar year. For example, many educational institutes use a July 1 to June 30 fiscal year. The U.S. Government uses October 1 to September 30 as a fiscal year.

Peachtree Complete Accounting makes it easy to change from one accounting period to the next.

CHANGING ACCOUNTING PERIODS

Step 3: Launch Peachtree Complete Accounting and load in "Softbyte Computer Software" from the previous chapter.

Step 4: From the Tasks menu, on the main menu bar, select System and then Change Accounting Period as shown in Figure 3.1.

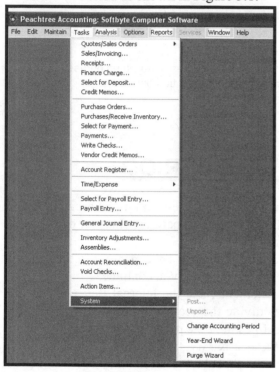

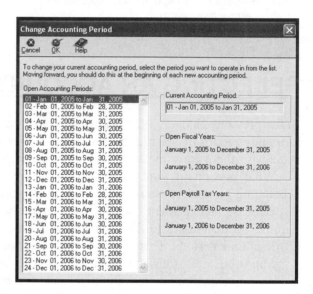

Figure 3. 1 Changing Accounting Periods period.

Figure 3. 2 Choosing a new accounting

Step 5: Select the accounting period required from the pop up menu as shown in Figure 3.2

Step 6: Change the period to your requirements and click OK.

Step 7: A message box appears asking if you would like to print reports before continuing. Select NO. If you were at the end of the accounting period for this company and wanted a full set of reports, then you would have selected the reports to be printed.

You can change the accounting period at will, moving back and forth in the fiscal years. The General Ledger will track balances as of the current period date. However, Peachtree Complete Accounting selects the period in which to post a transaction by the transaction date. You can enter a transaction in a future fiscal period but not in a prior accounting period.

BASICS OF ADJUSTING ENTRIES

In order for revenues to be recorded in the period in which they are earned and for expenses to be recognized in the period in which they are incurred, adjusting entries are made at the end of the accounting period. In short, adjusting entries are needed to ensure that the revenue recognition and matching principles are followed.

Adjusting entries make it possible to report on the balance sheet the appropriate assets, liabilities, and owner's equity at the statement date and to report on the income statement the proper net income (or loss) for the period.

Any prepaid asset account, such as Prepaid Insurance or Prepaid Rent (where more than a month has been paid), must be adjusted.

Supplies that have been used up will require an adjustment to the Supplies account. Depreciation on productive facilities (fixed assets), will have to be adjusted and expensed. Unearned revenue and accrued expenses, such as salaries and wages, must be adjusted.

These adjustments require General Journal entries, just like those you did in the first chapter.

PREPAID ASSETS (RENT AND INSURANCE)

Many companies pay their office rent and insurance premiums in advance. Insurance companies may require that an entire year of premiums be paid ahead and many landlords also require several months or more of rent to be paid in advance. As the month goes by, much of the insurance and rent payment becomes an expense instead of an asset.

First, you pay the rent in advance.

On January 1, 2005, Softbyte Computer Software pays the Phoenix Group $12,000 for office rent for the entire year, January 1 to December 31. This results in an initial debit of $12,000 to the asset account Prepaid Rent and a credit to Cash. Starting January 31, and at the end of each month following until December 31 you will debit Rent Expense for $1,000 ($12,000 / 12 months) and credit your asset account called Prepaid Rent. Because this is a prepaid expense, cash is not affected.

The same procedure is used for recording Insurance. On January 1, you pay J. Smith Lanier $6,000 for the insurance premium for a year's coverage - a debit to the asset Prepaid Insurance and a credit to cash. Each month during the year, you expense $500 as Insurance expense (a debit) and deduct that amount from the asset account Prepaid Insurance (a credit).

Make the entries:

Step 1: Launch Peachtree Complete Accounting and open "Softbyte Computer Software" if it is not already open.

Step 2: You will be required to create three new accounts. You learned how to create accounts in Chapter 2. Click on Maintain, on the main menu bar and then Chart of Accounts.

Step 3: Use account no. 130 for Prepaid Insurance, the Account Type is "Other Current Assets"; account no. 131 for Prepaid Rent, the Account Type is "Other Current Assets" and account no. 722 for Insurance Expense; the Account Type is "Expenses". (Rent Expense already exists.) The first account, Prepaid Insurance is shown in Figure 3.3.

56

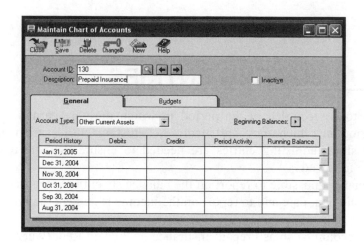

Figure 3. 3 New Account Creation - Prepaid Insurance

Step 4: After the accounts are created, use January 1, 2005, as the date and "Trans #5.1" as the transaction number in the reference box.

Step 5: Make the combination General Journal entry to record both the prepayment of Insurance for $6,000 and the prepayment of Rent for $12,000. The transaction is illustrated in Figure 3.4.

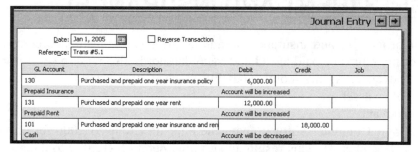

Figure 3. 4 Compound Journal Entry for prepaid assets.

A SPECIAL NOTE BEFORE CONTINUING

You used "Trans 5.1" for the transaction number because you wanted the entry to "fit in" the order of General Journal entries that have already been created for "Softbyte." If you looked at the "Edit" command while you were in the General Journal entry section, you would see where this entry was made.

Also, if you look at the General Ledger Report or the Balance Sheet, you will notice that the Cash account (#101) now has a credit balance. And, realize that because "Softbyte" is a new company, new accounts must be created along the way. You would only create the appropriate expense account once. You do not have to create new accounts every accounting period.

MAKING THE ADJUSTMENTS

On January 31, 2005, you must make the adjustment to recognize $500 of Prepaid Rent that was used up (expensed) and $500 of Prepaid Insurance that has expired (expensed). No cash was involved because the accounts were prepaid on January 1.

Open the General Journal entry window.

Step 1: Change the date to read January 31. The transaction number is "Trans #11".

Step 2: Debit the expense account #722, Insurance Expense for $500 and Credit the asset account #130 Prepaid Insurance for $500.

Step 3: Make sure your entry matches the one in Figure 3.5.

Step 4: Correct any errors and post your entry.

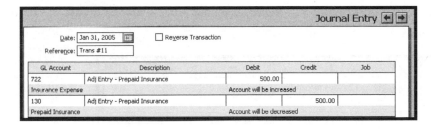

Figure 3. 5 Adjusting Journal entry for Prepaid Insurance

Follow the same procedure to post the adjusting entry for Prepaid Rent.

Step 1: Be sure the General Journal entry window is open and ready for the next transaction

Step 2: Make sure the date reads January 31. The transaction number is "Trans #12".

Step 3: Debit the expense account no. 729, Rent Expense for $1,000 and credit the asset account #131 Prepaid Rent for $1,000.

Step 4: Make sure your entry matches the one in Figure 3.6.

Step 5: If correct, post your entry.

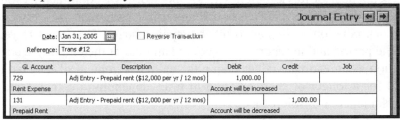

Figure 3. 6 Adjusting entry for Prepaid Rent

SUPPLIES

In Chapter 1, one of the entries you made for Softbyte Computer Software was the purchase of Supplies on account for $1,600. Normally, at the end of the interim fiscal periods and fiscal periods, the value of ending inventory is determined by an audit process. If the you find that there is $1,250 worth of supplies left in the supply closet. That means that $350 of your supplies has been used up, resulting in an expense.

An adjusting general journal entry needs to be made to reflect the correct balance of the asset Supplies for the beginning of February. The entry is simple: a debit (increasing) entry is made to the account Supplies Expense account and a credit is made (decreasing) to the Supplies (asset) account.

Step 1: Create the Supplies Expense account, Account No. 631, Account Type is "Expense".

Step 2: January 31, 2005, is the date. You are now on Transaction 13 (Trans #13).

Step 3: Create a General Journal entry to debit (increase) the Supplies Expense account by $350 and credit (decrease) the asset account Supplies by the same amount.

Step 4: The entry is shown in Figure 3.7. Make sure your work matches Figure 3.8 before posting the account.

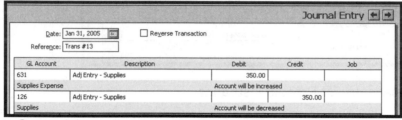

Figure 3. 7 General Journal entry adjusting supplies.

DEPRECIATION

Earlier in the Softbyte sequence, Softbyte purchased $7,000 worth of equipment. From an accounting standpoint, the equipment purchased is viewed as a long-term prepayment for services. The need for periodic adjustment for depreciation is similar to other prepaid entries. You need to recognize the cost that has expired during the period and to report the unexpired amount at the end of the accounting period.

Recognize depreciation as an estimate rather than a factual measurement of the cost that has expired. The asset may be useful for a longer or shorter period of time, depending on such factors as actual use, deterioration due to the elements or obsolescence.

A common procedure in computing depreciation expense is to divide the cost of the asset by its useful life. For example, the computer equipment the company purchased for $7,000 should last about four years before it becomes figuratively worthless. Therefore, the yearly depreciation for the equipment will be ($7,000 / 4 yrs) $1,750 a year or ($7,000 / 48 mos) $146 a month with a slightly different amount expensed the last month.

Two new accounts need to be created - Accumulated Depreciation – Equipment that will be a contra-asset account, and Depreciation Expense – Equipment, that will be an expense account.

Before making the entries, you must create the two new accounts.

Step 1: Since the Accumulated Depreciation – Equipment account is related to the asset account Equipment, use account number 158. The account type is "Accumulated Depreciation".

Step 2: Create the new account.

Step 3: The expense account, "Depreciation Expense – Equipment" is a regular expense account. Use account No. 617, the account type is "Expense".

Step 4: Create the new account.

The entries to record depreciation expense are similar to ones you have done before.

Step 1: January 31, 2005, is still the date. You are now on Transaction 14.

Step 2: Create a General Journal entry to debit (increase) the Depreciation Expense – Equipment account by $146 and credit (decrease) the contra asset account Accumulated Depreciation – Equipment by the same amount.

Step 3: The entry is shown in Figure 3.8. Make sure your work matches Figure 3.8 before posting the entry.

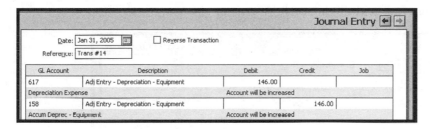

Figure 3. 8 Adjusting entry for depreciation of equipment

UNEARNED REVENUE

In the example of "Softbyte," several customers decided to enter into a contract agreement where they will pay $600 up front for six months of on site service. Five customers make their $600 payment, a total of $3,000. "Softbyte" recognizes the total amount as Unearned Revenue, a liability. When cash is received for a service not yet rendered the amount is considered a liability. Only after service has been performed will the liability be recognized as income or revenue. The service, represented by the $600 payment, is due to the client, thus the liability. The Unearned Revenue account is the only new account that must be created. Create the account using Account No. 209 for Unearned Service Revenues. Remember the 200 level of accounts represent liabilities. The account type is Other Current Liabilities.

Because cash was received for services yet to be rendered, you now must make a General Journal entry recognizing the $3,000. (Five Customers @ $600/ea = $3,000).

Step 1: Open the General Journal window.

Step 2: On January 1, 2005, the contracts were each signed and each customer wrote a check to "Softbyte" for $600. Since you are inserting another transaction, the transaction number will be 1.1 (putting the transaction near the top of the edit list).

Step 3: The Cash account, No. 101 will be debited (increased) by $3,000. Be sure to add the explanation.

Step 4: The Unearned Service Revenue account, No. 209 will be credited (also increased) by the same amount.

Step 5: Make sure your entries match the ones in Figure 3.8.

Step 6: Correct any mistakes and post your entry.

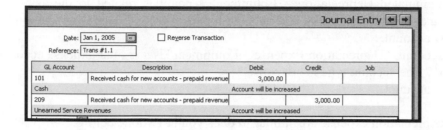

Figure 3. 9 Entry for receiving cash and recognizing unearned income.

At the end of January, "Softbyte" must make an adjusting entry to the revenue account recognizing the prepaid revenues earned. Make the entries:

Step 1: Change the date to January 31. Your transaction number is "15".

Step 2: The Unearned Revenue account, Account No. 209 must be debited (decreased) by $500.

Step 3: The Service Revenue account, Account No. 401, must be increased (credited) by $500.

Step 4: Check your entry with Figure 3.10.

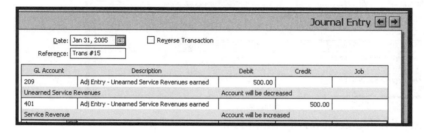

Figure 3. 10 Adjusting entry for Unearned Service Revenue.

ACCRUED SALARIES

There is one other adjusting entry to be considered before you wrap up Chapter 3. Most companies pay their employees every week or every two weeks. For accounting purposes it would be helpful if you paid your employees on Friday and the last day of every month ended on a Friday. But, it rarely happens that way. In fact, the last day of the month often falls in the middle of the week. To keep accurate accounting and payroll records (payroll will be covered in another chapter) you must recognize the payroll expenses when they occur even though you are not issuing a paycheck at that time. You recognize what is due as a liability. When the actual payroll is paid, the liability is eliminated and the total payroll is paid.

To illustrate - Looking at the calendar for January 2005, the last payday for Softbyte was Friday, January 28, 2005. The next payday will be in two weeks on Friday, February 11, 2005. The total payroll for Softbyte is $1,200 for a fourteen day pay period. Softbyte's employees only work five days a week. There are 14 total days in the last January 2005 pay period, which is not addressed here, and 1 day working day left in January which will be paid in the first pay period of February. If you divide the total payroll, $1,200, by the 10 working days in the pay period, you determine that the daily payroll cost is $120. So you have an adjusting entry for unpaid payroll obligations of $120. This is the amount that must be expensed in January and recognized as a payable until it is paid on the next payday, February 11, 2005.

To make the entry:

Step 1: For the General Journal entry, use the date January 31, 2005. Use transaction #16, (Trans #16), On January 31, the salaries for the last day of the month represent an accrued expense and a related liability. Although you call these entries *accruals* you do not put *accrual* in any of the account titles.

Step 2: The adjusting entry will be a debit to Account No. 726, Salaries Expense for $120.

Step 3: The corresponding credit will be to the liability Account No. 212, Salaries Payable for $120.

Step 4: The entry is shown below in Figure 3.10. Make sure your entry matches Figure 3.10.

Step 5: Correct any errors and post the entry.

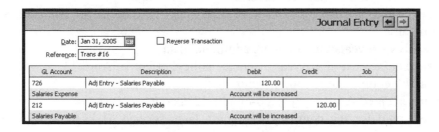

Figure 3. 11　Adjusting entry to recognize accrued payroll.

Since payroll for Softbyte is paid every two weeks, on February 11, 2005, employees will receive their paychecks. On that date, an entry will be made to debit (decrease) Salaries Payable by $120, debit (increase) Salaries Expense by $1,080 and credit (decrease) cash by $1,200.

Let's make the entry:

Step 1: Change the date to February 11, 2005. Ignore the entry for the transaction reference at this point.

Step 2: Make a compound General Journal entry:
  a.　Debiting (decrease) Salaries Payable by $120
  b.　Debiting (increase) Salaries Expense by $1,080.
  c.　Crediting (decrease) cash by $1,200.

Make sure your entries match those in Figure 3.12. Correct any errors and post your entry.

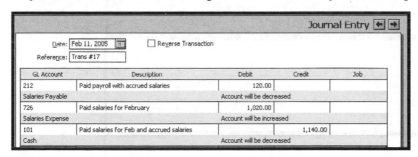

Figure 3. 12 Paying payroll Feb. 11, 2005

In Peachtree Complete Accounting, payroll is an automated process you will learn in a later chapter.

Demonstration Problem, Green Thumb Lawn Care Company, Directory "grethula"

Terry Thomas opened the Green Thumb Lawn Care Company on April 1st. At April 30th, the General Ledger Trial Balance reflected the following balances for selected accounts:

No. 120	Prepaid Insurance	$3,600
No. 157	Equipment	28,000
No. 201	Notes Payable	20,000
No. 209	Unearned Revenue	4,200
No. 400	Service Revenue	1,800

All beginning balances and all other accounts have been established in the Student Data Set for Green Thumb Lawn Care Company.

End of the month analysis reveals the following additional data:

1. Prepaid insurance is the cost of a 2-year insurance policy, effective April 1.
2. Depreciation on the equipment is $500 per month.
3. The note payable is dated April 1st. It is a 6-month, 12% note.
4. Seven customers paid for the company's 6-month lawn service package of $600 beginning in April. These customers were also serviced in April.
5. Lawn services provided other customers but not billed on April 30th totaled $1,500.

Instructions:

a. Open Green Thumb Lawn Care from your Student Data Set into Peachtree.
b. Journalize in the General Journal the adjusting entries for the month of April.

Solution to Demonstration Problem

Adjusting Entries #1 through 5:

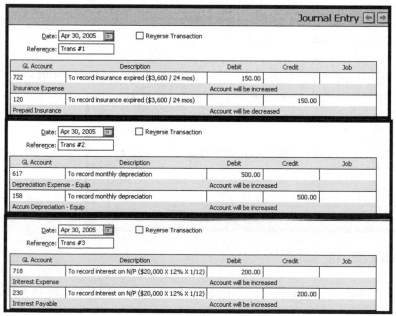

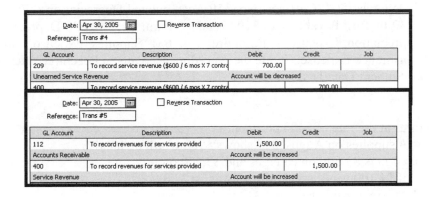

P3-2B, Spring River Resort, Directory "sprrivre"

Spring River Resort opened for business on June 1, 2005, with eight air-conditioned units. Its trial balance before adjustments on August 31st is as follows:

Spring River Resort

Trial Balance

August 31, 2005

Account No.		Debit	Credit
101	Cash	$19,600	
126	Supplies	3,300	
130	Prepaid Insurance	6,000	
140	Land	25,000	
143	Cottages	125,000	
149	Furniture	26,000	
201	Accounts Payable		6,500
208	Unearned Rent		7,400
275	Mortgage Payable		80,000
301	P. Orbis, Capital		100,000
306	P. Orbis, Drawing	5,000	
429	Rent Revenue		80,000
622	Repair Expense	3,600	
726	Salaries Expense	51,000	
732	Utilities Expense	9,400	
		$273,900	$273,900

In addition to those accounts listed on the trial balance above, the chart of accounts for Spring River Resort should also contain the following accounts and account numbers: No. 112 Accounts Receivable, No. 144 Accumulated Depreciation – Cottages, No. 150 Accumulated Depreciation – Furniture, No. 212 Salaries Payable, No. 230 Interest Payable, No. 310, Retained Earnings, No. 620 Depreciation Expense – Cottages, No. 621 Depreciation Expense – Furniture, No. 631 Supplies Expense, No. 718 Interest Expense, and No. 722 Insurance Expense. Create the preceding accounts in Peachtree after loading Spring River Resort from your Student Data Disk.

Other data:
1. Insurance expires at the rate of $400 per month.
2. The inventory of supplies on August 31st shows $900 worth on hand.
3. Annual depreciation is $3,600 on cottages and $2,400 on furniture.
4. Unearned rent of $4,100 was earned prior to August 31st
5. Salaries of $400 were unpaid at August 31st.
6. Rentals of $800 were due from tenants on August 31st. (Use Accounts Receivable)
7. The mortgage interest rate is 9% per year. It was taken out on August 1st.

Instructions:
a. Journalize the adjusting entries on August 31 for the 3-month period June 1 – August 31 in the General Journal using Peachtree Complete Accounting.
b. Print a general ledger, and trial balance after the adjusting entries are made.
c. Print an Income Statement, a Statement of Retained Earnings, and a Balance Sheet as of August 31st.

P3-5B, Beck Equipment Repair, Directory "becequre"

On September 1, 2005, the account balances of Beck Equipment Repair were as follows:

No.	Debits		No.	Credits	
101	Cash	4,880	154	Accumulated Depreciation	1,500
112	Accounts Receivable	3,520	201	Accounts Payable	3,400
126	Supplies	2,000	209	Unearned Service Revenue	1,400
153	Store Equipment	15,000	212	Salaries Payable	500
			301	J. Beck, Capital	18,600
		$25,400			$25,400

During September the following summary transactions were completed:

Sept 8 Paid $1,400 for salaries due employees, of which $900 is for September.
10 Received $1,200 cash from customers on account.
12 Received $3,400 cash for services performed in September.
15 Purchased store equipment on account $3,000.
17 Purchased supplies on account $1,200.
20 Paid creditors $4,500 on account.
22 Paid September rent $500.
25 Paid salaries $1,050.
27 Performed services on account and billed customers for services rendered $1,200.
29 Received $650 from customers for future service.

Adjustment data consists of:
1. Supplies on hand $1,700
2. Accrued salaries payable $400
3. Depreciation is $200 per month
4. Unearned service revenue of $1,450 is earned

Instructions:

a. Open Beck Equipment Repair in Peachtree from your Student Data Set.
b. Verify the beginning balances and the chart of accounts.
c. Journalize in Peachtree's General Journal the transactions for September.
d. Journalize in Peachtree's General Journal the adjusting entries for September.
e. Run a General Journal, an Income Statement, a Retained Earnings Statement, and a Balance Sheet for Beck Equipment Repair as of September 30th.

CHAPTER 4

Completion of the Accounting Cycle

OBJECTIVES

- State the required steps in the accounting cycle.
- Describe the content and purpose of a post closing trial balance

- Explain the process of changing the accounting period
- Explain the process of closing the books.

USING A WORK SHEET

Two somewhat different but similar trial balance reports are available in Peachtree. The General Ledger Trial Balance, Figure 4.2, shows each account and its balance as of the date or period you select. The Working Trial Balance, Figure 4.4, provides blank spaces so you can fill in any adjusting trial balance information. These reports are designed to help you make adjustments to account balances. These reports are simply devices used to make it easier to prepare adjusting entries and to guide you in the process of preparing your financial statements.

In the "manual" accounting process, financial statements are prepared directly from the worksheets prepared by the bookkeeper. The account balances of these worksheets are gathered directly from the General Ledger and the postings from the General Journal. In an automated system, such as Peachtree, the balances of the General Ledger accounts are continually updated as entries are made resulting in statement balances being continually updated. At the end of the accounting period however, general journal adjusting entries must be made as you did in the previous chapter.

THE GENERAL LEDGER TRIAL BALANCE

Step 1: Click on Reports on the Menu Bar, then General Journal. You will be presented with the Select A Report menu screen.

Step 2: General Ledger should be highlighted on the left side under Report Area by default. If not, make sure it is highlighted before selecting General Ledger Trial Balance as illustrated in Figure 4.1.

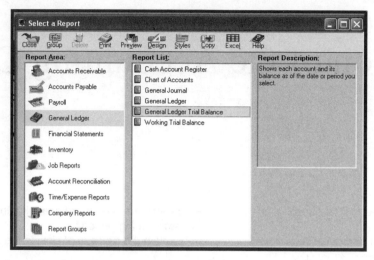

Figure 4. 1 Select a report menu screen.

Step 3: You may click the "Preview" icon on the tool bar to read the report on the screen or click the "Print" icon on the tool bar to produce a paper copy of the report.

The General Ledger Trial Balance for Softbyte Computer Company is shown in Figure 4.2.

Softbyte Computer Software
General Ledger Trial Balance
As of Jan 31, 2005

Filter Criteria includes: Report order is by ID. Report is printed in Detail Format.

Account ID	Account Description	Debit Amt	Credit Amt
101	Cash		6,950.00
112	Accounts Receivable	1,400.00	
126	Supplies	1,250.00	
130	Prepaid Insurance	5,500.00	
131	Prepaid Rent	11,000.00	
157	Equipment	7,000.00	
158	Accum Depreciation - Equi		146.00
201	Accounts Payable		1,600.00
209	Unearned Service Revenu		2,500.00
212	Salaries Payable		120.00
301	R. Neal, Capital		15,000.00
305	Ray Neal, Drawing	1,300.00	
401	Service Revenue		5,200.00
610	Advertising Expense	370.00	
631	Supplies Expense	350.00	
722	Insurance Expense	646.00	
726	Salaries Expense	900.00	
729	Rent Expense	1,600.00	
732	Utilities Expense	200.00	
	Total:	**31,516.00**	**31,516.00**

Figure 4. 2 The General Ledger Trial Balance.

THE WORKING TRIAL BALANCE

Step 1: Click on Reports on the Menu Bar, then General Journal. You will be presented with the "Select A Report" menu screen.

Step 2: General Ledger should be highlighted on the left side under Report Area by default. If not, make sure it is highlighted before selecting Working Trial Balance.

Step 3: You may click the "Preview" icon on the tool bar to read the report on the screen or click the "Print" icon on the tool bar to produce a paper copy of the report.

A portion of The Working Trial Balance for Softbyte Computer Software is shown below in Figure 4.3, below.

Softbyte Computer Software
Working Trial Balance
As of Jan 31, 2005

Filter Criteria includes: Report order is by ID. Report is printed with Accounts having Zero Amounts and in Detail Format.

Account ID Account Description	Last FYE Bal	Current Bal	Debit Adj	Credit Adj	End Bal	Reference
101 Cash	0.00	-6,950.00	_____	_____	_____	_____
112 Accounts Receivable	0.00	1,400.00	_____	_____	_____	_____
126 Supplies	0.00	1,250.00	_____	_____	_____	_____
130 Prepaid Insurance	0.00	5,500.00	_____	_____	_____	_____
131 Prepaid Rent	0.00	11,000.00	_____	_____	_____	_____
157 Equipment	0.00	7,000.00	_____	_____	_____	_____
158 Accum Depreciation - Equi	0.00	-146.00	_____	_____	_____	_____
201 Accounts Payable	0.00	-1,600.00	_____	_____	_____	_____
209 Unearned Service Revenu	0.00	-2,500.00	_____	_____	_____	_____

Figure 4. 3 Portion of the Working Trial Balance for Softbyte Computer Software.

CHANGING ACCOUNTING PERIODS

In Peachtree Complete Accounting, accounting periods are set up when you create a new company. Once you have set up accounting periods, you cannot change the structure of the periods. You must wait until the end of a fiscal year, year-end closing before those changes can be made. In other words, you can only change the current accounting period within the established structure.

There are 26 accounting periods that can be opened in Peachtree. For example, you may have last year's history available for editing or adjusting throughout the current year. Or, you can be in the next year without closing this year. The current period is shown in the status bar at the bottom right of the Peachtree window as shown in Figure 4.4.

70

Figure 4. 4   Bottom of the Peachtree window showing the Current Accounting Period on the far right.

Step 1: From the Tasks menu, select System, and then Change Account Period from the submenu as illustrated in Figure 4.5.

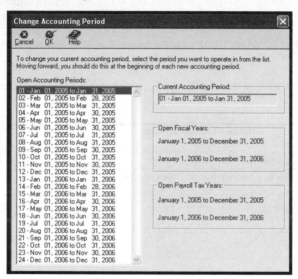

Figure 4. 5 Change Accounting Period submenu.

Step 2: Select the accounting you want to change to, and select OK.
Step 3: A message box will appear asking if you would like to print reports before continuing. Select "YES".
Step 4: A Print Reports window appears with the listing of suggested reports that you may wish to have printed paper copies. The window is shown in Figure 4.6.

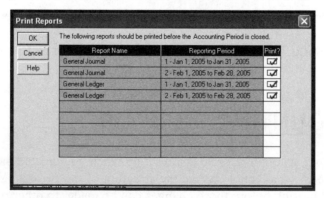

Figure 4. 6   The Print Reports menu.

In the sample company, Softbyte, you can select or deselect any of the default reports shown by allowing the checkmarks to remain or by clicking on them to remove one or more.

Step 5: In Softbyte, you can select or deselect any of the default reports shown by allowing the checkmarks to remain or by clicking on them to remove one or more.

Step 6: Select OK when you have chosen all the reports you want to print.

You can change the accounting period anytime you want by moving back and forth in the fiscal periods. The General Ledger will track your balances as of the current period dates. Peachtree Complete Accounting also will select the correct period in which to post a transaction by the transaction date. For example, you may enter a transaction in the future, but – you must change accounting periods to enter a "past" transaction.

AN ADDITIONAL WORD ABOUT CHANGING ACCOUNTING PERIODS

In the manual accounting process, it is necessary to distinguish between temporary and permanent accounts. Temporary (or nominal) accounts relate only to a given accounting period. For example, all income statement accounts, income or revenue accounts with account numbers in the 400 – 499 range and expense accounts with account numbers in the 500+ range, in a manual system would be closed. Their balances would be "zeroed out". The Owner's Drawing account, which in Peachtree is considered an equity account "that closes" also falls into that category – one that is closed each month in a manual system.

In a manual system permanent or real accounts are accounts which will relate to one or more future accounting periods. These accounts remain open through fiscal periods and carry their balances over to the next period. Those accounts consist of all balance sheet accounts including Owner's Capital.

As discussed earlier, Peachtree keeps a "running" balance of all accounts. However, in many of the Peachtree reports, account balances are shown both as cumulative balances – those where the totals are added together month after month and a current period balance.

Let's look at an example:

Step 1: Open the company "Bellwether Garden Supply" found within your Student Data Set. Bellwether Garden Supply is a generic company that Peachtree Complete Accounting uses for demonstration purposes.

Step 2: The company should open in the default accounting period of "Period 3 – March 1, 2007 – March 31, 2007. Make sure the accounting period is correct before continuing.

Step 3: Make a printed copy of "Bellwether's Income Statement. A portion, the revenue section, is shown in Figure 4.8, following.

Bellwether Garden Supply Income Statement For the Three Months Ending March 31, 2007					
	Current Month			Year to Date	
Revenues					
Sales	$ 5,175.00	7.83	$	8,250.95	10.16
Sales - Aviary	5,388.13	8.15		6,487.91	7.99
Sales - Books	149.75	0.23		3,654.60	4.50
Sales - Ceramics	0.00	0.00		0.00	0.00
Sales - Equipment	2,269.77	3.44		7,031.39	8.66
Sales - Food/Fert	367.60	0.56		697.24	0.86
Sales - Furntiture	30,000.00	45.41		30,000.00	36.96
Sales - Hand Tools	199.92	0.30		801.64	0.99
Sales - Landscape Services	2,059.53	3.12		2,939.34	3.62
Sales - Miscellaneous	18,199.98	27.55		18,199.98	22.42
Sales - Nursery	1,182.48	1.79		1,420.34	1.75
Sales - Pots	510.58	0.77		580.53	0.72
Sales - Seeds	223.17	0.34		766.24	0.94
Sales - Soil	351.48	0.53		365.46	0.45
Sales - Statuary	0.00	0.00		0.00	0.00
Sales - Topiary	0.00	0.00		0.00	0.00
Interest Income	0.00	0.00		0.00	0.00
Other Income	0.00	0.00		0.00	0.00
Finance Charge Income	0.00	0.00		0.00	0.00
Sales Returns and Allowances	0.00	0.00		0.00	0.00
Sales Discounts	(5.80)	(0.01)		(19.52)	(0.02)
Total Revenues	66,071.59	100.00		81,176.10	100.00

Figure 4. 7 Income Statement for Bellwether Garden Supply.

In the first column, each of the income sources for Bellwether is listed. The next columnar heading is for the current month, which is the 3rd accounting period ending on March 31, 2007. Each figure, going down the first column, is the monthly balance of that particular account. The second column shows the percentage of the total of that month.

The second set of columns, Year To Date, shows the balances of the accounts from January 1, 2007 up to when the statement was requested. If a previous accounting period had been selected, each of the columns would reflect balances based on that particular date.

Account balances are continually updated and carried over to Peachtree's balance sheet. A manual carryover of the previous month's balances is not needed for the balance sheet.

There is one section on a Peachtree balance sheet that required discussion. Look at the capital section of Bellwether's Balance sheet. It is illustrated below in Figure 4.8.

Capital		
Common Stock	5,000.00	
Paid-in Capital	100,000.00	
Retained Earnings	189,037.60	
Net Income	(3,052.23)	
Total Capital		290,985.37
Total Liabilities & Capital	$	354,718.91

Figure 4. 8   The Capital portion of Bellwether Garden Supply's balance sheet.

Bellwether is a corporation, which requires a section for Common Stock and Paid In Capital. Corporate accounting will be covered later. The Retained Earnings account is the amount of Net Income that has been retained by the company from prior periods. The Net Income figure represents the current net income which is the same net income figure shown on your print out of the income statement in the previous exercise. The figure will get added to the Retained Earnings figure in the next accounting period.

Demonstration Problem, Watson Answering Service, Directory "watansse"

Open Watson Answering Service on your Student Data Disk. Run a General Ledger Trial Balance. You will be presented with the following unadjusted General Ledger Trial Balance.

Watson Answering Service
General Ledger Trial Balance
As of Aug 31, 2005

Filter Criteria includes: Report order is by ID. Report is printed in Detail Format.

Account ID	Account Description	Debit Amt	Credit Amt
101	Cash	5,400.00	
112	Accounts Receivable	2,800.00	
120	Prepaid Insurance	2,400.00	
126	Supplies	1,300.00	
157	Equipment	60,000.00	
201	Notes Payable - Long term		40,000.00
202	Accounts Payable		2,400.00
301	Ray Watson, Capital		30,000.00
305	Ray Watson, Drawing	1,000.00	
400	Service Revenue		4,900.00
610	Advertising Expense	400.00	
726	Salaries Expense	3,200.00	
732	Utilities Expense	800.00	
	Total:	77,300.00	77,300.00

Other data consists of the following:

1. Insurance expires at the rate of $200 per month.
2. There is $1,000 of supplies on hand at August 31.
3. Monthly depreciation is $900 on the equipment.
4. Interest of $500 has accrued during August on the notes payable.

Instructions:

a. Based on the above data, enter the necessary General Journal transactions to adjust the August 2005 month end balances assuming $5,000 of the notes payable is now a current liability.
b. Check your work by printing a General Ledger Trial Balance.
c. Print an Income Statement, a Statement of Retained Earnings, and a Classified Balance Sheet for the month ended August 31, 2005.

Solution To Demonstration Problem

Adjusting Entries in the General Journal:

			Journal Entry ← →	

Date: Aug 31, 2005 ☐ Reverse Transaction
Reference: Trans #1

GL Account	Description	Debit	Credit	Job
718	Adj Entry - Prepaid insurance	200.00		
Interest Expense		Account will be increased		
120	Adj Entry - Prepaid insurance		200.00	
Prepaid Insurance		Account will be decreased		

Date: Aug 31, 2005 ☐ Reverse Transaction
Reference: Trans #2

GL Account	Description	Debit	Credit	Job
631	Adj Entry - Supplies Expense ($1,300 - $1,000)	300.00		
Supplies Expense		Account will be increased		
126	Adj Entry - Supplies Expense ($1,300 - $1,000)		300.00	
Supplies		Account will be decreased		

Date: Aug 31, 2005 ☐ Reverse Transaction
Reference: Trans #3

GL Account	Description	Debit	Credit	Job
615	Adj Entry - Depreciation Expense	900.00		
Depreciation Expense		Account will be increased		
158	Adj Entry - Depreciation Expense		900.00	
Accum Deprec - Equipment		Account will be increased		

Date: Aug 31, 2005 ☐ Reverse Transaction
Reference: Trans #4

GL Account	Description	Debit	Credit	Job
718	Adj Entry - Interest Expense	500.00		
Interest Expense		Account will be increased		
230	Adj Entry - Interest Expense		500.00	
Interest Payable		Account will be increased		

General Journal entry transferring $5,000 of Notes Payable from the Long Term Liability classification to the Notes Payable account classified as a Current Liability. This transaction makes $5,000 of Notes Payable a current liability, payable within a year.

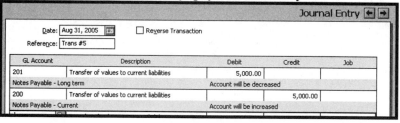

		Journal Entry ← →	

Date: Aug 31, 2005 ☐ Reverse Transaction
Reference: Trans #5

GL Account	Description	Debit	Credit	Job
201	Transfer of values to current liabilities	5,000.00		
Notes Payable - Long term		Account will be decreased		
200	Transfer of values to current liabilities		5,000.00	
Notes Payable - Current		Account will be increased		

General Ledger Trial Balance

Watson Answering Service
General Ledger Trial Balance
As of Aug 31, 2005

Filter Criteria includes: Report order is by ID. Report is printed in Detail Format.

Account ID	Account Description	Debit Amt	Credit Amt
101	Cash	5,400.00	
112	Accounts Receivable	2,800.00	
120	Prepaid Insurance	2,200.00	
126	Supplies	1,000.00	
157	Equipment	60,000.00	
158	Accum Deprec - Equipmen		900.00
200	Notes Payable - Current		5,000.00
201	Notes Payable - Long term		35,000.00
202	Accounts Payable		2,400.00
230	Interest Payable		500.00
301	Ray Watson, Capital		30,000.00
305	Ray Watson, Drawing	1,000.00	
400	Service Revenue		4,900.00
610	Advertising Expense	400.00	
615	Depreciation Expense	900.00	
631	Supplies Expense	300.00	
718	Interest Expense	700.00	
726	Salaries Expense	3,200.00	
732	Utilities Expense	800.00	
	Total:	**78,700.00**	**78,700.00**

The Income Statement

Watson Answering Service
Income Statement
For the Eight Months Ending August 31, 2005

	Current Month			Year to Date	
Revenues					
Service Revenue	$ 4,900.00	100.00	$	4,900.00	100.00
Total Revenues	4,900.00	100.00		4,900.00	100.00
Cost of Sales					
Total Cost of Sales	0.00	0.00		0.00	0.00
Gross Profit	4,900.00	100.00		4,900.00	100.00
Expenses					
Advertising Expense	400.00	8.16		400.00	8.16
Depreciation Expense	900.00	18.37		900.00	18.37
Supplies Expense	300.00	6.12		300.00	6.12
Interest Expense	700.00	14.29		700.00	14.29
Insurance Expense	0.00	0.00		0.00	0.00
Salaries Expense	3,200.00	65.31		3,200.00	65.31
Utilities Expense	800.00	16.33		800.00	16.33
Total Expenses	6,300.00	128.57		6,300.00	128.57
Net Income	$ (1,400.00)	(28.57)	$	(1,400.00)	(28.57)

The Statement of Retained Earnings

Watson Answering Service
Statement of Retained Earnings
For the Eight Months Ending August 31, 2005

Beginning Retained Earnings	$	0.00
Adjustments To Date		0.00
Net Income		(1,400.00)
Subtotal		(1,400.00)
Ray Watson, Drawing		(1,000.00)
Ending Retained Earnings	$	(2,400.00)

The Balance Sheet

```
                            Watson Answering Service
                                 Balance Sheet
                                August 31, 2005

                                    ASSETS

Current Assets
Cash                          $        5,400.00
Accounts Receivable                    2,800.00
Prepaid Insurance                      2,200.00
Supplies                               1,000.00

Total Current Assets                                    11,400.00

Property and Equipment
Equipment                             60,000.00
Accum Deprec - Equipment                (900.00)

Total Property and Equipment                            59,100.00

Other Assets

Total Other Assets                                           0.00

Total Assets                                    $       70,500.00


                            LIABILITIES AND CAPITAL

Current Liabilities
Notes Payable - Current       $        5,000.00
Accounts Payable                       2,400.00
Interest Payable                         500.00

Total Current Liabilities                                7,900.00

Long-Term Liabilities
Notes Payable - Long term             35,000.00

Total Long-Term Liabilities                             35,000.00

Total Liabilities                                       42,900.00

Capital
Ray Watson, Capital                   30,000.00
Ray Watson, Drawing                   (1,000.00)
Net Income                            (1,400.00)

Total Capital                                           27,600.00

Total Liabilities & Capital                     $       70,500.00
```

P4-2B, Mr. Watson Company, Directory "mrwatcom"

As of December 31, 2005, the adjusted trial balance of the "work sheet" for Mr. Watson Company is as follows:

Mr. Watson Company
Work Sheet
For the year ended December 31, 2005

Account No.	Account Titles	Adjusted Trial Balance Dr.	Cr.
101	Cash	20,800	
112	Accounts Receivable	16,200	
126	Supplies	2,300	
130	Prepaid Insurance	4,400	
151	Office Equipment	44,000	
152	Accumulated Depreciation – Office Equipment		18,000

200	Notes Payable - Noncurrent		20,000
201	Accounts Payable		8,000
212	Salaries Payable		2,600
230	Interest Payable		1,000
301	M. Watson, Capital		36,000
306	M. Watson, Drawing	12,000	
400	Service Revenue		79,800
610	Advertising Expense	12,000	
631	Supplies Expense	3,700	
711	Depreciation Expense	6,000	
722	Insurance Expense	4,000	
726	Salaries Expense	39,000	
905	Interest Expense	1,000	
		165,400	165,400

Instructions:

a. Run a General Ledger Balance Sheet to check the accuracy of the beginning balances.

b. Journalize the recognition of the current notes payable. Account 210 is Notes Payable - Current.

c. Run an Income Statement, Retained Earnings Statement and a Balance Sheet for the current period.

P4-5B, Young's Carpet Cleaners, Directory "youcarcl"

Mike Young opened Young's Carpet Cleaners on March 1, 2005. During March 2005, the following transactions were completed:

March	1	Invested $10,000 cash in the business.
	1	Purchased used truck for $6,000, paying $3,000 cash and the balance on account.
	3	Purchased cleaning supplies for $1,200 on account.
	5	Paid $1,800 cash on one-year insurance policy effective March 1.
	14	Billed customers $2,800 for cleaning services.
	18	Paid $1,500 cash on amount owed on truck and $500 on amount owed on cleaning supplies.
	20	Paid $1,800 cash for employee salaries.
	21	Collected $1,400 cash from customers billed on March 14.
	28	Billed customers $2,500 for cleaning services.
	31	Paid gas and oil for month on truck $200.
	31	Withdrew $700 cash for personal use.

The chart of accounts for Young's Carpet Cleaners includes: No. 101 Cash, No. 112 Accounts Receivable, No. 128 Cleaning Supplies, No. 130 Prepaid Insurance, No. 157 Equipment, No. 158 Accumulated Depreciation – Equipment, No. 201 Accounts Payable, No. 212 Salaries Payable, No. 301 M. Young, Capital, No. 306 M. Young, Drawing, No. 310 Retained Earnings, No. 400 Service Revenue, No. 633 Gas & Oil Expense, No. 634 Cleaning Supplies Expense, No. 711 Depreciation Expense, No. 722 Insurance Expense, No. 726 Salaries Expense.

The chart of accounts has been created and the beginning balances have been entered. Print a Trial Balance and verify the beginning balances.

78

Instructions:

a. Journalize and post the March transactions as presented above.

b. Prepare a General Ledger Trial Balance as of March 31, 2005.

c. Enter the following adjusting entries:

1. Earned but unbilled revenue at March 31st was $700.
2. Depreciation on equipment for the month was $250.
3. One-twelfth of the insurance expired.
4. An inventory count shows $600 of cleaning supplies on hand at March 31st.
5. Accrued, but unpaid employee salaries were $500.

d. Print the General Journal showing your adjusting entries.

e. Prepare an Income Statement, Statement of Retained Earnings, and a Balance Sheet as of March 31, 2005.

CHAPTER 5

Accounting for Merchandising Operations

OBJECTIVES

- Identify the differences between a service enterprise and a merchandiser.
- Explain the entries for purchases under a perpetual inventory system.
- Explain the entries for sales revenues under a perpetual inventory system.

- Explain the steps in the accounting cycle for a merchandiser.
- Distinguish between a multiple step and a single step income statement.
- Explain the computation and the importance of gross profit.

MERCHANDISING OPERATIONS

Merchandisers are companies that purchase and sell directly to consumers. There are two types of merchandisers, retailers and wholesalers. Kmart, Safeway, and Toys "R" Us are retailers. On the other hand, merchandisers that sell to retailers are known as wholesalers. Walgreen's might buy goods from McKesson & Robbins, which is a wholesaler. The wholesaler United Stationers might sell office supplies to Office Depot. Walgreen's and Office Depot sell their goods to the consumer.

The steps in the accounting cycle for a merchandising company are the same as for a service enterprise with the addition of several additional accounts and entries.

Measuring net income for a merchandiser is similar as a service enterprise. For example, net income results from the matching of expenses with revenue. The primary source of revenue for a merchandiser is often referred to as sales revenue or just plain sales. There are two different expense categories in a merchandising enterprise: (1) The cost of goods sold and (2) operating expenses.

The cost of goods sold is the total cost of merchandise sold during the period. This expense is directly related to the revenue recognized when goods are sold. Sales revenue less cost of goods sold is called gross profit on sales. For example, when a calculator that costs $15 is sold for $25, the gross profit would be $10 on that item. Gross profit for a merchandise company is reported on the income statement. After gross profit is calculated, operating expenses are totaled and deducted to determine net income or loss.

In Peachtree Complete Accounting, following some preliminary effort, most of the work is done for you.

ENTERING VENDOR INFORMATION

A vendor is the seller, the merchant, the retailer, or the manufacturer that has goods, products or merchandise that you plan to buy, increase the price, and resale to your customers. In Peachtree Complete Accounting, before you can enter any merchandise to be sold, you must have a record of your vendors.

Step 1: Open the company "Beyer Video" from within your Student Data Set.

Step 2: Click on "Maintain" from the menu bar and then click on "Vendors" from the pull down menu. You should see the "Maintain Vendors" screen as shown in Figure 5.1 below.

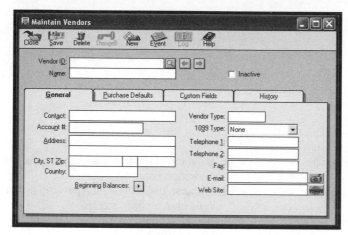

Figure 5. 1 Maintain Vendors window.

Each vendor selling to your company should be listed by Vendor ID and their company name.

Step 3: Enter the following information in the appropriate boxes. The first Vendor ID is V101. The vendor's name is Columbus Import Company.

The next set of text boxes on the left side of the form under the "General" tab include a contact name, usually your salesperson, a resource person you can talk with at the company, your account number, and the address information of the vendor.

Step 4: Enter the following information on the left side of the form: Alyce Merchant is your contact person, your account number at Columbus Import is 1347, Columbus Import's address is 1492 Queen Isabella Way in Madrid, GA 30341. Enter 555.555.1492 as the phone number.

For Vender Type you may assign a "type" such as "Utilities" for the phone company or the electric company and "Whlsler" for your vendors.

Next, it is particularly important to check to see if the vendor requires a Form 1099. An outside contractor earning more than $600 would require an IRS Form 1099. Columbus Import is not an outside contractor.

On the right side of the form, under the "General" tab you may include any additional information you may feel is necessary. It is not entered here to preclude unnecessary key strokes. If you do enter a URL or Web page information you may then click on the icon to send e-mail to a vendor or visit their Web site.

Step 5: Enter the following additional information on the left side of the form: the vendor type is "Wholesaler." You may abbreviate it as "Whlsler." Make sure every other wholesaler listed uses exactly the same abbreviation. Columbus Imports will not receive a 1099. The phone number for Columbus Imports is 555.555.1492.

Step 6: Your entry should match the one in Figure 5.2. Make any corrections before continuing.

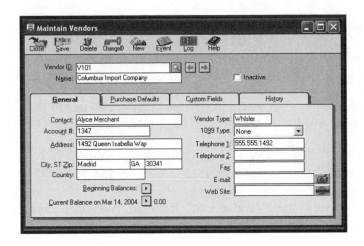

Figure 5. 2 The completed Maintain Vendors window.

Before continuing to enter additional information, you must assign a purchasing account to the vendor. Because your vendors are only wholesalers, you will assign the "Cost of Goods Sold," account no. 505 to the vendor.

Step 7: Click on the "Purchase Defaults" tab and enter account number 120 in the "Purchase Acct" text box as shown in Figure 5.3.

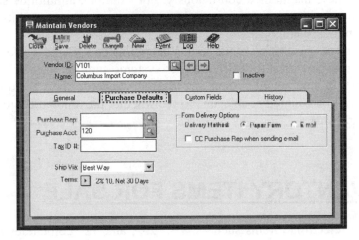

Figure 5. 3 Assigning a purchase account to the vendor.

Step 8: Click the "Save" icon on the toolbar to save your work.
Step 9: Using the information in Table 5.1, continue entering the three additional vendors.

Table 5. 1 Data for Vendors

Vendor ID	V102	V103	V104
Company	Southern Video	Atlanta Television	Ivory Group
Contact	John Pack	Peter Bell	Larry Ivory
Account #	1397	5812	9174
Address	753 Northside Dr.	99 Spring St.	23 Tuxedo Dr.
City/State/Zip	Atlanta, GA 30340	Alpharetta, GA 30041	Buckhead, GA 30300
Vendor Type	Whlsler	Whlsler	Whlsler
1099?	None	None	None
Telephone	555.555.4900	555.555.9713	555.555.3732

Step 10: When finished, review the "Vendor List" from the Accounts Payable report group to check for errors. Make any corrections before continuing.

THE PERPETUAL INVENTORY SYSTEM

The merchandise company keeps track of its inventory to determine what is available for sale and what has been sold. Most companies using an automated system such as Peachtree will very likely use a perpetual inventory system – one that is maintained continuously. For example, an antique store such as Great Gatsby's in Atlanta will keep individual inventory records for each item, its cost, and its retail price, either on their showroom floor or in their warehouse.

Under a perpetual inventory system, the cost of goods sold is determined each time a sale occurs. This system provides much better control over inventories than other systems such as the Periodic System, which is also discussed in your text. In a perpetual system, the inventory records show the quantities that should be on hand, the goods that can be counted at any time to see whether the amount of goods actually on hand agrees with the inventory records.

MAINTAINING INVENTORY ITEMS FOR SALE

Beyer Video sells several different electronic items such as: 19," 25", and 32" color televisions, DVD players, stereo VCRs, standard home stereo component units, surround/sound entertainment units, computer monitors, 52" projection televisions, and 74" flat screen wall entertainment centers. They also sell furniture for the three smaller models of color televisions. Each of these inventory items will have a specific inventory identification number and each is sold to Beyer Video through the vendors entered earlier. All of these items are considered stock items, meaning that Beyer Video carries these items on a continuous basis. Occasionally there will be some special items sold, but let's keep it simple for now.

Also notice that you are concerned here only with the sales price of an item and not the actual cost. You will concern yourself with cost when an actual purchase has been made. As you continue, each inventory item above must be documented in the system.

Step 1: On the menu bar, click on "Maintain," and then click "Inventory Items" on the pull down menu. You will be presented with the screen as shown in Figure 5.4 on the next page.

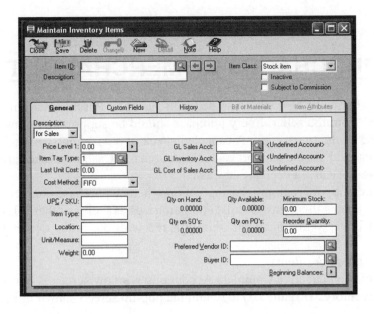

Figure 5. 4 Maintain Inventory Items window.

Step 2: The first item to be entered is the 19" Color TV. Enter TV19 as the Item ID. The description would be, of course, 19" Color TV. Leave the larger description box blank for now.

Step 3: In Peachtree, your items for retail may have five different pricing levels. In the example you will use only one. The sales price for the 19" Color TV is $225.

Step 4: Leave the units of measurement, item type and location blank. Those fields are not needed at this time.

Step 5: Enter 401 as the GL Sales Acct, enter 120 as the GL Inventory Acct, and 505 as the GL Cost of Sales Acct.

Step 6: Leave everything below the bar in its default state.

Step 7: Use Table 5.2 to continue entering inventory items. You have already completed the first entry.

Inventory Item	ID Number	Description	Sales Price
19" Color TV	TV19	19" Color TV	$225
25" Color TV	TV25	25" Color TV	$275
32" Color TV	TV32	32" Color TV	$325
DVD Player	DV01	DVD Player	$199
Stereo VCR	VC23	Stereo VCR	$299
Home Stereo	ST61	Home Stereo	$750
Surround Sound	SU85	Surround Sound	$950
Computer Monitor	MO17	Computer Monitor	$345
Projection System	PROJ	Projection System	$999
Flat Screen System	FLAT	Flat Screen System	$999
19" Cabinet	CAB19	19" Cabinet	$35
25" Cabinet	CAB25	25" Cabinet	$45
32" Cabinet	CAB32	32" Cabinet	$49

Table 5.2 Inventory Items

Step 7: Check your work for errors by running an "Item Price List" under the "Inventory Reports" heading.

RECORDING PURCHASES OF MERCHANDISE

Purchases of inventory may be made for cash or on accounts payable. Purchases are normally recorded when the goods are received from the seller. Every purchase should be supported by business documents that provide written evidence of the transaction. A canceled check or a cash register receipt indicating the items purchased and amounts paid should support each cash purchase. Cash purchases are recorded by an increase in Merchandise Inventory and a decrease in Cash.

A Purchase Order should support each purchasing action whether purchases on account or payment with cash. This document indicates the items, details, and purchases as well as other relevant information agreed to by the seller and buyer. This document should agree with the Sales Order generated by the seller.

To enter the purchase of inventory items:

Step 1: At the bottom of the Peachtree Complete Accounting window screen is a row of "Navigator" icons, click "Inventory" (Figure 5.5) to obtain the pop-up screen shown in Figure 5.6.

Figure 5. 5 Inventory Icon at bottom of Peachtree screen.

If the Navigator is not visible at the bottom of the screen you can invoke it through "Options" and select "View Navigation Aid".

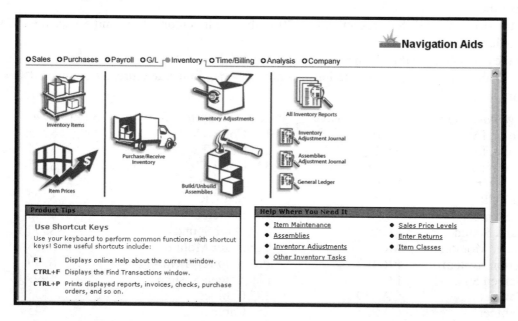

Figure 5. 6 Inventory Navigator icons

Step 2: Click on the "Purchases/Receive Inventory" icon (the back of the truck) in the middle section. You will then be presented with the form pictured in Figure 5.7.

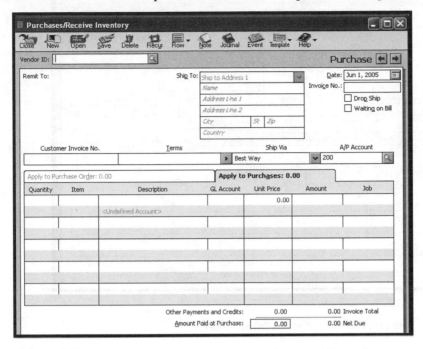

Figure 5. 7 Purchase/Receive Inventory form..

On June 3, 2005, Beyer Video purchased: two "19 Color TV's for $175/ea, six 25" Color TV's for $225/ea and four 32" color TV's for $300/ea from Southern Video. The Invoice Number is 0603 and the GL Account is the Merchandise Inventory Account No. 120. The Accounts Payable Account No. 200 has been defaulted for you.

Step 1: Referring to Figure 5.7, click on the magnifying glass at the vendor ID text box to get a pull-down listing of all of the available vendors. This is the list you composed earlier.

Step 2: Find and double click on vendor V102, Southern Video. Notice all of the information that has now been entered on the form for you, including billing and shipping addresses.

Step 3: Enter 0603 as the invoice number. Note that this is the invoice to be issued from the vendor.

Step 4: You will enter the purchasing information on the main body of the form. You'll be ordering three items from Southern Video. Under "quantity" enter 2.0. Again, the decimal must be entered.

Step 5: Tab to the next space, "Item," and click on the magnifying glass. The pull-down menu is a listing of all of the items available for your company, Beyer Video, to purchase and sell. Find and click on ID No. TV19, which is the 19" color TV. The General Ledger account number for Merchandise Inventory will be automatically entered for you. However, because the cost may change at will by the vendor, you must enter the individual item cost $175.00. The extended cost will be figured for you.

Step 6: Repeat the same procedure entering the order for six 25" Color Televisions and four 32" color TV's.

Step 7: Your entry should look like Figure 5.8. Make any necessary changes before saving your order.

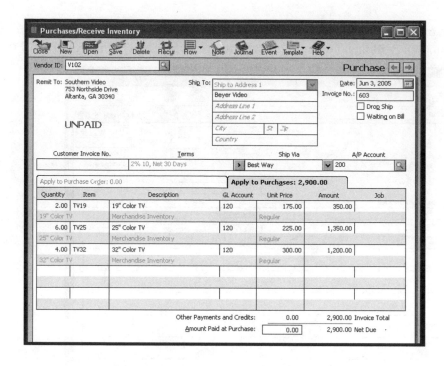

Figure 5. 8 Completed Purchase/Receive Inventory form.

Some of the prices that Beyer will pay for items will change. When you enter cost information into the system, it will be automatically default to that cost the next time you enter the item. If it is the same, no changes are needed. If the price (cost) does change, however, the new price must be entered for accurate accounting.

Table 5.3 Additional inventory purchases

Vendor	Date Purchased	Additional Purchases Invoice Number	Quantity	ID No.	Inventory Item	Cost
Ivory	June 10, 2005	610	30	DV01	DVD Player	$145
			30	VC23	Stereo VCR	$200
			10	ST61	Home Stereo	$500
			25	SU85	Surround Sound	$500
			5	MO17	Computer Monitor	$200
Atlanta Television	June 15, 2005	615	1	PROJ	Projection System	$750
			1	FLAT	Flat Screen System	$750
Columbus Imports	June 18, 2005	618	5	CAB19	19" Cabinet	$10
			10	CAB25	25" Cabinet	$20
			5	CAB32	32" Cabinet	$22
Southern Video	June 19, 2005	619	3	TV19	19" Color TV	$165
			2	TV25	25" Color TV	$230
			1	TV32	32" Color TV	$275

Ivory	June 21, 2005	621	5	ST61	DVD Player	$150
			2	VC23	Stereo VCR	$225
Columbus Imports	June 27, 2005	627	3	CAB19	19" Cabinet	$10
			2	CAB25	25" Cabinet	$20
			1	CAB32	32" Cabinet	$30

In order to check your work, run an inventory valuation report. A portion of the report is shown in Figure 5.9. The total value of inventory should be $36,140.

Beyer Video
Inventory Valuation Report
As of Jun 30, 2005
Filter Criteria includes: 1) Stock/Assembly. Report order is by ID. Report is printed with Truncated Long Descriptions.

Item ID Item Class	Item Description	Unit	Cost Method	Qty on Hand	Item Value	Avg Cost	% of Inv Value
CAB19 Stock item	19" Cabinet		FIFO	8.00	80.00		0.22
CAB25 Stock item	25" Cabinet		FIFO	12.00	240.00		0.66
CAB32 Stock item	32" Cabinet		FIFO	6.00	140.00		0.39
DV01 Stock item	DVD Player		FIFO	30.00	4,350.00		12.04
FLAT Stock item	Flat Screen System		FIFO	1.00	750.00		2.08
MO17 Stock item	Computer Monitor		FIFO	5.00	1,000.00		2.77
PROJ Stock item	Projection System		FIFO	1.00	750.00		2.08
ST61 Stock item	Home Stereo		FIFO	15.00	5,750.00		15.91
SU85 Stock item	Surround Sound		FIFO	25.00	12,500.00		34.59
TV19 Stock item	19" Color TV		FIFO	5.00	845.00		2.34

Figure 5. 9 Inventory Summary Valuation Report

ENTERING INVENTORY ADJUSTMENTS

Occasionally, you may need to record adjustments to on-hand quantities of inventory items. The inventory adjustment task makes it easy to make and track these adjustments.

There are two types of inventory adjustments, increases in quantity and decreases in quantity. For an increasing adjustment you will enter a positive quantity and can also enter a unit cost. This will increase your quantity on hand and total inventory value much as a purchase would. If you previously miscounted your inventory and now have more units on hand than recorded you would adjust up.

For a decreasing adjustment you will enter a negative quantity. You can not enter a unit cost. Peachtree will compute the cost value that these units are being removed in the same manner as a sale. A decreasing inventory adjustment will decrease the quantity on hand as well as the total value. For example, if something was stolen or broken, or, if inventory was previously over stated, you would adjust down.

When you make an adjustment, the Cost of Goods Sold, Inventory Total Value, and Inventory G/L accounts are all updated.

To record an inventory adjustment

Step 1: From the Tasks menu, select Inventory Adjustments or click on Inventory Adjustments in the center section of the Inventory Navigator.. Peachtree displays the inventory adjustment window as shown in Figure 5.10.

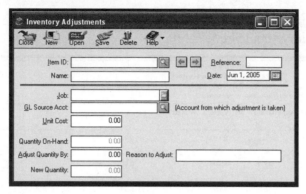

Figure 5. 10 Inventory Adjustment Window.

Step 2: Enter or select the Item ID you want to adjust. To display a list of existing items, type **?** in the field, or click on the magnifying glass. This can only be done if an item is classified as a stock item.

Step 3: The Reference field is for your use. The window is limited to 20 alphanumeric characters.

Step 4: Enter the date that the change in inventory occurred (or the date of the physical inventory count).

Step 5: The GL Source Account should be the Cost of Goods Sold Account. The other account affected by adjustments will be the Merchandise Inventory account.

Step 6: The Unit Cost default is the current cost of the item and must be positive.

Step 7: Enter the amount by which to adjust the quantity. The Quantity on Hand is already filled in, and Peachtree Complete Accounting calculates the New Quantity after you enter the adjustment.

Step 8: If you know the reason for the adjustment, for example, "Found in warehouse" or "Theft", you can enter it. Save the adjustment by selecting the appropriate button.

NOTE: If you made entries in the previous section, do not save (post) your work. Cancel the form and continue to the next activity. If you saved it, utilize OPEN to select and delete it.

ENTER AND APPLY A VENDOR CREDIT MEMO

Occasionally, a vendor may issue a credit to a purchaser. This happens when the purchaser is dissatisfied with the merchandise received or if the goods are damaged or defective. When a credit is issued the purchaser may keep the goods or return the goods to the seller, and get partial or full credit, as the seller and buyer both agree. The purchaser is then issued a Credit Memo (credits sellers A/R accounts) if the sale was made on credit or a cash refund if the purchase was for cash. This transaction is known as a Purchase Return and Allowance by the purchaser and a Sales Return and Allowance by the seller.

To record Purchases Returns and Allowances for credits use the Vendor Credit Memos form under Tasks or click on Purchases in the Purchases Navigator and then click on Credit Memos. Use the Apply to Invoice No. section of the form if merchandise is returned and use the Apply to Purchases if merchandise is not returned. In this example you will return the Projection System purchased from Atlanta Television on June 15th on June 29th for a credit on your account.

Step 1: From the Tasks menu, select Vendor Credit Memos form from either path option.

Step 2: Then enter the vendor ID, V103 for Atlanta Television.

Step 3: Enter the date of the credit, June 29, 2005, in the date window.

Step 4: Peachtree requires a value be entered in the Credit No. window, enter "1".

Step 5: There are text windows for the Terms, Return Authorization, and A/P Account. Default entries in light gray text are supplied by Peachtree and cannot be changed.

Step 6: When the vendor ID is entered, Peachtree will fill the Apply to Invoice No.: window on the Apply to Invoice No. panel with available invoices for the specific vendor. When the drop down arrow is clicked and an invoice is selected, all items on the invoice will appear available for adjustment. Select Invoice No. 0615 in this window and the Apply to Invoice No. panel will be populated with Invoicc 0615 data.

Step 7: In the Returned window on the line for Projection System enter a "1". Peachtree will extend the value into the Amount window when the active window is advanced.

Step 8: Since this is the only item requiring attention, click on the Save icon to save and post the credit memo.

Step 9: Check your work for any errors with the completed form shown in Figure 5.11.

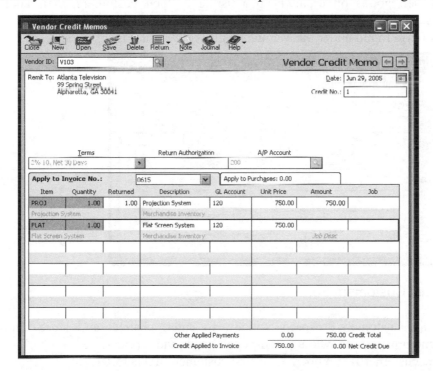

Figure 5. 11 Completed Vendor Credit Memo returning goods to the supplier for credit on account.

Had the vendor issued an allowance, he did not require the return of the merchandise, you would have used the Apply to Purchases panel and simply entered the GL Account for inventory, 120 in Beyer Video, and an amount as shown in Figure 5.12.

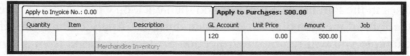

Figure 5. 12 Completed Vendor Credit Memo returning goods to the supplier for credit on account.

RECORDING THE SALES OF MERCHANDISE

Sales revenue, like service revenues, are recorded when earned. This is in accordance with the revenue recognition principle. Typically, sales revenues are earned when the goods are transferred from the seller to the buyer. At this point the sales transaction is completed and the sales price has been established.

Sales may be made on credit or for cash. Every sales transaction should be supported by a business document that provides written evidence of the sale. Cash register tapes provide evidence of cash sales. A sales invoice, such as the one generated by Peachtree and signed by the buyer provides support for a credit sale. The original copy of the invoice remains with the seller and the customer receives the copy. The invoice shows the date of sale, customer name, items sold, total sales price, and other relevant information.

Companies that sell goods on credit keep a listing of their customers, their addresses, contact information, credit limits, etc. Those entries are made in Peachtree using the Maintain Customer/Prospects Form found under the Maintain path as shown in Figure 5.13.

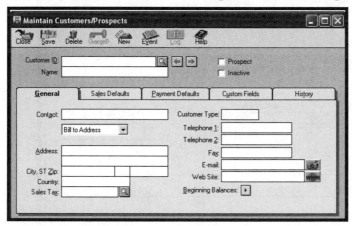

Figure 5. 13 Maintain Customers Form

Use the Maintain Customers/Prospects window to enter, change, and store information about customers, clients, and prospects to whom you may sell goods and services.

Step 1: Enter the customer ID number. Your first customer's ID is C101.

Step 2: Enter the customer's name in the Name box: Adam Zoula. The contact, in the next box is the same as the customer, Adam Zoula.

Step 3: Enter Mr. Zoula's address in the proper boxes: 347 Appling Drive., Atlanta, GA 30300.

Step 4: Ignore the Sales Tax box. That will be updated in the next chapter.

Step 5: For the sake of time and typing, you will leave the phone numbers, beginning balances, e-mail, Web sites and fax numbers blank for now.

Step 6: Click on the Sales Default tab and change the GL/Sales Account to Acct # 401/Sales.

Step 7: At the bottom of the form, click on the "Terms" button to get the window shown in Figure 5.13.

Step 8: Delete the check mark at "Use Standard Terms." Click on "Due in # days" and enter 30 in the net due days box and remove the values from the Discount in --- days and Discount percentage windows. See Figure 5.14.

Step 9: Change the credit limit to $5000.

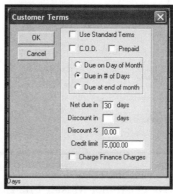

Figure 5. 14 Customer terms

Step 10: On the Sales Defaults tab select or enter 401 for the GL Sales Account value.

Step 11: Check your work with the completed forms below in Figure 5.15 before continuing with the remaining three customers in Table 5.4. Remember to change the terms and the credit limit under the "Sales Default" tab.

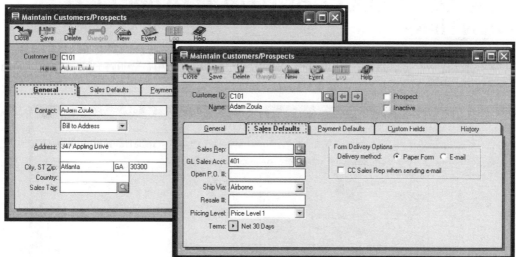

Figure 5. 15 Completed Customer entry.

Table 5.4 Additional customers to be included on Customer list.

	Additional Customers		
Customer ID	C102	C103	C104
Name	Betty Young	Cathy Xao	Donald Walace
Contact	Betty Young	Cathy Xao	Donald Walace
Address	987 Amigos Dr.	513 Lake Cir.	1397 Toyta Dr.
	Atlanta, GA 30300	Atlanta, GA 30340	Atlanta, GA 30302

After entering the customers above, run the Customer Master File list. The report is shown in Figure 5.16, following.

Beyer Video			
Customer Master File List			

Filter Criteria includes: Report order is by ID.

Customer ID Customer	Address line 1 Address line 2 City ST ZIP	Contact Telephone 1 Telephone 2 Fax Number	Tax Code Resale No Terms Cust Since
C101 Adam Zoula	347 Appling Drive Atlanta, GA 30300	Adam Zoula	 Net 30 Days 3/14/04
C102 Betty Young	987 Amigos Dr Atlanta, GA 30300	Betty Young	 Net 30 Days 3/14/04
C103 Cathy Xao	513 Lake Circle Atlanta, GA 30340	Cathy Xao	 Net 30 Days 3/14/04
C104 Donald Wallace	1397 Toyta Drive Atlanta, GA 30302	Donald Wallace	 Net 30 Days 3/14/04

Figure 5. 16 Customer Master File List Report

MAKING SALES IN PEACHTREE COMPLETE ACCOUNTING

Step 1: Click on the "Sales" icon on the navigation bar to get the "Sales" Navigation Aid shown in Figure 5.17.

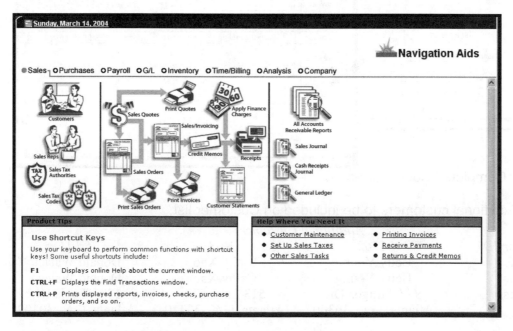

Figure 5. 17 Sales Navigation Aids.

Step 2: Click on the Sales/Invoices icon in the center screen or active the same dialog box through Tasks and Sales/Invoicing to get the Sales/Invoice form, as shown in Figure 5.18. The form is similar to the form used to enter inventory items into the system.

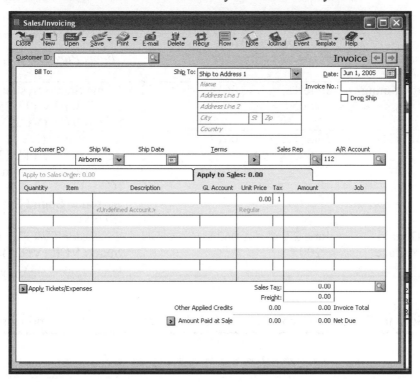

Figure 5. 18 The Sales/Invoice Form

Step 3: Enter the customer ID number for "Adam Zoula." C101 is the number. The invoice number is 0612. Information such as billing address will be entered by the default information entered earlier in the Customer Entry procedure.

Step 4: On June 12, 2005, Mr. Zoula is buying a 25" Color TV with the matching cabinet and a VCR. Enter the information on the form. It is correctly filled out in Figure 5.19. Suggestion: take advantage of the magnifying glass that gives you the drop down list of required information.

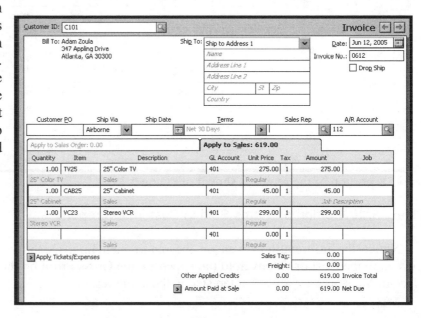

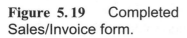

Figure 5.19 Completed Sales/Invoice form.

Table 5.5 lists the other items customers purchased during this accounting period. Make the entries for each customer following the previous instructions.

Table 5. 5 Additional Customer Purchases

Customer ID	Customer Name	Date of Purchase	Invoice Number	Items Purchased
C102	Betty Young	June 15, 2005	0615	1. Home Stereo System (ST61) 2. 25" Color TV (TV25) 3. Stereo VCR (VC23)
C103	Cathy Xao	June 17, 2005	0617	1. DVD Player (DV01) 2. 32" Color TV (TV32) 3. 32" Color TV Cabinet (CAB32) 4. Surround Sound System (SU85)
C104	Donald Wallace	June 27, 2005	0627	1. 25" Color TV (TV25) 2. Stereo VCR (VC23) 3. DVD Player (DV01)

Run a "Items Sold to Customers" report under the "Accounts Receivable" report list to check your

```
                                    Beyer Video
                               Items Sold to Customers
                       For the Period From Jun 1, 2005 to Jun 30, 2005
Filter Criteria includes: Report order is by Customer ID, Item ID. Report is printed in Detail Format.

Customer ID      Item ID         Qty      Amount    Cost of Sales  Gross Profit   Gross Margin
Name

C101             CAB25           1.00       45.00                       45.00       100.00
Adam Zoula       TV25            1.00      275.00       225.00          50.00        18.18
                 VC23            1.00      299.00       200.00          99.00        33.11

                                 3.00      619.00       425.00         194.00        31.34


C102             ST61            1.00      750.00       500.00         250.00        33.33
Betty Young      TV25            1.00      275.00       225.00          50.00        18.18
                 VC23            1.00      299.00       200.00          99.00        33.11

                                 3.00    1,324.00       925.00         399.00        30.14


C103             CAB32           1.00       49.00                       49.00       100.00
Cathy Xao        DV01            1.00      199.00       145.00          54.00        27.14
                 SU85            1.00      950.00       500.00         450.00        47.37
                 TV32            1.00      325.00       300.00          25.00         7.69

                                 4.00    1,523.00       945.00         578.00        37.95


C104             DV01            1.00      199.00       145.00          54.00        27.14
Donald Wallace   TV25            1.00      275.00       225.00          50.00        18.18
                 VC23            1.00      299.00       200.00          99.00        33.11

                                 3.00      773.00       570.00         203.00        26.26
```

work. A portion of the report is shown in Figure 5.19.

Figure 5. 20 Portion of "Items Sold to Customers" report.

Notice the information given on the report including: Quantity of Items Sold, the Total Amount (revenue), the Cost of Goods Sold (an expense), the Gross Profit on the item(s) sold, and the Gross Profit Margin. Managers are always interested in those figures.

MULTIPLE STEP INCOME STATEMENT

The multiple step income statement is so named because it shows the steps in determining net income (or net loss). Two steps are shown, (1.) Cost of Sales which is subtracted from Total Revenues and results in Gross Profit, and (2.) Operating Expenses which are deducted from the Gross Profit and results in Net Income.

The top portion of the multiple step income statement, through Gross Profit, for the data entered in this chapter, is shown on 5.20.

	Current Month			Year to Date	
Revenues					
Sales	$ 4,239.00	100.00	$	4,239.00	100.00
Total Revenues	4,239.00	100.00		4,239.00	100.00
Cost of Sales					
Cost of Goods Sold	2,907.00	68.58		2,907.00	68.58
Total Cost of Sales	2,907.00	68.58		2,907.00	68.58
Gross Profit	1,332.00	31.42		1,332.00	31.42

Beyer Video — Income Statement — For the Six Months Ending June 30, 2005

Figure 5. 21 Top portion of Income Statement showing Sales and Cost of Sales.

Demonstration Problem, Falcetto Company, Chapter 5, Directory "falcomp Chap 5"

The adjusted trial balance for the year ended December 2005, for Falcetto Company, Chapter 5, is shown below. Open the company from within your Student Data Set.

Falcetto Company
General Ledger Trial Balance
As of Dec 31, 2005

Filter Criteria includes: Report order is by ID. Report is printed in Detail Format.

Account ID	Account Description	Debit Amt	Credit Amt
101	Cash	14,500.00	
112	Accounts Receivable	11,100.00	
120	Merchandise Inventory	29,000.00	
130	Prepaid Insurance	2,500.00	
153	Store Equipment	95,000.00	
154	Accum Deprec - Store Equi		18,000.00
200	Notes Payable		25,000.00
201	Accounts Payable		10,600.00
301	Larry Falcetto, Capital		81,000.00
305	Larry Falcetto, Drawing	12,000.00	
401	Sales		536,800.00
410	Interest Revenue		2,500.00
412	Sales Returns and Allowa	6,700.00	
414	Sales Discounts	5,000.00	
505	Cost of Goods Sold	363,400.00	
610	Advertising Expense	12,000.00	
615	Depreciation Expense	9,000.00	
644	Freight-out	7,600.00	
718	Interest Expense	3,600.00	
722	Insurance Expense	4,500.00	
729	Rent Expense	24,000.00	
731	Store Salaries Expense	56,000.00	
732	Utilities Expense	18,000.00	
	Total:	**673,900.00**	**673,900.00**

Instructions:

a. Verify the beginning balances.
b. Prepare an Income Statement based on the above data.

Solution to Demonstration Problem
Income Statement:

Falcetto Company					
Income Statement					
For the Twelve Months Ending December 31, 2005					
	Current Month			**Year to Date**	
Revenues					
Sales	$ 536,800.00	101.74	$	536,800.00	101.74
Interest Revenue	2,500.00	0.47		2,500.00	0.47
Sales Returns and Allowances	(6,700.00)	(1.27)		(6,700.00)	(1.27)
Sales Discounts	(5,000.00)	(0.95)		(5,000.00)	(0.95)
Total Revenues	527,600.00	100.00		527,600.00	100.00
Cost of Sales					
Cost of Goods Sold	363,400.00	68.88		363,400.00	68.88
Total Cost of Sales	363,400.00	68.88		363,400.00	68.88
Gross Profit	164,200.00	31.12		164,200.00	31.12
Expenses					
Advertising Expense	12,000.00	2.27		12,000.00	2.27
Depreciation Expense	9,000.00	1.71		9,000.00	1.71
Freight-out	7,600.00	1.44		7,600.00	1.44
Interest Expense	3,600.00	0.68		3,600.00	0.68
Insurance Expense	4,500.00	0.85		4,500.00	0.85
Rent Expense	24,000.00	4.55		24,000.00	4.55
Store Salaries Expense	56,000.00	10.61		56,000.00	10.61
Utilities Expense	18,000.00	3.41		18,000.00	3.41
Total Expenses	134,700.00	25.53		134,700.00	25.53
Net Income	$ 29,500.00	5.59	$	29,500.00	5.59

P5-2B, Shmi Distributing Company, Directory "shmdisco"

Shmi Distributing Company completed the following merchandising transactions in the month of April 2005. At the beginning of April, the ledger of Shmi showed Cash of $9,000 and O. Shmi, Capital of $9,000. Inventory items, clients and customer accounts have been established within the Student Data Set. For all transactions use the date in a 04/XX/05 format as invoice number, reference, or receipt number.

April 2 Use the Purchases/Receive Inventory form to purchase 59 pieces of Item "04/02/05" on account, for $100 each from Wookie Supply Co., terms 1/10,n/30, the Invoice No. is 04/02/05

4 Use the Sales/Invoicing form to record the sale of 100 pieces of Item "04/04/05" at $52 each, FOB destination, $5,200 total, to Empire Exterminators on account with terms 1/10, n/30. Verify that Peachtree calculates the cost of goods sold at $4,100 through the general ledger account.

5 Use the Write Checks form to pay freight-out of $240 on the April 4th sale. Use "Cash" as the payee and check number 102.

6 Use the Vendor Credit Memo form to receive a credit from Wookie Supply Co. for 5 pieces of Item "04/02/05".

11 Use the Payments form to pay Wookie Supply Co. in full, less discount. Ensure that you take advantage of the proper discount and use account 120, Merchandise Inventory for the discount.

13 Use the Receipts form for collections in full, less discounts, from Empire Exterminators billed on April 4.

14 Use the Purchases/Receive Inventory form to purchase 38 pieces of inventory Item "04/14/05" for **_cash_** $100 each, $3,800 total, from Tatooine Supply Co. Use check reference 103 and insure that "Amount paid at purchase" is entered.

16 Use the Vendor Credit Memo to receive a refund from Tatooine on cash purchase of April 14, for 5 pieces at $100 each. Ensure that Cash, account 101, is in the A/P account window.

18 Use the Purchase/Receive Inventory for to purchase 60 pieces of Item "04/18/05" from Skywalker Distributors at $70 each, $4,200 total, terms 2/10,n/30

20 Use the Write Check form to pay the freight in of $100 on April 18th purchase. Use check number 104 and insure that the Expense window is set to Merchandise Inventory account, 120.

23 Use the Receipts form to record the sale of 640 pieces of Inventory Item "04/23/05" for $10 each in cash, a total of $6,400. Verify through the general ledger that Peachtree calculates the cost of goods sold at $5,120.

26 Use the Payments form to record the purchase of 46 pieces of Inventory Item "04/26/05" for $50 each, totaling a cash payment of $2,300 from Wookie Supply Co.

27 Use the Payments form and check 105 to pay Skywalker Distributors in full, less discount.

29 Use the General Journal to make refunds to cash customers for defective Item "04/23/05", $90, 9 pieces of material were returned. The returned merchandise had a scrap value of $30. Use a debit to Cost of Goods Sold and a credit to Inventory.

30 Use the Sales/Invoicing form to record the sale of 400 pieces of Inventory Item "04/30/05" at $9.25 each on account to the Mos Eisley Club, $3,700 total, terms n/30. Verify that Peachtree calculates the cost of goods sold at $2,800.

Shmi Distributing Company's chart of accounts includes the following: No. 101 Cash, No. 112 Accounts Receivable, No. 120 Merchandise Inventory, No. 201 Accounts Payable, No. 301 O. Shmi, Capital, No. 401 Sales, No. 412 Sales Returns and Allowance, No. 414 Sales Discounts, No. 505 cost of Goods Sold and No. 644 Freight-out.

Instructions:
   a. Verify the beginning balances and the chart of accounts.
   b. Record the events as instructed. (Note: All events can be recorded in the general journal but this will preclude the use of the various Peachtree forms and screens.)
   c. Print the General Journal, Cash Receipts Journal, Sales Journal, Cash Disbursements Journal, Check Register, Purchases Journal, General Ledger, and the Income Statement.
   d. Verify all information is correct and proper.

P5-4B, Ackbar's Tennis Shop, Directory "acktensh"

J. Ackbar, a former professional tennis star, operates Ackbar's Tennis Shop at the Miller Lake Resort. At the beginning of the current season, the ledger of Ackbar's Tennis Shop showed Cash $2,500, Merchandise Inventory $1,700 and J. Ackbar, Capital $4,200. The following transactions were completed during April 2005. For all transactions use the date in a 04/XX/05 format as invoice number, reference, or receipt number.

April 4 Purchased 16 inventory items "Tennis Racquets" at $40 each from Jay-Mac Co. for a total of $640, terms FOB shipping point, 2/10, n/30. Use Invoice No. "04/04/05"

     6 Paid freight on purchase from Jay-Mac Co. $40. Write check 101 to Cash Vendor to record this.

8   Sold 10 inventory item "Play the Game" to Club Members for $115 each, terms n/30, Invoice No. "04/08/05". Verify in the general ledger that the cost of goods sold is $790.

10   Received credit from Jay-Mac Co. for one damaged racquet that was returned, $40, use Credit No. 04/10/05. Use Vendor Memo to record the event.

11   Purchased 42 pairs of inventory item "Shoes" from Venus Sports for cash, at $10 each. Use the Purchase/Receive Inventory form with check 102 and remember to record amount paid at the time of purchase.

13   Use the Payments form to pay Jay-Mac Co. in full with check no. 103. Ensure the discount is correct.

14   Purchased 10 sets of inventory item "Sportswear Set" from Serena's Sportswear at $70 per set, $700 total, terms are FOB shipping point, 3/10, n/30, use invoice 04/14/05

15   Received cash refund of $50 for 5 pairs of shoes at $10 each from Venus Sports for damaged merchandise that was returned, credit no 04/15/05. Use the Vendor Credit Memo form and change the A/P account to Cash, 101.

17   Paid freight on Serena's Sportswear purchase of $30. Write a check for this event.

18   Sold 20 sets of "Shirts" to club members for $38 per shirt on account. Terms are n/30. Verify in the general ledger that the cost of goods sold at $530.

20   Received $500 from various members on their accounts. Use the Receipts form for this event.

21   Paid Serena's Sportswear in full. Use the Payments form and ensure that the discount is correct.

27   Granted an allowance of $30 to members in settlement of their accounts. Use the Credit Memo form and account 412 for this event.

30   Received an additional $660 from various members on their accounts. This may be split between two sales events on the Receipts form.

The chart of accounts includes the following: No. 101 Cash, No. 112 Accounts Receivable, No. 120 Merchandise Inventory, No. 201 Accounts Payable, No. 301 J. Ackbar, Capital, No. 401 Sales, No. 412 Sales Returns and Allowance, No. 505 Cost of Goods Sold, and No. 644 Freight Out.

Instructions:

a. Verify the beginning balances and the chart of accounts.
b. Record the events as instructed. (Note: All events can be recorded in the general journal but this will preclude the use of the various Peachtree forms and screens.)
c. Print the General Journal, Cash Receipts Journal, Sales Journal, Cash Disbursements Journal, Check Register, Purchases Journal, General Ledger, and the Income Statement.
d. Verify all information is correct and proper.

CHAPTER 6

Inventories

OBJECTIVES

- Be able to determine the various cost methods involved in inventory valuation: LIFO, FIFO and Average Cost.
- Explain the advantages of using an automated inventory system.
- Be able to recognize inventory default information
- Understand cost of goods sold, including Freight, tax and shipping

- Be able to prepare a history of inventory items; "what has come in and what has gone out."
- Be able to make Inventory adjustments in an automated system.
- Be able to prepare the various Inventory reports

ADVANTAGES OF USING THE PEACHTREE INVENTORY SYSTEM

Peachtree Complete Accounting automatically keeps track of each of the inventory items bought and sold. The quantities are updated after each posted purchase and sale. The three-step process in tracking inventory in Peachtree involves:

1. Entering the item information, which includes the Sales account, the Inventory account, and the Cost of Sales account.
2. Using the "item codes" whenever a purchase or a sale is made.
3. Entering adjustments to the inventory, through the Inventory Adjustments Task.

The inventory navigation aid, found at the bottom of the main Peachtree window can be used to complete many of those tasks. It is shown in Figure 6.1.

As you saw in the previous chapter, through Maintain Inventory items you can set up your system with the goods and/or services you sell. A unit price (or a different pricing scale) can be set up and adjusted. When you enter a purchase or a sale of an item, everything is automatically updated for you. All totals are computed on the sales invoice.

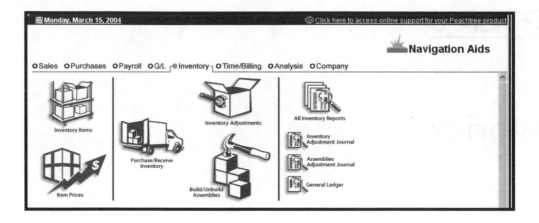

Figure 6. 1 The Inventory Navigation Aid

COST METHODS

Three different cost methods for inventory are available to use as shown in Figure 6.2. The cost methods, shown on the pull-down menu, are:
- Average Cost
- LIFO (Last In, First Out)
- FIFO (First In, First Out)

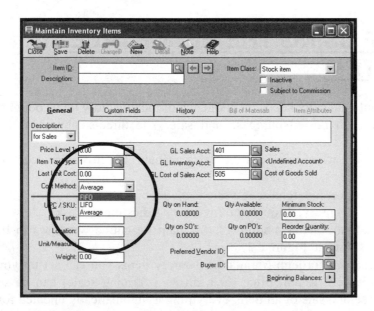

Figure 6. 2 The Maintain Inventory Items form.

AVERAGE COST

The average cost method calculates an average cost upon each acquisition of inventory. Each time you make a purchase, the average cost for that item is recalculated.

Whenever you sell an inventory item that has an average cost type, Peachtree Complete Accounting uses the average cost it has been tracking to compute the Cost of Goods Sold. The Cost of Goods Sold is the average cost times the quantity of the item sold. On a daily basis, an entry is made to the Cost of Goods Sold account that encompasses the sales for the day.

Please refer back to your text for additional details and examples.

Example – Average Cost
The company, Average Sales Company, on January 1, 2005, buys three AVGUNITS for $1/ea from Vendor 1. On January 15, 2005, three more are purchased for $2.00/each. The average cost thus far would be $1.50 ({[$1 X 3 units] + [$2 X 3 units]} / 6 units). Record these events in Average Sales Company.

Run an Item Costing Report:

Step 1: From within your Student Data Set, open the "Average Sales Company."

Step 2: From the reports menu, select "Inventory" then double click on "Item Costing Report".

The Item Costing Report, shown in Figure 6.3, shows the acquisition of inventory by date, quantity, unit cost, and extended cost as well as aggregate cost of inventory.

Average Sales Company **Item Costing Report** **For the Period From Jan 1, 2005 to Dec 31, 2006**									
Filter Criteria includes: Report order is by ID.									
Item ID **Item Description**	**Date**	**Qty Received**	**Item Cost**	**Actual Cost**	**Assembly Qty** **Assembly ($)**	**Adjust Qty** **Adjust ($)**	**Quantity Sold** **Cost of Sales**	**Remaining Qty**	**Remain Value**
AVGUNITS Average Cost Units									
	1/1/05	3.00	1.00	3.00				3.00	3.00
	1/15/05	3.00	2.00	6.00				6.00	9.00

Figure 6. 3 The Item Costing Report.

Example – Adjustments to Inventory
Peachtree Complete Accounting makes it easy to conduct a physical inventory count by providing a form listing all of the inventory items and providing blanks to the side for an employee to write in the specific count of an inventory item.

Run a Physical Inventory report:

Step 1: From the reports area menu, choose "Inventory."

Step 2: From the reports list click on "Physical Inventory." It is a short list, since you have only one inventory item. The report is shown in Figure 6.4 below with the inventory count already completed.

102

Average Sales Company
Physical Inventory List
As of Jan 31, 2005

Filter Criteria includes: 1) Stock/Assembly. Report order is by ID. Report is printed with Truncated Long Descriptions.

Item ID	Item Description	Unit	Location	Count	By
AVGUNITS	Average Cost Units			5	Brad

Figure 6. 4 Physical Inventory List

Based on Brad's January 20, 2005, report (Figure 6.4) from a "cycle count" it appears that one of the Average Units are missing from the warehouse. To recognize the shortage an inventory adjustment must be made. This can be done through the Inventory Adjustments under the Tasks menu.

Step 1: From the "Tasks" menu, click on "Inventory Adjustments." The completed entry window is shown in Figure 6.5.

Step 2: In the blank window, enter the Item ID. Once the Item ID is entered the cost information is automatically generated.

Step 3: The reference number is "0120." Change the date to January 20, 2005.

Step 4: Enter "-1" (a negative number) in the "Adjust Quantity By" text box.

Step 5: Click "Save" to save your work.

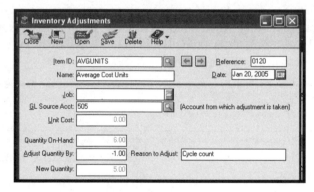

Figure 6. 5 Inventory Adjustments window.

The average cost of our units will remain at $1.50 because this is a mathematical calculation of total acquisition cost divided by total units.

Example – Cost of Goods Sold

On January 25, 2005, Cindi Customer buys three of the remaining AVGUNITS for $6/each. The cost of goods sold would be $4.50 (Average Cost * Quantity Sold or $1.50 * 3 units).

Record Cindy's Purchase:

Step 1: Click on the Sales navigation aid. Click on "Sales Invoicing" in the middle section.

Step 2: Complete the invoice (refer back to Chapter 5, if necessary). Cindy purchases three units at $6/each.

Step 3: Check your work for errors before continuing. The completed invoice is illustrated in Figure 6.6.

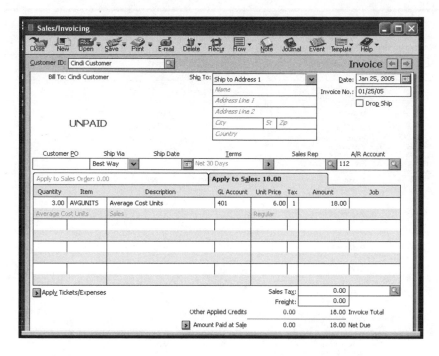

Figure 6. 6 Cindi Customer's invoice.

To see how accounts are affected, run another Item Costing Report and compare it to Figure 6.7,

Average Sales Company
Item Costing Report
For the Period From Jan 1, 2005 to Dec 31, 2006

Filter Criteria includes: Report order is by ID.

Item ID Item Description	Date	Qty Received	Item Cost	Actual Cost	Assembly Qty Assembly ($)	Adjust Qty Adjust ($)	Quantity Sold Cost of Sales	Remaining Qty	Remain Value
AVGUNITS Average Cost Units									
	1/1/05	3.00	1.00	3.00				3.00	3.00
	1/15/05	3.00	2.00	6.00				6.00	9.00
	1/20/05					-1.00 -1.50		5.00	7.50
	1/25/05						3.00 4.50	2.00	3.00

shown here. Notice on the report each affect each transaction has on the inventory value.

Figure 6. 7 Item Costing Report.

To see the "Big Picture" and how accounts have been affected, run a General Ledger Report, shown in Figure 6.8.

Average Sales Company
General Ledger
For the Period From Jan 1, 2005 to Jan 31, 2005
Filter Criteria includes: Report order is by ID. Report is printed with Truncated Transaction Descriptions and in Detail Format.

Account ID / Account Description	Date	Reference	Jrnl	Trans Description	Debit Amt	Credit Amt	Balance
112	1/1/05			Beginning Balanc			
Accounts Receivable	1/25/05	01/25/05	SJ	Cindi Customer	18.00		
				Current Period Ch	18.00		18.00
	1/31/05			**Ending Balance**			**18.00**
120	1/1/05			Beginning Balanc			
Merchandise Invento	1/1/05	01/01/05	PJ	Vendor 1 - Item: A	3.00		
	1/15/05	01/15/05	PJ	Vendor 1 - Item: A	6.00		
	1/20/05	0120	INAJ	Average Cost Unit		1.50	
	1/25/05	01/25/05	COG	Cindi Customer - I		4.50	
				Current Period Ch	9.00	6.00	3.00
	1/31/05			**Ending Balance**			**3.00**
201	1/1/05			Beginning Balanc			
Accounts Payable	1/1/05	01/01/05	PJ	Vendor 1		3.00	
	1/15/05	01/15/05	PJ	Vendor 1		6.00	
				Current Period Ch		9.00	-9.00
	1/31/05			**Ending Balance**			**-9.00**
401	1/1/05			Beginning Balanc			
Sales	1/25/05	01/25/05	SJ	Cindi Customer - I		18.00	
				Current Period Ch		18.00	-18.00
	1/31/05			**Ending Balance**			**-18.00**
505	1/1/05			Beginning Balanc			
Cost of Goods Sold	1/20/05	0120	INAJ	Average Cost Unit	1.50		
	1/25/05	01/25/05	COG	Cindi Customer - I	4.50		
				Current Period Ch	6.00		6.00
	1/31/05			**Ending Balance**			**6.00**

Figure 6. 8 General Ledger report.

Print out the income statement and evaluate the performance of Average Sales Company through Gross Profit. The income statement is shown in figure 6.9.

Average Sales Company
Income Statement
For the One Month Ending January 31, 2005

	Current Month			Year to Date	
Revenues					
Sales	$ 18.00	100.00	$	18.00	100.00
Sales Discounts	0.00	0.00		0.00	0.00
Total Revenues	18.00	100.00		18.00	100.00
Cost of Sales					
Cost of Goods Sold	6.00	33.33		6.00	33.33
Total Cost of Sales	6.00	33.33		6.00	33.33
Gross Profit	12.00	66.67		12.00	66.67
Expenses					
Freight-out Expense	0.00	0.00		0.00	0.00
Total Expenses	0.00	0.00		0.00	0.00
Net Income	$ 12.00	66.67	$	12.00	66.67

Figure 6. 9 Average Sales Company Income Statement.

LAST IN, FIRST OUT (LIFO)

The LIFO method keeps track of the cost you paid for each item. LIFO costs your sales and cost of goods sold as if the item you are selling is the most recently received item.

Select the LIFO method when you charge the most recent inventory costs against revenue. LIFO yields the lowest possible amount of net income in periods of constantly rising costs because the cost of the most recently acquired item more closely approximates the replacement cost of the item. Of course, in periods of declining costs, the effect is reversed.

Please refer back to your text for additional explanation and examples.

Example – LIFO

LIFO Sales Company, on January 1, 2005, buys 3 LIFOUNITS for $1/each from Vendor 1. On January 5, 2005 and 3 more are purchased for $2/each on January 15, 2005.

Run an Item Costing Report as explained in Average Sale Company, shown in Figure 6.10. Note its similarity to the same report under the Average Sales Company.

			LIFO Sales Company Item Costing Report For the Period From Jan 1, 2005 to Dec 31, 2006						
Filter Criteria includes: Report order is by ID.									
Item ID Item Description	Date	Qty Received	Item Cost	Actual Cost	Assembly Qty Assembly ($)	Adjust Qty Adjust ($)	Quantity Sold Cost of Sales	Remaining Qty	Remain Value
LIFOUNITS LIFO Units									
	1/1/05	3.00	1.00	3.00				3.00	3.00
	1/15/05	3.00	2.00	6.00				6.00	9.00

Figure 6. 10 Item Costing Report for LIFO Sales Company.

As shown in the Average Sales Company, complete an adjustment for one LIFOUNITS revealed in a cycle count by Brad on January 20, 2005 using a reference of 0120. This is shown in figure 6.11.

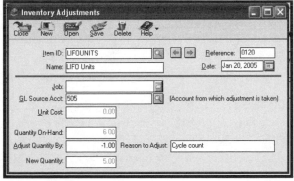

Figure 6. 11 Inventory Adjustments form for LIFO Sales Company.

The affect of this adjustment is shown in figure 6.12.

					LIFO Sales Company				
					Item Costing Report				
					For the Period From Jan 1, 2005 to Dec 31, 2006				

Filter Criteria includes: Report order is by ID.

Item ID Item Description	Date	Qty Received	Item Cost	Actual Cost	Assembly Qty Assembly ($)	Adjust Qty Adjust ($)	Quantity Sold Cost of Sales	Remaining Qty	Remain Value
LIFOUNITS LIFO Units									
	1/1/05	3.00	1.00	3.00				3.00	3.00
	1/15/05	3.00	2.00	6.00				6.00	9.00
	1/20/05					-1.00 -2.00		5.00	7.00

Figure 6. 12 Inventory Adjustments form for LIFO Sales Company after inventory adjustment.

Just as in Average Sales Company Cindi Customer purchases 3 LIFOUNITS on January 25, 2005, for $6 each. Use the form in Average Sales Company as a model to record the sale. As a result, the remaining value of inventory for LIFO Sales Company is $2 for two $1 units. In Average Sales Company it was $3 for two average costed units at $1.50 each. The LIFO Sales Company Item Costing Report, figure 6.13, and the General Ledger, figure 6.14, follow for comparison to Average Sales Company.

					LIFO Sales Company				
					Item Costing Report				
					For the Period From Jan 1, 2005 to Dec 31, 2006				

Filter Criteria includes: Report order is by ID.

Item ID Item Description	Date	Qty Received	Item Cost	Actual Cost	Assembly Qty Assembly ($)	Adjust Qty Adjust ($)	Quantity Sold Cost of Sales	Remaining Qty	Remain Value
LIFOUNITS LIFO Units									
	1/1/05	3.00	1.00	3.00				3.00	3.00
	1/15/05	3.00	2.00	6.00				6.00	9.00
	1/20/05					-1.00 -2.00		5.00	7.00
	1/25/05						3.00 5.00	2.00	2.00

Figure 6. 13 Item Costing Report after sale to Cindi Customer.

```
                                  LIFO Sales Company
                                   General Ledger
                          For the Period From Jan 1, 2005 to Jan 31, 2005
Filter Criteria includes: Report order is by ID. Report is printed with Truncated Transaction Descriptions and in Detail Format.
```

Account ID Account Description	Date	Reference	Jrnl	Trans Description	Debit Amt	Credit Amt	Balance
112	1/1/05			Beginning Balanc			
Accounts Receivable	1/25/05	01/25/05	SJ	Cindi Customer	18.00		
				Current Period Ch	18.00		18.00
	1/31/05			**Ending Balance**			**18.00**
120	1/1/05			Beginning Balanc			
Merchandise Invento	1/1/05	01/01/05	PJ	Vendor 1 - Item: LI	3.00		
	1/15/05	011505	PJ	Vendor 1 - Item: LI	6.00		
	1/20/05	0120	INAJ	LIFO Units		2.00	
	1/25/05	01/25/05	COG	Cindi Customer - I		5.00	
				Current Period Ch	9.00	7.00	2.00
	1/31/05			**Ending Balance**			**2.00**
201	1/1/05			Beginning Balanc			
Accounts Payable	1/1/05	01/01/05	PJ	Vendor 1		3.00	
	1/15/05	011505	PJ	Vendor 1		6.00	
				Current Period Ch		9.00	-9.00
	1/31/05			**Ending Balance**			**-9.00**
401	1/1/05			Beginning Balanc			
Sales	1/25/05	01/25/05	SJ	Cindi Customer - I		18.00	
				Current Period Ch		18.00	-18.00
	1/31/05			**Ending Balance**			**-18.00**
505	1/1/05			Beginning Balanc			
Cost of Goods Sold	1/20/05	0120	INAJ	LIFO Units	2.00		
	1/25/05	01/25/05	COG	Cindi Customer - I	5.00		
				Current Period Ch	7.00		7.00
	1/31/05			**Ending Balance**			**7.00**

Figure 6. 14 General Ledger for LIFO Sales Company after sale to Cindi Customer.

Print the income statement for LIFO Sales Company. It is presented in figure 6.15 for comparison.

```
                              LIFO Sales Company
                                Income Statement
                      For the One Month Ending January 31, 2005
```

	Current Month		Year to Date	
Revenues				
Sales	$ 18.00	100.00	$ 18.00	100.00
Sales Discounts	0.00	0.00	0.00	0.00
Total Revenues	18.00	100.00	18.00	100.00
Cost of Sales				
Cost of Goods Sold	7.00	38.89	7.00	38.89
Total Cost of Sales	7.00	38.89	7.00	38.89
Gross Profit	11.00	61.11	11.00	61.11
Expenses				
Freight-out Expense	0.00	0.00	0.00	0.00
Total Expenses	0.00	0.00	0.00	0.00
Net Income	$ 11.00	61.11	$ 11.00	61.11

Figure 6. 15 LIFO Sales Company Income Statement.

FIRST IN, FIRST OUT (FIFO)

The FIFO method is similar to LIFO and keeps track of the price you paid for each group of units received at the same time at the same unit cost.

Select FIFO when you charge costs against revenue in the order in which costs occur. This method generally yields the highest possible amount of net income during periods of constantly rising prices. Costs increase regardless of whether you have received merchandise prior to the cost increase. In periods of declining cost, the effect is reversed.

Example – FIFO

The company, FIFO Sales Company, on January 1, 2005 buys 3 FIFOUNITS for $1/ea from Vendor 1. On January 15, 2005, 3 more FIFOUNITS units were purchased at a cost of $2/each. As shown in the Average Sales Company, complete an adjustment for one FIFOUNITS revealed in a cycle count by Brad on January 20, 2005 using a reference of 0120.

Preview the Item Costing Report and compare it to figure 6.16

FIFO Sales Company
Item Costing Report
For the Period From Jan 1, 2005 to Dec 31, 2006

Filter Criteria includes: Report order is by ID.

Item ID Item Description	Date	Qty Received	Item Cost	Actual Cost	Assembly Qty Assembly ($)	Adjust Qty Adjust ($)	Quantity Sold Cost of Sales	Remaining Qty	Remain Value
FIFOUNIT FIFO Unit									
	1/1/05	3.00	1.00	3.00				3.00	3.00
	1/15/05	3.00	2.00	6.00				6.00	9.00

Figure 6. 16 Item Costing Report for FIFO Sales Company

Cindi Customer purchases 3 FIFOUNITS for $6 each, just like in Average Sales Company and LIFO Sales Company. Record this event and compare your Item Costing Report and General Ledger to figures 6.17 and 6.18.

FIFO Sales Company
Item Costing Report
For the Period From Jan 1, 2005 to Dec 31, 2006

Filter Criteria includes: Report order is by ID.

Item ID Item Description	Date	Qty Received	Item Cost	Actual Cost	Assembly Qty Assembly ($)	Adjust Qty Adjust ($)	Quantity Sold Cost of Sales	Remaining Qty	Remain Value
FIFOUNIT FIFO Unit									
	1/1/05	3.00	1.00	3.00				3.00	3.00
	1/15/05	3.00	2.00	6.00				6.00	9.00
	1/20/05					-1.00 -1.00		5.00	8.00
	1/25/05						3.00 4.00	2.00	4.00

Figure 6. 17 Item Costing Report for FIFO Sales Company after Cindi Customer sale.

```
                              FIFO Sales Company
                                General Ledger
                    For the Period From Jan 1, 2005 to Jan 31, 2005
Filter Criteria includes: Report order is by ID. Report is printed with Truncated Transaction Descriptions and in Detail Format.

Account ID        Date     Reference   Jrnl   Trans Description   Debit Amt   Credit Amt   Balance
Account Description

112               1/1/05                      Beginning Balanc
Accounts Receivable 1/25/05 01/25/05  SJ      Cindi Customer        18.00
                                              Current Period Ch     18.00                   18.00
                  1/31/05                      Ending Balance                                18.00

120               1/1/05                       Beginning Balanc
Merchandise Invento 1/1/05  01/01/05  PJ       Vendor 1 - Item: FI   3.00
                  1/15/05  011505    PJ        Vendor 1 - Item: FI   6.00
                  1/20/05  0120      INAJ      FIFO Unit                         1.00
                  1/25/05  01/25/05  COG       Cindi Customer - I                4.00
                                              Current Period Ch      9.00        5.00        4.00
                  1/31/05                      Ending Balance                                4.00

201               1/1/05                       Beginning Balanc
Accounts Payable  1/1/05   01/01/05  PJ        Vendor 1                          3.00
                  1/15/05  011505    PJ        Vendor 1                          6.00
                                              Current Period Ch                  9.00       -9.00
                  1/31/05                      Ending Balance                               -9.00

401               1/1/05                       Beginning Balanc
Sales             1/25/05  01/25/05  SJ        Cindi Customer - I               18.00
                                              Current Period Ch                 18.00      -18.00
                  1/31/05                      Ending Balance                              -18.00

505               1/1/05                       Beginning Balanc
Cost of Goods Sold 1/20/05 0120      INAJ      FIFO Unit             1.00
                  1/25/05  01/25/05  COG       Cindi Customer - I    4.00
                                              Current Period Ch      5.00                    5.00
                  1/31/05                      Ending Balance                                5.00
```

Figure 6. 18 Item Costing Report for FIFO Sales Company after Cindi Customer sale.

Print the income statement. Look at the effect on our income and profits. Run a copy of the Income Statement, which is shown in Figure 6.19. Notice how the costs have been reflected in Cost of Goods Sold and in Revenue. Compare the FIFO income statement with the one previously generated from LIFO sales.

```
                          FIFO Sales Company
                           Income Statement
                   For the One Month Ending January 31, 2002

                          Current Month                Year to Date

Revenues
Sales            $      225.00    100.00    $      225.00    100.00

Total Revenues          225.00    100.00           225.00    100.00

Cost of Sales
Purchases               160.00     71.11           160.00     71.11

Total Cost of Sales     160.00     71.11           160.00     71.11

Gross Profit             65.00     28.89            65.00     28.89

Expenses
Theft                     0.00      0.00             0.00      0.00

Total Expenses            0.00      0.00             0.00      0.00

Net Income       $       65.00     28.89   $        65.00     28.89
```

Figure 6. 19 FIFO Income Statement after sale to Cindi Customer.

INVENTORY DEFAULT INFORMATION

Peachtree Complete Accounting lets you set up default information for inventory items. This feature is like a template or model in which you "build" your inventory item records. You enter the most common information; then, when you set up new inventory items and enter transactions, the default information is automatically included.

To set up or review inventory item defaults

Step 1: Select Default Information from the Maintain menu and choose Inventory Item Defaults.

Step 2: You have a choice of several tabs, as shown in Figure 6.20. Look at the GL Accts/Costing tab.

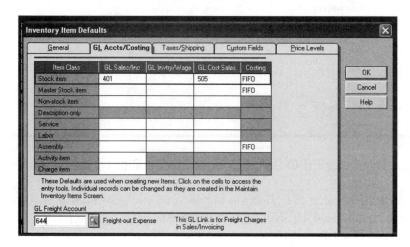

Figure 6. 20 Inventory Items Default

Step 3: Enter "401" for the General Ledger Sales account and "505" for the Cost of Sales account and "644" at the bottom, for Freight-out. Entering this data here will preclude entering it each time inventory items are built. Also on this tab you can control FIFO, LIFO, and Average Costing as a global default while you can change this default during specific builds.

Step 4: The "Taxes/Shipping" tab, not shown, contains the taxing structures as well as the shipping methods. No changes are normally made to this tab.

Step 5: The "Custom Fields" tab allows additional messages and fields to be added to the inventory data files.

Step 6: The "Price Levels" tab allows numerous pricing levels to be established for a single item. These levels can be calculation controlled rather than absolute values. So Price Level 2 can be 10% off of Price Level 1 while Price Level 3 is 10% above Price Level 1. Useful in business but not required for accomplishments of textbook accounting.

Step 7: The "General" tab controls warning messages of inventory levels and other actions not relevant to textbook accounting.

Step 5: You may change these fields to meet your needs. For now, you'll leave them as they are.

Step 6: Click "OK" to return to the main screen.

INVENTORY REPORTS

Peachtree Complete Accounting provides you with a variety of default reports for organizing and monitoring the inventory process. These reports include listing inventory items, cost, quantity on hand, assembly components, adjustments, and general ledger activity.

To obtain Inventory Reports:

Step 1: Under the "Reports" heading on the menu bar, click on "Inventory."

Step 2: You are presented with the "Inventory" reports selection menu as shown in Figure 6.21.

Step 3: Select the report required.

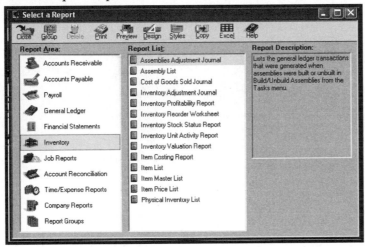

Figure 6. 21 Available Inventory reports.

P6-1A, Kananaskis Country Limited, Directory "kancouli"

Kananaskis Country Limited is trying to determine the value of its ending inventory as of February 28, 2004, the company's year-end. The following transactions occurred, and the accountant asked your help in determining whether they should be recorded or not.

(a) On February 26, Kananaskis shipped goods costing $800 to a customer and charged the customer $1,000. The goods were shipped with terms FOB destination and the receiving report indicates that the customer received the goods March 2.

(b) On February 26, Seller Inc. shipped goods to Kananaskis under terms FOB shipping point. The invoice price was $350 plus $25 for freight. The receiving report indicates that the goods were received by Kananaskis on March 2.

(c) Kananaskis had $500 of inventory isolated in the warehouse. The inventory is designated for a customer who has requested that the goods be shipped on March 10.

(d) Also included in Kananaskis' warehouse is $400 of inventory that Craft Producers shipped to Kananaskis on consignment.

(e) On February 26, Kananaskis issued a purchase order to acquire goods costing $750. The goods were shipped with terms FOB destination on February 27. Kananaskis received the goods March 2.

(f) On February 26, Kananaskis shipped goods to a customer under terms FOB shipping point. The invoice price was $350 plus $25 for freight; the cost of the items was $280. The receiving report indicates that the goods were received by the customer on March 7.

Instructions:

On a sheet of paper, specify whether each item in question should be included in ending inventory, and if so, at what amount. There is no Peachtree data set for this problem.

CHAPTER 7

Accounting Information Systems

OBJECTIVES

- Identify the basic principles of accounting information systems.
- Explain the major phases in the development of an accounting system.
- Describe the nature and purpose of a subsidiary ledger.

- Explain how special journals are used in journalizing.
- Indicate how a multicolumn journal is posted.

BASIC CONCEPTS OF ACCOUNTING INFORMATION SYSTEMS

The accounting information system is the system of collecting and processing transaction data and distributing financial information to interested parties. An Accounting Information System (AIS for short) includes each of the steps in the accounting cycle you have studied in your text. The documents providing evidence of the transactions and events and the records, trial balances, work sheets and financial statements are a result of a solid Accounting Information System. It may be either manual or computerized.

An efficient and effective accounting information system is based on certain principles:

- Cost effectiveness
- Usefulness
- Flexibility

In a manual accounting system, the debits and credits for each transaction were first entered in a book called a journal. The journal record for each transaction is called a journal entry, or simply an entry. Later the journal entries are copied, or posted, to another book called the ledger.

The journal lists the transactions in the order in which they occur, somewhat like a diary; the ledger contains a page for each account and a running balance total. In a manual system, the journal tells the bookkeeper which accounts are to be debited and credited. The bookkeeper carries out these instructions by posting these journal entries to the ledger.

MANUAL VERSES COMPUTERIZED SYSTEMS

In a manual accounting system, each of the steps in the accounting cycle is performed by hand. For example, each accounting transaction is entered manually in a journal and each is posted manually to the ledger. To obtain a trial balance or financial statements, manual computations must be made.

In a computerized accounting system, the program is performing these steps in the accounting cycle such as posting and preparing trial balances. Once the journal entry is entered into the application, the software carries out the posting and report generation process. Functions such as billing customers, preparing the payroll, and budgeting are also accomplished inside the computerized system.

Both manual and computerized systems rely on a chart of accounts and account classifications such as assets, liabilities, owner's equity, revenues, and expenses. These accounts are usually identified by a text title and number. Several major advantages are apparent in the computerized system. Unbalanced journal entries generally cannot be posted, posting is automatic, reports are available at the click of a button with little delay, and, with networking, numerous accountants can be working on the books at one time. The disadvantage of computerized accounting systems is the degree of trust without review that is placed on generated information because of the "computer" process.

SUBSIDIARY LEDGERS AND PEACHTREE REPORTS

Imagine a business that has several thousand charge (credit) customers and shows the transactions with these customers using only one general ledger account – Accounts Receivable. It would be impossible to determine the balance owed by a single customer at any specific time. Similarly, the amount you need to pay to a creditor would also be difficult to locate quickly from a single Accounts Payable account in the general ledger. This is why companies use subsidiary ledgers to keep track of individual balances.

A subsidiary ledger, or reports as they are called in Peachtree, is a group of accounts with a common characteristic. For example, all Accounts Receivable (money owed to you by your customers) are contained in one report. The subsidiary ledger frees the general ledger from the details of individual balances. A subsidiary ledger simply is an addition to a second volume or an expansion of the general ledger.

The two most common subsidiary ledgers in Peachtree are as follows:
- The Accounts Receivable Ledger - contains information about the transactions affecting the company's customers. A listing of who owes the company money.
- The Accounts Payable Ledger - contains information about the transactions affecting the company's creditors. A listing of those to whom the company owes money.

THE ACCOUNTS RECEIVABLE LEDGER

The Accounts Receivable Ledger is found under the Reports heading of the menu bar.
Run a copy of the Accounts Receivable Ledger for "Bellwether Garden Supply."
Step 1: Open "Bellwether Garden Supply" on your student disk.

Step 2: Click on "Reports" on the reports menu and then click on "Accounts Receivable." You will be presented with the complete listing of reports pertaining to "Accounts Receivable" as shown in Figure 7.1.

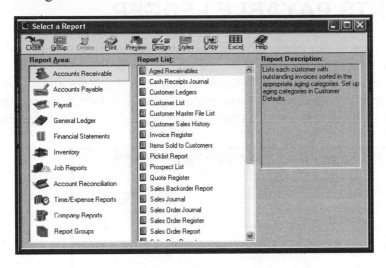

Figure 7. 1 Select A Report window (Accounts Receivable)

Step 3: Click on "Customer Ledgers" under the Report List to obtain a listing of "Bellwether's" customers and balances, and such. A portion of the report is shown in Figure 7.2.

Bellwether Garden Supply						
Customer Ledgers						
For the Period From Mar 1, 2007 to Mar 31, 2007						
Filter Criteria includes: Report order is by ID. Report is printed in Detail Format.						
Customer ID Customer	**Date**	**Trans No**	**Type**	**Debit Amt**	**Credit Amt**	**Balance**
ALIGOOD-01 Aligood Chiropractic	3/4/07	10332	SJ	129.97		129.97
ARCENEAUX-01 Arceneaux Software	3/4/07	10329	SJ	59.98		59.98
	3/17/07	CCM4008	SJ		49.99	9.99
	3/18/07	10317	SJ	49.99		59.90
ARMSTRONG-01 Armstrong Consulting	3/1/07	Balance Fwd				99.97
	3/2/07	CCM4002	SJ		99.97	0.00
	3/17/07	CCM4007	SJ		49.99	-49.99
	3/18/07	10314	SJ	49.99		0.00
	3/21/07	10336	SJ	63.49		63.49
CHAPMAN-MURPHY-01 Chapman-Murphy Law O	3/16/07	CC0001	CRJ	40.25	40.25	0.00
	3/18/07	10313	SJ	199.96		199.96
COMMON-01 Common Heathcare Cen	3/17/07	CC0002	CRJ	6.35	6.35	0.00
	3/20/07	10321	SJ	49.99		49.99
	3/21/07	10335	SJ	635.90		685.89
CUNNINGHAM-01 Cunningham Constructio	3/13/07	10307	SJ	180.18		180.18
	3/15/07	CASH-31503	CRJ	423.89	423.89	180.18
	3/17/07	CCM4005	SJ		49.99	130.19

Figure 7. 2 Portion of Customer Ledgers for "Bellwether Garden Supply"

Look at the information provided for "Armstrong Consulting." Each date on which business was conducted with "Armstrong" is listed, including the beginning balance for the period of $99.97, Credit Memos for $99.97 and $49.99, and Sales Invoices for $49.99 and $63.49 resulting in a period end balance of $63.49.

THE ACCOUNTS PAYABLE LEDGER

The Accounts Payable Ledger is also found under the Reports heading of the menu bar.

Run a copy of the Accounts Payable Ledger for "Bellwether Garden Supply".

Step 1: Open "Bellwether Garden Supply" on your student disk if it is not already open.

Step 2: Click on "Reports" on the reports menu bar and then click on "Accounts Payable." You will be presented with the complete listing of reports pertaining to "Accounts Payable" as shown in Figure 7.3.

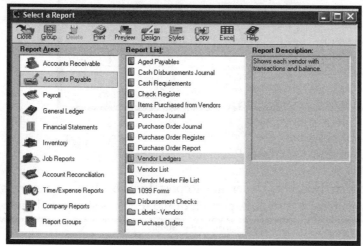

Figure 7. 3 Report listing for Accounts Payable

Step 3: Click on "Vendor Ledgers" under the Report List to obtain a listing of "Bellwether's" creditors and balances, and such. A portion of the report is shown in Figure 7.4.

Bellwether Garden Supply
Vendor Ledgers
For the Period From Mar 1, 2007 to Mar 31, 2007

Filter Criteria includes: Report order is by ID.

Vendor ID Vendor	Date	Trans No	Type	Paid	Debit Amt	Credit Amt	Balance
AARON-01	3/1/07	B1000	PJ			75.00	75.00
Aaron and Son Contracto	3/9/07	B1015	PJ	*		195.65	270.65
	3/12/07	VCM30001	PJ	*	195.65		75.00
ANDERSON-01	3/14/07	B1016	PJ	*		27.20	27.20
Anderson Distribution	3/17/07	VCM30002	PJ	*	27.20		0.00
	3/17/07		CDJ		1,000.00	1,000.00	0.00
CLOWNEY-01	3/1/07	Balance Fwd					124.68
Clowney Chemical Suppl	3/12/07	116655	PJ			297.60	422.28
	3/12/07	10201	CDJ		124.68		297.60
	3/24/07	B1021	PJ			23.85	321.45
CLUNE-01	3/15/07	B1006	PJ			400.00	400.00
Clune Construction, Inc.	3/26/07	B1023	PJ			55.65	455.65
CORCORAN-01	3/4/07	B1004	PJ			90.00	90.00
Corcoran Consulting Co	3/16/07	B1017	PJ	*		45.90	135.90
	3/19/07	VCM30003	PJ	*	45.90		90.00
DEJULIO-01	3/1/07	Balance Fwd					2,663.00
DeJulio Wholesale Supp	3/10/07	22113	PJ			64.80	2,727.80
	3/13/07	AR1303	PJ			1,192.50	3,920.30
	3/24/07	B1020	PJ			13.50	3,933.80

Figure 7. 4 Portion listing of Vendor Ledger (Accounts Payable)

Look at the information provided for "Clowney Chemical Supply." The detail shows a period beginning balance of $124.68, a purchase for $297.60, a payment for 124.68, and a purchase for $23.85 resulting in an ending balance of $321.45.

SPECIAL JOURNALS

In addition to these two subsidiary ledgers there are other special journals such as the sales journal, the cash receipts journal, the purchases journal, and the cash payments journal.

SALES/INVOICE JOURNAL

The Sales/Invoicing Journal is used to record sales of merchandise on account. This form allows the processing of sales orders which were taken earlier and are now being filled as a sale as well as sales in which the entire process is occurring in one event such as a customer approaching a sales counter for an inventoried item and accepting the material at the time of sale on an account arrangement. Within Peachtree the Apply to Sales tab of the Sales/Invoicing Journal is driven by inventory items but text can be placed in the Description windows and values can be entered into the Amount field without an inventory item being identified. If inventory items are identified, inventory and cost of goods sold are updated when the form is saved.

From the Sales/Invoicing Journal you can use the arrows near the upper right corner to move through the available forms that have been saved or recorded. These forms can be edited or deleted as required. Through an option towards the bottom of the form you can receive cash at the time of sale if appropriate. You can use this form for cash sales if desired but unnecessary additional lines will appear in the general ledger if that is accomplished. Cash sales should be entered in the Cash Receipts Journal. Credit sales of assets other than merchandise would be entered through a General Journal entry.

Run a copy of the Sales Journal:

Step 1: Continue to use the Peachtree demo company, "Bellwether Garden."

Step 2: Click on "Reports" and "Accounts Receivable".

Step 3: On the Report listing, click on (highlight) the sales journal. A portion of the journal is shown in Figure 7.5.

Bellwether Garden Supply
Sales Journal
For the Period From Mar 1, 2007 to Mar 31, 2007
Filter Criteria includes: Report order is by Invoice/CM Date. Report is printed in Detail Format.

Date	Account ID	Invoice/CM #	Line Description	Debit Amnt	Credit Amnt
3/1/07	40000-LS	10327	Lawn and Turf Care Service		39.99
	11000		Dashevskaya Business Systems	39.99	
3/2/07	40000-LS	CCM4002	Lawn and Turf Care Service	39.99	
	40000-LS		Group Prep and Cultivation Service	59.98	
	11000		Armstrong Consulting		99.97
3/3/07	23100	10301	GEORGIA: Georgia State Sales Tax		7.19
	23100		GWINNETT: Gwinnett County Sales Tax		3.60
	40000-EQ		Bell-Gro Impulse Sprinkler		59.98
	50000-EQ		Cost of sales	23.90	
	12000		Cost of sales		23.90
	40000-FF		Bell-Gro Lawn Fertilizer 5 lb. Bag; All-Organic		59.94
	50000-FF		Cost of sales	23.70	
	12000		Cost of sales		23.70
	40000-HT		Bell-Gro Long-Handled Tined Garden Cultivator 4-prong		19.99
	50000-HT		Cost of sales	7.95	
	12000		Cost of sales		7.95
	40000-EQ		Bell-Gro Fertilizer Compression Pump Hand Sprayer - 3 Gallon		39.99
	50000-EQ		Cost of sales	15.95	
	12000		Cost of sales		15.95

Figure 7. 5 Sales Journal for Bellwether Garden Supply.

Look at the entry for Invoice 10301 made on March 3, 2007. The 23100 accounts are Sales Taxes Payable accounts related to sales tax liability, the 40000 series accounts are Sales revenue accounts, the 50000 series accounts are Cost of Goods Sold accounts, the 12000 series accounts are Inventory accounts being relieved by COGS, and the 11000 account is Accounts Receivable showing the total value of the sale - $190.69. This can be verified or clarified by reading Bellwether's chart of accounts within the Reports of General Ledger. By placing your cursor over an item which results in a magnifying glass as a cursor and double clicking you will be taken to the original entry for that data.

THE RECEIPTS JOURNAL

The cash receipts within Peachtree are handled through the Receipts Journal which can be accessed through Tasks. Almost all cash receipts are recorded through the Receipts Journal. If the customer has outstanding invoices for payments Peachtree will present these on the Apply To Invoices tab. The Apply To Revenues tab can be used for cash sales. This tab can be driven by inventory items. However, it will allow you to text into the Description window and values in the Amount window without identifying an inventory item.

When using the Apply To Invoices tab Peachtree will generally calculate a discount if applicable but this value should be checked before accepted.

The Receipts form creates the Cash Receipts Journal. A portion of this report for Bellwether is shown in figure 7.6. To generate a Cash Receipts Journal:

Step 1: Click on Reports.

Step 2: Click on Accounts Receivable.

Step 3: Click on Cash Receipts Journal.

Bellwether Garden Supply
Cash Receipts Journal
For the Period From Mar 1, 2007 to Mar 31, 2007

Filter Criteria includes: Report order is by Check Date. Report is printed in Detail Format.

Date	Account ID	Transaction Ref	Line Description	Debit Amnt	Credit Amnt
3/3/07	23100	4452	GEORGIA: Georgia State Sales Tax		8.23
	23100		FULTON: Fulton County Sales Tax		4.12
	23100		MARTA: Transportation Tax		2.06
	40000-HT		Bell-Gro Wheelbarrow - Green Metal; Holds 6 cubic feet		49.99
	50000-HT		Cost of sales	19.95	
	12000		Cost of sales		19.95
	40000-EQ		Bell-Gro Heavy Duty Garden Hose - 75 ft. x 5/8 in. hose		39.99
	50000-EQ		Cost of sales	15.95	
	12000		Cost of sales		15.95
	40000-PO		Bell-Gro Cedar Window/Trough Box Planter - 33.5 in. long x 11.5 in. wide x 8.75 in. high w/brackets		79.98
	50000-PO		Cost of sales	31.90	
	12000		Cost of sales		31.90
	40000-FF		Bell-Gro Azalea and Evergreen Food 4 lb. Bag		35.94
	50000-FF		Cost of sales	14.10	
	12000		Cost of sales		14.10
	10200		Williamson Industries	220.31	

Figure 7. 6 Portion of Cash Receipts Journal for Bellwether Garden Supply

By reading and being familiar with the chart of accounts you can gain insight as to the actual events of the journal. The first transaction, dated March 3, 2007 with an Account ID of 23100 indicates that sales tax was collected since cash was debited and the Sales Tax Payable account credited for the amount of $8.23.

THE PURCHASES/RECEIVE INVENTORY JOURNAL

Within Peachtree you can issue Purchase Orders and then receive those ordered items through the Purchases/Receive Inventory form found under Tasks on the menu bar. This is accomplished through the Apply To Purchase Orders Tab. For the problems of the text book, this form is utilized to purchase and receive inventory at the same time through the Apply To Purchases tab. As with other forms, this form can be inventory item driven or you can enter text into the Description window and value into the Amount window for a one time or seldom acquired item.

While this form is usually used for purchases and receipts of merchandise on Accounts Payable, there is a options button at the bottom of the form which allows you to pay some or all of the amount due at the time of recording.

The Purchases/Receive Inventory form generates the Purchases Journal which is found under Accounts Payable within Reports. A portion of Bellwether's Purchases Journal is shown in Figure 7.7, below.

Bellwether Garden Supply
Purchase Journal
For the Period From Mar 1, 2007 to Mar 31, 2007

Filter Criteria includes: Report order is by Date. Report is printed in Detail Format.

Date	Account ID Account Description	Invoice/CM #	Line Description	Debit Amount	Credit Amount
3/1/07	74500 Repairs Expense	B1000	Minor repairs on shop entrance	75.00	
	20000 Accounts Payable		Aaron and Son Contractors		75.00
3/3/07	61000 Auto Expenses	26171	radial tires for landscape truck	274.56	
	20000 Accounts Payable		Jones Memorabilia		274.56
3/3/07	12000 Inventory	B1003	Catalog #: 101030: Rose - Red Seeds	25.50	
	12000 Inventory		Catalog #: 101040: Rose - Yellow Seeds	25.50	
	12000 Inventory		Catalog #: 101050: Rose - White Seeds	25.50	
	20000 Accounts Payable		DPH Web Design		76.50
3/3/07	74000 Rent or Lease Expense	LS-6341	Landscape Equipment Rental	550.00	
	20000 Accounts Payable		Miller Leasing Corp.		550.00
3/4/07	12000 Inventory	11544	Wooden Trellises	95.70	
	57200 Materials Cost		Park Bench - Cedar	159.95	

Figure 7. 7 Portion of Purchases Journal.

Notice that there is both a debit and credit column on the report and Account ID explains the depicted information.

THE CASH PAYMENTS JOURNAL

Cash payments are made through the Payments form under Tasks. This form resembles a check with additional information and fields. If the payment is being made to a party in the vendor or customer data base, you can select that party through the Vendor ID or Customer ID window. If the check is being written to a party without a data record, you can enter the payee's data directly into the Pay To The Order Of fields. If you select a vendor, Peachtree will offer outstanding invoices on the Apply to Invoices tab. Peachtree will also calculate applicable discounts, these values need to be verified.

If the Apply To Expenses tab is selected, you can designate the account that will be credited in the lower portion of the form. While the tab is titled Apply To Expenses, all accounts within the chart of accounts are available in the GL Account window. Again, while this appears to be inventory item driven, you can enter text into the Description windows and values into the Amount windows without selecting inventory items.

The Payments form generates the Cash Disbursements Journal found under Accounts Payable within Reports. A portion of Bellwether's Cash Disbursements Journal is presented in figure 7.8.

Bellwether Garden Supply
Cash Disbursements Journal
For the Period From Mar 1, 2007 to Mar 31, 2007
Filter Criteria includes: Report order is by Date. Report is printed in Detail Format.

Date	Check #	Account ID	Line Description	Debit Amount	Credit Amount
3/12/07	10201	20000	Invoice: 33112	124.68	
		10200	Clowney Chemical Supply		124.68
3/12/07	10202	20000	Invoice: 44555	360.00	
		10200	Gunter, Wilson, Jones, & Smith		360.00
3/12/07	10203	20000	Invoice: LS-6211	550.00	
		10200	Miller Leasing Corp.		550.00
3/12/07	10204	57300-LS	Ground Prep: Chapman Job	215.70	
		57300-LS	Lawn Prep: Hensley Job	119.80	
		10200	Duffey Lawn Pro, Inc.		335.50
3/14/07	10205	89500	Discounts Taken		3.00
		20000	Invoice: 3445574	150.00	
		10200	Gwinnett County License Board		147.00
3/14/07	10206	20000	Invoice: 26171	274.56	
		10200	Jones Memorabilia		274.56
3/14/07	10207	20000	Invoice: LS-6341	550.00	
		10200	Miller Leasing Corp.		550.00
3/14/07	10208	89500	Discounts Taken		5.11

Figure 7. 8 Portion of the Cash Disbursements Journal.

As with some of the other special journals, this journal has a debit and credit column. A good general knowledge of the chart of accounts helps to read the information.

Demonstration Problem, The Celine Dion Company, Directory "theceldi"

The Celine Dion Company uses the Receipts Journal to receive cash. The chart of accounts has been constructed but should be verified prior to use. Record the following transactions in the Celine Dion Company within your Peachtree Student Data Set:

July   3   Cash sale totaled $5,800 for "Bath Towel Set". Verify within the General Ledger that cost of goods sold is $3,480. There is a "Cash Customer" in the database.

        5   A check for $6,370 is received from the Jeltz Co. in payment of an invoice dated June 26 for $6,500, terms 2/10, n/30.

        9   An additional investment of $5,000 in cash is made in the business by Celine Dion, the proprietor. Place Celine Dion in the Name window of the form.

      10   Cash sale totaled $12,519 for "Touring Dress". Verify within the General Ledger that cost of goods sold is $7,511.

      12   A check is received for $7,275 from R. Elliot & Co. in payment of a $7,500 invoice dated July 3, terms 3/10, n/30.

      15   Fast Freddy sent an advance of $700 cash for future sales.

      20   Cash sale total $15,472 for a "Performance Outfit". Verify that the cost of goods sold is $9,283 within the general ledger.

      22   A check for $5,880 is received from Beck Company in payment of $6,000 invoice dated July 13, terms 2/10, n/30.

      29   Cash sale totaled $17,660 for "Baby Clothes". Verify in the general ledger the cost of goods sold of $10,596.

      31   Cash of $200 is received from the Bank of Vegas as interest earned for July.

Instructions:

a. Use the date in the format of 070305 for July 3, 2005, as all invoice and reference requirements.

b. Journalize the above transactions in the Peachtree Receipts form.

c. Run the following reports to check your work:
  1. Cash Receipts Journal
  2. Sales Journal
  3. General Ledger
  4. Income Statement

Sample entry for July 3, 2005 transaction - Receipts form for Cash Sales

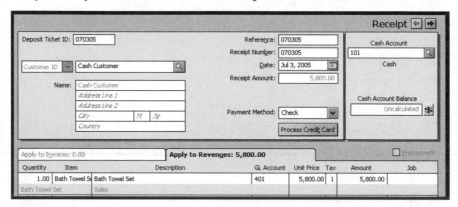

Sample entry for July 5, 2005 transaction - Receipts form for payment on account

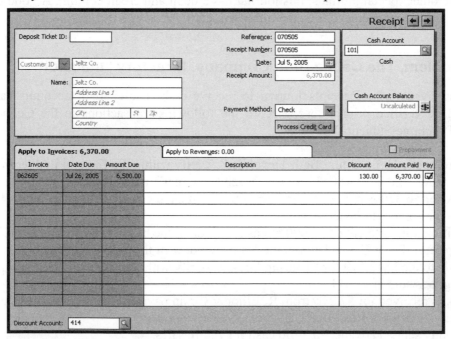

Sample entry for July 9, 2005 transaction – Additional investment in business

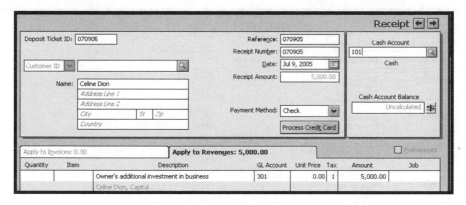

Sample entry for July 15, 2005 transaction – Receipt of advance

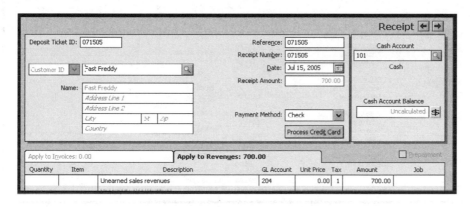

Sample entry for July 31, 2005 transaction – Receipt of interest revenue

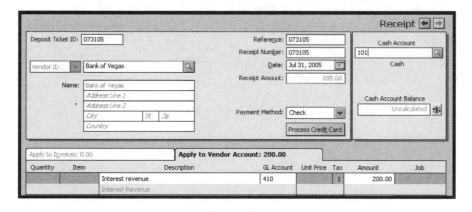

124

Cash Receipts Journal

<table>
<tr><td colspan="6" style="text-align:center">The Celine Dion Company
Cash Receipts Journal
For the Period From Jul 1, 2005 to Jul 31, 2005</td></tr>
<tr><td colspan="6">Filter Criteria includes: Report order is by Check Date. Report is printed in Detail Format.</td></tr>
</table>

Date	Account ID	Transaction Ref	Line Description	Debit Amnt	Credit Amnt
7/3/05	401	070305	Bath Towel Set		5,800.00
	505		Cost of sales	3,480.00	
	120		Cost of sales		3,480.00
	101		Cash Customer	5,800.00	
7/5/05	414	070505	Discounts Taken	130.00	
	112		Invoice: 062605		6,500.00
	101		Jeltz Co.	6,370.00	
7/9/05	301	070905	Owner's additional investment in business		5,000.00
	101		Celine Dion	5,000.00	
7/10/05	401	071005	Touring Dress		12,519.00
	505		Cost of sales	7,511.00	
	120		Cost of sales		7,511.00
	101		Cash Customer	12,519.00	
7/12/05	414	071205	Discounts Taken	225.00	
	112		Invoice: 070305		7,500.00
	101		R. Elliot & Co.	7,275.00	
7/15/05	204	071505	Unearned sales revenues		700.00
	101		Fast Freddy	700.00	
7/20/05	401	072005	Performance Outfit		15,472.00
	505		Cost of sales	9,283.00	
	120		Cost of sales		9,283.00
	101		Cash Customer	15,472.00	
7/22/05	414	072205	Discounts Taken	120.00	
	112		Invoice: 071305		6,000.00
	101		Beck Company	5,880.00	
7/29/05	401	072905	Baby Clothes		17,660.00
	505		Cost of sales	10,596.00	
	120		Cost of sales		10,596.00
	101		Cash Customer	17,660.00	
7/31/05	410	073105	Interest revenue		200.00
	101		Bank of Vegas	200.00	
				108,221.00	108,221.00

General Ledger

The Celine Dion Company
General Ledger
For the Period From Jul 1, 2005 to Jul 31, 2005

Filter Criteria includes: Report order is by ID. Report is printed with Truncated Transaction Descriptions and in Detail Format.

Account ID / Account Description	Date	Reference	Jrnl	Trans Description	Debit Amt	Credit Amt	Balance
101	7/1/05			Beginning Balanc			
Cash	7/3/05	070305	CRJ	Cash Customer	5,800.00		
	7/5/05	070505	CRJ	Jeltz Co.	6,370.00		
	7/9/05	070905	CRJ	Celine Dion	5,000.00		
	7/10/05	071005	CRJ	Cash Customer	12,519.00		
	7/12/05	071205	CRJ	R. Elliot & Co.	7,275.00		
	7/15/05	071505	CRJ	Fast Freddy	700.00		
	7/20/05	072005	CRJ	Cash Customer	15,472.00		
	7/22/05	072205	CRJ	Beck Company	5,880.00		
	7/29/05	072905	CRJ	Cash Customer	17,660.00		
	7/31/05	073105	CRJ	Bank of Vegas	200.00		
				Current Period Ch	76,876.00		76,876.00
	7/31/05			**Ending Balance**			**76,876.00**
112	7/1/05			Beginning Balanc			6,500.00
Accounts Receivable	7/3/05	070305	SJ	R. Elliot & Co.	7,500.00		
	7/5/05	070505	CRJ	Jeltz Co. - Invoice:		6,500.00	
	7/12/05	071205	CRJ	R. Elliot & Co. - Inv		7,500.00	
	7/13/05	071305	SJ	Beck Company	6,000.00		
	7/22/05	072205	CRJ	Beck Company - I		6,000.00	
				Current Period Ch	13,500.00	20,000.00	-6,500.00
	7/31/05			**Ending Balance**			
120	7/1/05			Beginning Balanc			-3,750.00
Merchandise Invento	7/3/05	070305	COG	R. Elliot & Co. - Ite		4,500.00	
	7/3/05	070305	COG	Cash Customer - I		3,480.00	
	7/10/05	071005	COG	Cash Customer - I		7,511.00	
	7/13/05	071305	COG	Beck Company - It		3,250.00	
	7/20/05	072005	COG	Cash Customer - I		9,283.00	
	7/29/05	072905	COG	Cash Customer - I		10,596.00	
				Current Period Ch		38,620.00	-38,620.00
	7/31/05			**Ending Balance**			**-42,370.00**
204	7/1/05			Beginning Balanc			
Unearned Sales Rev	7/15/05	071505	CRJ	Fast Freddy - Une		700.00	
				Current Period Ch		700.00	-700.00
	7/31/05			**Ending Balance**			**-700.00**
301	7/1/05			Beginning Balanc			
Celine Dion, Capital	7/9/05	070905	CRJ	Celine Dion - Own		5,000.00	
				Current Period Ch		5,000.00	-5,000.00
	7/31/05			**Ending Balance**			**5,000.00**
401	7/1/05			Beginning Balanc			-6,500.00
Sales	7/3/05	070305	SJ	R. Elliot & Co. - Ite		7,500.00	
	7/3/05	070305	CRJ	Cash Customer - I		5,800.00	
	7/10/05	071005	CRJ	Cash Customer - I		12,519.00	
	7/13/05	071305	SJ	Beck Company - It		6,000.00	
	7/20/05	072005	CRJ	Cash Customer - I		15,472.00	
	7/29/05	072905	CRJ	Cash Customer - I		17,660.00	
				Current Period Ch		64,951.00	-64,951.00
	7/31/05			**Ending Balance**			**-71,451.00**
410	7/1/05			Beginning Balanc			
Interest Revenue	7/31/05	073105	CRJ	Bank of Vegas - In		200.00	
				Current Period Ch		200.00	-200.00
	7/31/05			**Ending Balance**			**-200.00**
414	7/1/05			Beginning Balanc			
Sales Discounts	7/5/05	070505	CRJ	Jeltz Co. - Invoice:	130.00		
	7/12/05	071205	CRJ	R. Elliot & Co. - Inv	225.00		
	7/22/05	072205	CRJ	Beck Company - I	120.00		
				Current Period Ch	475.00		475.00
	7/31/05			**Ending Balance**			**475.00**
505	7/1/05			Beginning Balanc			3,750.00
Cost of Goods Sold	7/3/05	070305	COG	R. Elliot & Co. - Ite	4,500.00		
	7/3/05	070305	COG	Cash Customer - I	3,480.00		
	7/10/05	071005	COG	Cash Customer - I	7,511.00		
	7/13/05	071305	COG	Beck Company - It	3,250.00		
	7/20/05	072005	COG	Cash Customer - I	9,283.00		
	7/29/05	072905	COG	Cash Customer - I	10,596.00		
				Current Period Ch	38,620.00		38,620.00
	7/31/05			**Ending Balance**			**42,370.00**

Income Statement

	The Celine Dion Company					
	Income Statement					
	For the Seven Months Ending July 31, 2005					
	Current Month			Year to Date		
Revenues						
Sales	$	64,951.00	100.43	$	71,451.00	100.39
Interest Revenue		200.00	0.31		200.00	0.28
Sales Discounts		(475.00)	(0.73)		(475.00)	(0.67)
Total Revenues		64,676.00	100.00		71,176.00	100.00
Cost of Sales						
Cost of Goods Sold		38,620.00	59.71		42,370.00	59.53
Total Cost of Sales		38,620.00	59.71		42,370.00	59.53
Gross Profit		26,056.00	40.29		28,806.00	40.47
Expenses						
Freight-out Expense		0.00	0.00		0.00	0.00
Total Expenses		0.00	0.00		0.00	0.00
Net Income	$	26,056.00	40.29	$	28,806.00	40.47

P7-1B, Iqbal Company, Directory "iqbcompa"

Iqbal Company's chart of accounts includes the following selected accounts already set up within your Student Data Set.

101	Cash	401	Sales
112	Accounts Receivable	414	Sales Discounts
120	Merchandise Inventory	505	Cost of Goods Sold
301	O. Iqbal, Capital		

On April 1, the accounts receivable ledger of Iqbal Company showed the following balances: Naper $1,550, Chelsea $1,200, Finlandia Co. $2,900 and Baez $1,400. The chart of accounts and the beginning balances have been entered into the Peachtree so they do not need to be inserted or established. An inventory item of General Merchandise (Gen Merchandise) has been created for inventory transactions.

The April transactions involving the receipt of cash were as follows:

April	1	The owner, O. Iqbal, invested additional cash in the business, $7,200.
	4	Received check for payment of account from Baez less 2% cash discount.
	5	Received check for $620 in payment of invoice no. 307 from Finlandia Co.
	8	Made cash sales of General Merchandise totaling $7,245. The cost of the merchandise sold was $4,347.
	10	Received check for $600 in payment of invoice no. 309 from Naper.
	11	Received cash refund from a supplier for damaged General Merchandise $740.
	23	Received check for $1,500 in payment of invoice no. 310 from Finlandia Co.
	29	Received check for payment of account from Chelsea.

Instructions:
a. Verify the chart of accounts and the beginning balances.
b. Journalize and post the above transactions.
c. Run the following reports to check your work:
   1. Cash Receipts Journal
   2. Customer Ledger
   3. Income Statement

P7-3B, Odeon Company, Directory "odecompa"

The Chart of Accounts for Odeon Company includes the following selected accounts that have already been set up on your Student Data Set:

112	Accounts Receivable	401	Sales
120	Merchandise Inventory	412	Sales Returns and Allowances
126	Supplies	505	Cost of Goods Sold
157	Equipment	610	Advertising Expense
201	Accounts Payable		

In July, the following selected transactions were completed. All purchases and sales were on account. The cost of all merchandise sold was 70% of the sales price. There are two inventory items set up for purchases and sales. The "Pur Gen Inv" item should be used for all inventory purchasing events while the "Sales Gen Inv" should be used for all inventory sales events. All invoices and references should be in the format of 07/01/05, as dictated by date – this example for July 1, 2005.

July	1	Purchased merchandise from Gucci Company $5,000
	2	Received freight bill from Wayward Shipping on Denton purchase $400.
	3	Made sales to Marion Company $1,300 and to Wayne Bros. $1,500.
	5	Purchased merchandise from Lee Company $3,200.
	8	Received credit on merchandise returned to Lee Company $300.
	13	Purchased store supplies from Boyd Supply $720.
	15	Purchased merchandise from Gucci Co. $3,600 and from Anton Co. $3,300.
	16	Made sales to Rowen Co. $3,450 and to Wayne Bros. $1,570.
	18	Received bill from advertising from Lynda Advertisements $600.
	21	Sales were made to Marion Co. $310 and to Haddad Co. $2,300.
	22	Granted allowance to Marion Co. for merchandise damaged in shipment $40.
	24	Purchased merchandise from Lee Co. $3,000.
	26	Purchased equipment from Boyd Supply $600.
	28	Received freight bill from Wayward Shipping on Grant purchase of July 24th, $380.
	30	Sales were made to Rowen Co., $5,600.

Instructions:
a. Journalize and post the above transactions in Peachtree.
b. Run the following reports to check your work:
   1. Aged Accounts Payable Journal
   2. Invoice Register
   3. Sales Journal
   4. Income Statement
   5. Cash Flows Statement

P7-5B, Scott Co. Directory "scoco"

Presented below are the handwritten purchases and cash payments journals for Scott Co. for its first month of operation, July 2005.

Purchases Journal			
Date	Account Credited	Ref.	Merchandise Inventory, Dr. Accounts Payable, Cr.
July 4	G. Bashful		6,800
5	A. Doc		8,100
11	J. Happy		3,920
13	C. Sleepy		15,300
20	M. Sneezy		7,900
			42,020

Cash Payments Journal					
Date	Account Debited	Other Accounts Dr.	Accounts Payable Dr.	Merchandise Inventory Cr.	Cash Cr.
July 4	Store Supplies	600			600
10	A. Doc		8,100	81	8,019
11	Prepaid Rent	6,000			6,000
15	G. Bashful		6,800		6,800
19	Scott, Drawing	2,500			2,500
21	C. Sleepy		15,300	153	15,147

In addition, the following transactions have not been journalized and posted for July. The cost of all merchandise sold was 65% of the sales price. There are two inventory items set up for purchases and sales. Pur Item should be used for all inventory purchasing events while Sales Item should be used for all inventory sales events. All invoices and references should be in the format of 070105, as dictated by date – this example for July 1, 2005.

July 1 The founder, D. Scott, invests $80,000 in cash in the business.
6 Sell 6,200 Sales Items on account to Dopey Co. for $1 each, terms 1/10, n/30, verify the cost of goods sold in the General Ledger of $4,030.
7 Make a cash sale of 4,000 Sales Items at $1 each, verify the cost of goods sold of $2,600
8 Sell 3,600 Sales Item on account to S. Beauty for $1 each, terms 1/10, n/30
10 Sell 4,900 Sales Item on account to W. Queen for $1 each, terms 1/10, n/30
13 Receive payment in full from S. Beauty
16 Receive payment in full from W. Queen
20 Receive payment in full from Dopey Co.
21 Sell 4,000 Sales Item on account to H. Prince for $1 each, terms 1/10, n/30
29 Returned 420 Pur Item to G. Bashful and received cash refund of $420, use the General Journal..

Instructions:

a. Open the company Scott Company and verify the beginning balances and the chart of accounts.

b. Journalize and post the transactions that have not been journalized. Utilize the Pur Item and Sales Item at the cost of $1 each for all purchasing and selling events. Sales Item's cost has been set at $.65 each.

c. Prepare a trial balance as of July 31, 2005.

d. Determine whether the subsidiary ledgers agree with the control accounts in the general ledger.

e. Make the following adjustments in the General Journal:
   1. A count of supplies indicates that $140 is still on hand.
   2. Recognize rent expense for July, $500.

f. Prepare a General Ledger Trial balance and check your work for errors.

g. Prepare a complete set of Financial Statements including:
   1. Income Statement
   2. Retained Earnings Statement
   3. Balance Sheet

Mini Practice Set

A Financial Reporting Problem

Cedzo Co. uses a perpetual inventory system and both an Accounts Receivable and an Accounts Payable subsidiary ledger. Balances related to both the general ledger and the subsidiary ledger for Cedzo are indicated in the Peachtree Student Data Set for Cedzo. Presented below are a series of transactions for Cedzo Co. for the month of January 2005. Credit sales terms are 2/10, n/30. The cost of all merchandise sold was 60% of the sales price.

Jan 3   Use Sales/Invoicing to record the sale of 4,100 "Sales Item" at $1 each to B. Stahre on account with Invoice # 510, and 1,800 "Sales Item" at $1 each to J. Eppler on account with Invoice #511.

5   Use Purchase/Receive Inventory to purchase 3,000 units of "Pur Item" from S. Wong, in Invoice #010505A for $1 each and 2,200 units of "Pur Item" from D. Lynch for $1 each on Invoice #010505B, terms n/30.

7   Received checks from S. LaDew, $4,000 and B. Garcia, $2,000. The discount period has elapsed. There are invoices that these can be received against.

8   Use Payments to pay freight-in on merchandise purchased, $235, remember to leave the Quantity and Item blank and set the GL account to 120.

9   Use Payments to send checks for payment on account to S. Jung for $9,000 less the 2% cash discount, and on account to D. Norby for $11,000 less a 1% cash discount. Ensure that proper discount is taken.

9   Use Credit Memo to issue a credit memo for $300 to J. Eppler for 300 units of "Sales Item" merchandise returned, Credit Memo #010905A.

10   Use Receipts to record the sale of 15,500 units of "Sales Item" as daily cash sales totaling $15,500, receipt 011005.

11   Use Sales/Invoicing to record the sale of 1,600 units of "Sales Item" on credit to R. Dvorak for $1,600 with Invoice No. 512, and 900 units of "Sale Item" on credit to S. LaDew totaling $900, Invoice No. 513.

12   Use Payments to record the payment of January's rent to landlord, $1,000. Remember to use the Apply to Expenses tab and set the GL account to Rent Expense.

13	Use Receipts to receive payment in full from B. Stahre and J. Eppler less their cash discounts.
15	Use Payments to record M. Cedzo withdrawing $800 cash for his personal use.
16	Use Purchase/Receive Inventory to record the purchase of 16,000 units of "Pur Item" on account from D. Norby for $1 each, terms 1/10, n/30; S. Jung, 14,200 units of "Pur Item" for $1 each, terms 2/10, n/30 and 1,500 units of "Pur Item" from S. Wong for $1 each, terms n/30
17	Use Payments to record the payment of $400 cash for office supplies.
18	Use Vendor Credit Memo to record the return of 200 units of "Pur Item" at $1 each as defective merchandise to S. Jung.
20	Use Receipts to record the sale of 18,100 units of "Sales Item" as daily cash sales totaling $18,100, receipt 012005.
21	You can use Payments to record the issuance of a $15,000 note to R Moses in payment of balance due. This will allow you to "apply" the note to payable invoices. Remember to set the Cash Account to Notes Payable.
21	Received payment in full from S. LaDew less the cash discount.
22	Sold 2,700 units of "Sales Item" for $1 each on credit to B. Stahre, invoice no. 514, and 800 units of "Sale Item" for $1 each to R. Dvorak $800, invoice no. 515.
23	Sent check to D. Norby and S. Jung in full payment on account less the cash discounts.
25	Sold 3,500 units of "Sales Item" merchandise on account to B. Garcia, $3,500, invoice no. 516 and 6,100 units of "Sales Item" for $1 each to J. Eppler on invoice no. 517.
27	Purchased 14,500 units of "Pur Item" for $1 each from D. Norby, terms 1/10, n/30; 1,200 units of "Pur Item" for $1 each from D. Lynch, terms n/30; and 5,400 units of "Pur Item" from S. Wong, terms n/30.
28	Paid $200 cash for office supplies.
31	Summary of daily cash sales is 21,300 units of "Sales Item" for $1 each.
31	Paid sales salaries $4,300 and office salaries $2,800

Instructions:

a. Using the proper subsidiary ledgers for sales, purchases and expenses record the January transactions in Peachtree Complete Accounting.

b. Prepare a working trial balance as of January 31, 2005. The trial balance total should equal $199,400.

c. The following notes will help you make adjusting entries:
1. Office supplies inventory on January 31st totaled $900.
2. Insurance coverage expires on October 31, 2005.
3. Annual depreciation on equipment is $1,500.
4. Interest of $50 has accrued on the note payable.

d. Prepare an Income Statement, Statement of Retained Earnings, Balance Sheet, and a Statement of Cash Flows for the month.

CHAPTER 8

Internal Control and Cash

OBJECTIVES

- Define internal control.
- Explain the applications of internal control to principles to cash receipts.
- Identify the principles of internal control.
- Explain the application of internal control principles to cash disbursements.

- Describe the operation of a petty cash fund.
- Indicate the control features of a bank account.
- Prepare a bank reconciiation.
- Explain the reporting of cash.

INTERNAL CONTROL

Internal control consists of the plan of organization and all the related methods and measures adopted within a business to:

- Safeguard its assts from employee theft, robbery, and unauthorized use.
- Enhance the accuracy and reliability of its accounting records.
- Reduce the risk of errors and irregularities in the accounting process.

PEACHTREE COMPLETE ACCOUNTING REPORTS THAT AID IN THE CONTROL OF CASH

Segregation of duties involving cash is paramount in assuring an accurate cash flow. For example, one employee may be responsible for cash register receipts. That worker in turn gives the receipts and all paperwork to a second worker who double checks the receipts and records them into Peachtree.

Look at the cash receipts journal for High Cotton Farms.

Step 1: Open "High Cotton Farms" from within your Student Data Set and familiarize yourself with the chart of accounts.

Step 2: Review the "Cash Receipts Journal" report found under "Reports" and "Accounts Receivable", shown in figure 8.1.

High Cotton Farms
Cash Receipts Journal
For the Period From Jan 1, 2005 to Jan 31, 2005
Filter Criteria includes: Report order is by Check Date. Report is printed in Detail Format.

Date	Account ID	Transaction Ref	Line Description	Debit Amnt	Credit Amnt
1/10/05	401	011005	Cash Sales		586.10
	101			586.10	
1/16/05	401	011605	Cash Sales		476.58
	101			476.58	
1/30/05	401	013005	Cash Sales		214.10
	101			214.10	
				1,276.78	1,276.78

Figure 8. 1 Cash Receipts Journal from High Cotton Farms.

Notice the date(s) for each transaction along with the Account Number, in your case Sales (#401) and Cash (#101). The Transaction Reference refers to Cash Register Sales (Reg Sales). The line description refers either to cash receipts or cash sales. The amount on the debit side increases the asset cash whereas the amount on the credit side increases the revenue account, sales. This is just opposite of the cash disbursements journal, which was discussed in the previous chapter. Here is the Cash Disbursements Journal for High Cotton Farms.

High Cotton Farms
Cash Disbursements Journal
For the Period From Jan 1, 2005 to Jan 31, 2005
Filter Criteria includes: Report order is by Date. Report is printed in Detail Format.

Date	Check #	Account ID	Line Description	Debit Amount	Credit Amount
1/1/05	147	610	Advertising Expense	1,259.95	
		101	Atlanta Journal/Constitution		1,259.95
1/7/05	148	636	Auto Expense	568.14	
		101	Bob's Exxon		568.14
1/8/05	149	733	Telephone Expense	289.74	
		101	Bell South		289.74
1/14/05	150	680	Travel Expense	398.99	
		101	Delta Airlines		398.99
1/15/05	151	607	Legal & Accounting	1,200.00	
		101	Pam Collins		1,200.00
1/15/05	152	755	Feed & Grain Expense	235.75	
		101	Cobb Feed and Seed		235.75
1/16/05	153	734	Rent - Office	3,200.00	
		101	Pope and Land Realty		3,200.00
1/17/05	154	739	Laundry & Cleaning	72.00	
		101	Chung Xao Pan		72.00
1/18/05	155	655	Entertainment Expense	53.89	
		101	Gold Club		53.89
1/20/05	156	722	Insurance Expense	750.00	
		101	J Smith Lanier		750.00
1/31/05	157	105	Petty Cash	15.00	
		101	Petty Cash Fund		15.00
	Total			8,043.46	8,043.46

Figure 8. 2 Cash Disbursements Journal.

Each check is listed as written for the current period. The appropriate expense account number along with the cash account number follows with the line description. Because these are all paid expense items, the debit amount will be for the expense and the credit amount will be for the decrease in the asset Cash. The Check Register is the next report.

Look at the Check Register Journal for High Cotton Farms.

Step 1: If not already open, open "High Cotton Farms" from within your Student Data Set.

Step 2: Run the "Check Register" report found under "Reports" on the menu bar, and click on Accounts Payable.

Step 3: Click on "Check Register" to obtain the report shown in Figure 8.3.

High Cotton Farms
Check Register
For the Period From Jan 1, 2005 to Jan 31, 2005

Filter Criteria includes: Report order is by Date.

Check #	Date	Payee	Cash Account	Amount
147	1/1/05	Atlanta Journal/Constitut	101	1,259.95
148	1/7/05	Bob's Exxon	101	568.14
149	1/8/05	Bell South	101	289.74
150	1/14/05	Delta Airlines	101	398.99
151	1/15/05	Pam Collins	101	1,200.00
152	1/15/05	Cobb Feed and Seed	101	235.75
153	1/16/05	Pope and Land Realty	101	3,200.00
154	1/17/05	Chung Xao Pan	101	72.00
155	1/18/05	Gold Club	101	53.89
156	1/20/05	J Smith Lanier	101	750.00
157	1/31/05	Petty Cash Fund	101	15.00
Total				8,043.46

Figure 8. 3 Check Register Report

Each check that has been written during this accounting period is listed along with to whom it was paid, the cash account charged, and the amount of the check. Remember that a company may have several checking accounts. If the total amount is deducted from the cash receipts journal, you should have your cash balance for the company.

ESTABLISHING THE PETTY CASH FUND

Better internal control over cash disbursements is possible when payments are made by check. However, writing a check for small amounts can be impractical and inconvenient. Many businesses handle the situation by setting up a petty cash fund which is a fund used to pay relatively small amounts. It is technically called an imprest system that involves a three-step process:

1. Establishing the fund.
2. Making payments from the fund.
3. Replenishing the fund.

The two essential steps in establishing a petty cash fund are: (1.) appointing a petty cash custodian who will be responsible for the fund and (2.) determining the size of the fund. Normally, the amount would be set to cover anticipated expenses over the monthly accounting period. To establish the account, you will write a check for $15 directly to the account. Writing a check is easy in Peachtree. In fact, you'll be doing a lot of check writing in the accounts payable section.

To write a check to the Petty Cash Fund:

Step 1: On the navigation bar, click on "Purchases."

Step 2: In the middle of the "Navigation Aid", Figure 8.4, click on "Write Checks".

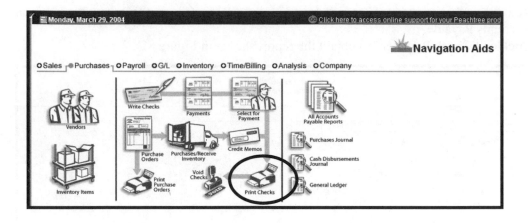

Figure 8. 4 Purchases "Navigation Aid"

Step 3: The Check Writing form, Figure 8.5, will appear.
Step 4: On January 31, 2005, make the check payable to "Cash" or the name of the Petty Cash Custodian; the "Expense Account" will be Account No. 105, the Petty Cash Fund for $15.

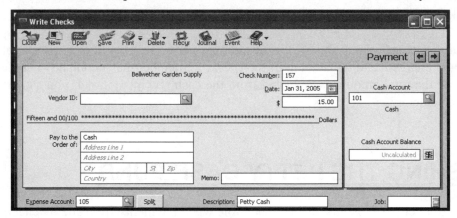

Figure 8. 5 Check Writing Form

Often when a check is written it would be charged to or debited to an expense, thus increasing the expense item (a debit) and decreasing (a credit) cash, an asset. If you were to increase a cash account, such as Petty Cash, that account would have to be debited also.

MAKING PAYMENTS FROM THE PETTY CASH FUND

The custodian of the petty cash fund has the authority to make payments from the fund. Usually, management limits the size of expenditures that may be made. Each payment from the fund must be documented on a prenumbered petty cash receipt or voucher. This would be an internal system that is not available in Peachtree.

REPLENISHING THE PETTY CASH FUND

When the funds in the petty cash fund reach a minimum level, the fund is replenished. The Petty Cash account, number 105, will not be affected by the reimbursement entry. Utilize the Write Check form to write a check to Petty Cash Fund. However, this time use the "Split" function to document the actual expenditures. On February 1, 2005 it is determined that the petty cash fund must be replenished.

Step 1: To write the check, open the Write Checks form under Tasks.

Step 2: On February 1, 2005, it is determined the fund needs replenishing because it is discovered that the fund contains $2. There is a receipt indicating that $5 was spent for postage and that $8 spent for office supplies.

Step 3: Utilize the "Split" function of Write Checks to record the Postage Expense of $5 and the Office Supplies Expense of $8. This is shown in Figure 8.6.

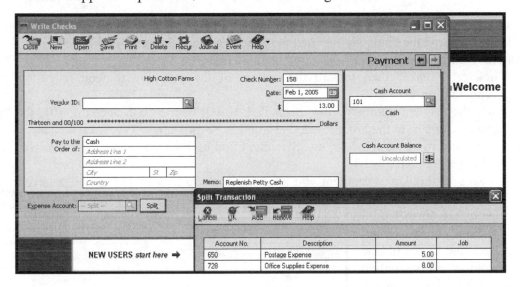

Figure 8. 6 Write Check form to replenish the Petty Cash Fund.

RECONCILING THE BANK ACCOUNT

The bank and the depositor always maintain independent records of the checking account. The two balances are seldom the same at any given time. It is then necessary to make the balance in the books agree with the balance according to the bank. This process is called reconciling the bank account and is an easy automated step in Peachtree.

During the current accounting period, High Cotton had 15 banking transactions; 12 checks numbered 147 – 158 were written and three bank deposits were made. According to High Cotton's books, the Cash account balance is $14.82 as of January 31, 2005. This can be verified in the General Ledger as shown in Figure 8.7.

High Cotton Farms
General Ledger
For the Period From Jan 1, 2005 to Jan 31, 2005
Filter Criteria includes: Report order is by ID. Report is printed with Truncated Transaction Descriptions and in Detail Format.

Account ID Account Description	Date	Reference	Jrnl	Trans Description	Debit Amt	Credit Amt	Balance
101	1/1/05			Beginning Balance			6,781.50
Cash	1/1/05	147	CDJ	Atlanta Journal/Const		1,259.95	
	1/7/05	148	CDJ	Bob's Exxon		568.14	
	1/8/05	149	CDJ	Bell South		289.74	
	1/10/05	011005	CRJ		586.10		
	1/14/05	150	CDJ	Delta Airlines		398.99	
	1/15/05	151	CDJ	Pam Collins		1,200.00	
	1/15/05	152	CDJ	Cobb Feed and Seed		235.75	
	1/16/05	011605	CRJ		476.58		
	1/16/05	153	CDJ	Pope and Land Realty		3,200.00	
	1/17/05	154	CDJ	Chung Xao Pan		72.00	
	1/18/05	155	CDJ	Gold Club		53.89	
	1/20/05	156	CDJ	J Smith Lanier		750.00	
	1/30/05	013005	CRJ		214.10		
	1/31/05	157	CDJ	Petty Cash Fund		15.00	
				Current Period Chang	1,276.78	8,043.46	-6,766.68
	1/31/05			Ending Balance			14.82

Figure 8. 7 Cash Account from the General Ledger

When you received your bank statement, the balance was $792.13. Checks 151 for $1,200.00 and 155 for $53.89 had not cleared the bank. Neither had the deposit on January 16th for $476.58.

To reconcile your bank account.

Step 1: Click on "Tasks" then toward the bottom of the pull down menu, click on "Account Reconciliation,"

Step 2: Enter the account number being reconciled. It will be the Cash account, 101, the Peachtree account number, in the box provided just under the tool bar.

Step 3: At the bottom of the window, by "Statement Ending Balance" enter the balance as shown on the bank statement $792.13.

Step 4: Looking at the bank statement you know all but two checks 151 and 155 have cleared the bank. The deposit on January 16 for $476.58 did not clear either. Check the boxes on the account reconciliation form by clicking in the box for those items *that have* cleared the bank.

Step 5: Your completed reconciliation should look like that shown in Figure 8.8. Notice the tally at the bottom of the window. Also, bear in mind that not all information will be shown because scroll boxes (list boxes) are utilized.

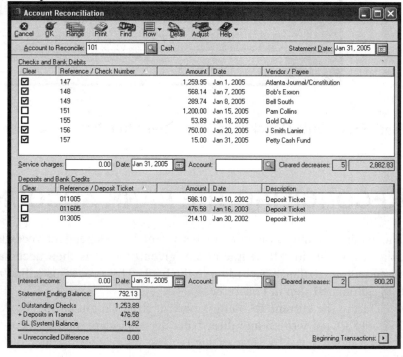

Figure 8. 8 The completed Account Reconciliation window.

In the bottom left corner of the Account Reconciliation form Peachtree shows you the mathematics of the reconciliation. From the bank's balance it subtracts outstanding checks, adds deposits in transit, and subtracts the GL balance for the account. The difference must equal zero before the account is "reconciled". Ensure that you print the reconciliation report through the "Print" option. These prints are kept in the files for reference and support later.

With the delay in the deposit of January 16, 2005 now in excess of 14 days, this deposit must be investigated. This is an excessive time delay.

Demonstration Problem, K. Poorten Company, Directory "kpoocomp"

K. Poorten Company's bank statement for May 2005 shows the following data:

Balance May 1st	$12,650	Balance May 31st	$14,280
Debit Memorandum:		Credit Memorandum	
NSF Check	$175	Collection of note receivable	$505

The cash balance per books at May 31 is $13,319. Your review of the data reveals the following:

1. The NSF check was received from Copple Co., a customer on May 15 2005 on account, use a general journal entry to reinstate this accounts receivable.
2. The note collected by the bank was a $500, 3-month, 12% note. The bank charged a $10 collection fee. No interest has been accrued. Use the general journal to record this issue.
3. Outstanding Checks at May 31st are numbers 510 and 512 totaling $2,410.
4. There is one Deposit in Transit at May 31st, it is Deposit 05/30/05 for $1,752.
5. A K. Poorten Company check, number 503, dated May 10, 2005, cleared the bank on May 25, 2005. This check, which was payment on account, was journalized for $325. Use the Payments task form to pay the additional amount so you can apply it to Accounts Payable. Use "Adj 503" as the number.

Instructions:

a. Use Peachtree Complete Accounting to prepare a bank reconciliation on May 31, 2005, for the K Poorten Company.
b. Journalize any entries as directed
c. Print the Account Reconciliation form.

138

Solution:

Page: 1

K. Poorten Company
Account Reconciliation - Deposits and Bank Credits
For Account 101 - Cash
Statement Date May 31, 2005

Filter Criteria includes: All Deposits and Bank Credits for 101 - Cash

Clear Status	Reference Number	Amount	Date	Description
Yes	051205	2,500.00	May 12, 2005	Deposit Ticket
Yes	051505	175.00	May 15, 2005	Deposit Ticket
Yes	052405	2,450.00	May 24, 2005	Deposit Ticket
No	053005	1,752.00	May 30, 2005	Deposit Ticket
Yes	Bank Rec 2	505.00	May 31, 2005	N/R collection

		7,382.00		Sub Total
		0.00		Interest Income

		7,382.00		Total
		========		

Page: 1

K. Poorten Company
Account Reconciliation - Checks and Bank Debits
For Account 101 - Cash
Statement Date May 31, 2005

Filter Criteria includes: All Checks and Bank Debits for 101 - Cash

Clear Status	Reference Number	Amount	Date	Vendor / Payee
Yes	503	325.00	May 10, 2005	Vendor
No	510	1,000.00	May 15, 2005	Vendor
No	512	1,410.00	May 17, 2005	Vendor
Yes	515	1,500.00	May 22, 2005	Vendor
Yes	518	2,520.00	May 25, 2005	Vendor
Yes	Adj	27.00	May 31, 2005	Vendor
Yes	Bank Rec 1	175.00	May 31, 2005	NSF Check, Copple Co.

		6,957.00		Sub Total
		0.00		Service Charge

		6,957.00		Total
		========		

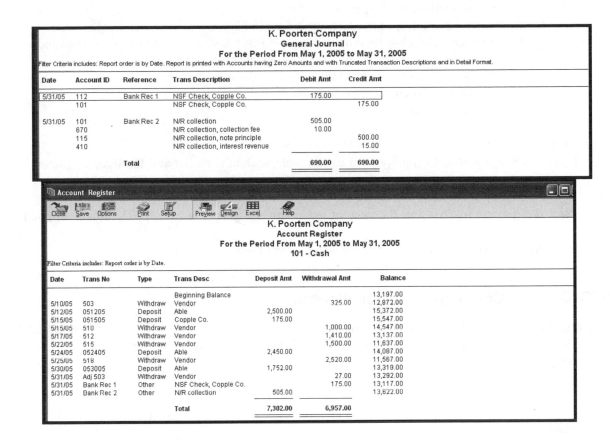

K. Poorten Company
General Journal
For the Period From May 1, 2005 to May 31, 2005
Filter Criteria includes: Report order is by Date. Report is printed with Accounts having Zero Amounts and with Truncated Transaction Descriptions and in Detail Format.

Date	Account ID	Reference	Trans Description	Debit Amt	Credit Amt
5/31/05	112	Bank Rec 1	NSF Check, Copple Co.	175.00	
	101		NSF Check, Copple Co.		175.00
5/31/05	101	Bank Rec 2	N/R collection	505.00	
	670		N/R collection, collection fee	10.00	
	115		N/R collection, note principle		500.00
	410		N/R collection, interest revenue		15.00
		Total		690.00	690.00

Account Register

Close Save Options Print Setup Preview Design Excel Help

K. Poorten Company
Account Register
For the Period From May 1, 2005 to May 31, 2005
101 - Cash

Filter Criteria includes: Report order is by Date.

Date	Trans No	Type	Trans Desc	Deposit Amt	Withdrawal Amt	Balance
			Beginning Balance			13,197.00
5/10/05	503	Withdraw	Vendor		325.00	12,872.00
5/12/05	051205	Deposit	Able	2,500.00		15,372.00
5/15/05	051505	Deposit	Copple Co.	175.00		15,547.00
5/15/05	510	Withdraw	Vendor		1,000.00	14,547.00
5/17/05	512	Withdraw	Vendor		1,410.00	13,137.00
5/22/05	515	Withdraw	Vendor		1,500.00	11,637.00
5/24/05	052405	Deposit	Able	2,450.00		14,087.00
5/25/05	518	Withdraw	Vendor		2,520.00	11,567.00
5/30/05	053005	Deposit	Able	1,752.00		13,319.00
5/31/05	Adj 503	Withdraw	Vendor		27.00	13,292.00
5/31/05	Bank Rec 1	Other	NSF Check, Copple Co.		175.00	13,117.00
5/31/05	Bank Rec 2	Other	N/R collection	505.00		13,622.00
			Total	7,382.00	6,957.00	

P8-2B, Sammy Sosa Company, Directory "samsosco"

Sammy Sosa Company maintains a petty cash fund for small expenditures. The following transactions occurred over a 2-month period.

July 1 Established a petty cash fund by writing a check for $200.

15 Replenished the petty cash fund by writing a check for $198.00. On this date, the fund consisted of $2.00 in cash and the following petty cash receipts:
- Freight out, $94.00
- Postage Expense, $42.40
- Entertainment Expense, $46.60
- Miscellaneous Expense, $11.20

31 Replenished the petty cash fund by writing a check for $192.00. On this date, the fund consisted of $8.00 in cash and the following petty cash receipts:
- Freight out, $82.10
- Charitable Contributions, $45.00
- Postage Expense, $25.50
- Miscellaneous expense, $39.40

August 15 Replenished the petty cash fund by writing a check for $187.00. On this date, the fund consisted of $13.00 in cash and the following petty cash receipts:
- Freight out, $74.60
- Entertainment Expense, $43.00
- Postage Expense, $33.00

- Miscellaneous Expense, $37.00
16 Increased the amount of the petty cash fund to $300 by writing a check for $100.
31 Replenished petty cash fund by writing a check for $284.00. On this date, the fund consisted of $16.00 in cash and the following petty cash receipts:
   - Postage Expense, $140.00
   - Travel Expense, $95.60
   - Freight out, $47.10

Instructions:
a. Open the Sammy Sosa Company from within your Student Data Set and familiarize yourself with the chart of accounts.
b. Using the General Journal, journalize the petty cash transactions.
c. Print the general journal and the general ledger for the period July 1, 2005 through August 31, 2005.
d. What internal control features exist in this petty cash fund?

P8-5B, Cell Ten Company, Directory "celten"

Cell Ten Company maintains a checking account at the Commerce Bank. At July 21, 2005, selected data from the ledger balance and the bank statement are as follows: The bank statement for July 2005 shows the following data.

	Cash in Bank	
	Per Books	**Per Bank**
Balance, July 1, 2005	$17,600	$18,800
July receipts	81,400	
July credits		80,470
July disbursements	77,150	
July debits		74,756
Balance, July 31, 2005	$21,850	$24,514

Analysis to the bank data reveals that the credits consist of $79,000 of July deposits and a credit memorandum of $1,470 for the collection of a $1,400 note plus interest revenue of $70. The July debits per bank consist of checks cleared $74,700 and a debit memorandum of $56 for printing additional company checks.

You also discover the following errors involving July checks: (1) A check for $230 to a creditor on account that cleared the bank in July was journalized and posted as $320, (2) A salary check to an employee for $255 was recorded by the bank for $155.

The June 30 bank reconciliation contained only two reconciling items: (1) deposits in transit $5,000, and (2) outstanding checks of $6,200.

Instructions:
a. Open the Cell Ten Company from within your Student Data Set and familiarize yourself with the chart of accounts.
b. Utilize the General Journal to journalize the events known by the bank but not known by you until this statement's receipt.

c. Use Peachtree Complete Accounting to prepare a bank reconciliation on July 31 for Cell Ten Company. Assume that interest has been accrued. Note: the check can be adjusted in its recording process.

d. Utilize the Account Reconciliation capability of Peachtree Complete Accounting under Tasks.

e. Print out the Reconciliation Report and the General Journal.

CHAPTER 9

Accounting for Receivables

OBJECTIVES

- Explain how accounts receivable are recognized in accounts
- Identify the different types of receivables
- Distinguish between the methods and basics used to value accounts receivable.
- Describe the entries to record the disposition of accounts receivable.

- Explain how notes receivable are recognized in the accounts.
- Describe how notes receivable are valued.
- Describe the entries to record the disposition of notes receivable.
- Explain the statement presentation and analysis of receivables.

TYPES OF RECEIVABLES

The term *receivable* refers to amounts due from individuals and other companies. They are claims that are expected to be collected in cash. Receivables are frequently classified as: Accounts; Notes; and Other.

ACCOUNTS RECEIVABLE

Accounts receivable are the amounts owed by customers on their account. They result from the sale of goods and services. These receivables generally are expected to be collected within 30 to 60 days. They are the most significant type of claim held by a company.

NOTES RECEIVABLE

Notes receivables are claims for which formal instruments of credit are issued as proof of the debt. A note receivable normally requires the debtor to pay interest. Notes and accounts receivable that results from sales transactions are often called trade receivables.

OTHER RECEIVABLES

Other receivables include nontrade receivables such as interest receivable, loans to company officers, advances to employees, and income taxes refundable. These are unusual and are generally classified and reported as separate items on the balance sheet.

Three primary accounting issues are associated with accounts receivable:
- Recognizing the receivable
- Valuing the accounts receivable
- Disposing of accounts receivable.

RECOGNIZING ACCOUNTS RECEIVABLE

Recognizing accounts receivable is relatively straightforward; most of the work was done in Chapter 5. To review, let's work through a sale using a simple company.

Step 1: From within your Student Data Set, open "Jordache Co."

Step 2: Click on the "Sales Navigation Aid" at the bottom of the Peachtree window

Step 3: Click on "Sales/Invoicing" about midway on the navigation aid.

Step 4: You will be presented with the blank sales invoice.

Step 5: On January 1, 2005, use C101, the Customer ID for the Polo Co and invoice number 010105.

Step 6: Make the "Apply to Sales" entry area to sell Polo 100 pairs of Jeans at $10/each..

Step 7: Make sure the terms read: 2/10, net/30.

Step 8: Check your work with the completed form as shown in Figure 9.1.

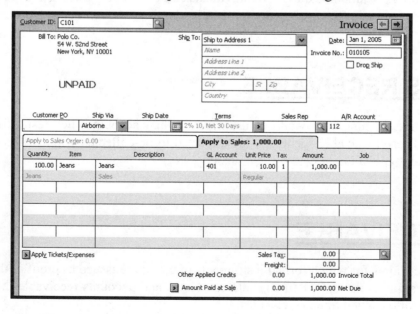

Figure 9. 1 Completed sales invoice.

On January 8, payment from Polo is received for the balance due which should include a $20 discount because they paid within the 10-day time limit.

Step 1: Click on "Sales" on the navigation bar.
Step 2: Click on "Receipts" to get the window.
Step 3: Click on the "Customer ID" and you are presented with all of the open invoices for that specific customer as shown in Figure 9.2.
Step 4: Use Deposit Ticket Number, Reference, and Receipt Number 010805.

<u>***Note:***</u> Because you are within the discount period, the discount (2% of the total invoice) is automatically recognized and posted to the proper account when the account is posted.

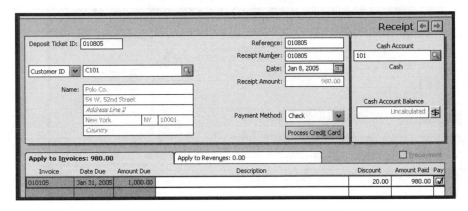

Figure 9. 2 The completed Receipts window.

WRITE OFF OF A CUSTOMER BAD DEBT

In some cases customers will not pay money owed, and the accounts receivable must be written off to bad debt expense. There are two methods for writing off bad debts.

Direct Method: Each invoice that is a bad debt is posted to Bad Debt Expense (an expense account) as the bad debt is recognized.

Allowance Method: A percentage of your accounts receivables is written off periodically or at the end of each fiscal year. The amount that is written off depends on the percentage of bad debt you believe your company incurs throughout the year. Normally, you would make a General Journal entry affecting an accounts receivable (used as a contra-asset) account titled "Allowance for Doubtful Accounts" and Bad Debt Expense (an expense account). Then, each invoice is written off to Allowance for Doubtful Accounts as the bad debt is recognized.

To directly write off an invoice(s) whether partially paid or not paid at all in Accounts Receivable as a bad debt, follow the procedure below.

On January 5, 2005, Zaxby's Restaurant, Customer ID ZAXB01, purchased 50 table clothes for $15 each. Record these event through the Sales/Invoice form, use invoice and reference numbers 010505..

On March 20, 2005, it was determined that the restaurant went out of business and would not be paying their bill. Thus, it is to be written off as a bad debt

Step 1: Open "Jordache Co." from within your Student Data Set, if it is not already open.

Step 2: From the "Navigation Aid," select "Sales" then "Receipts." Peachtree displays the receipts window.

Step 3: Identify and click on Zaxby's Customer ID, ZAXB01. There is only one invoice, number 010505, for Zaxby to be written off as a bad debt.

Step 4: Peachtree displays the outstanding invoice that is due.

Step 5: Enter the reference number 032005.

Step 6: In the Cash Account list, select "Bad Debt Expense" from the pull down menu

Step 7: On the "Apply to Invoices" tab, select the "Pay" check box next to the invoice you wish to write off. The completed form is shown in Figure 9.3.

Step 8: Then save the form.

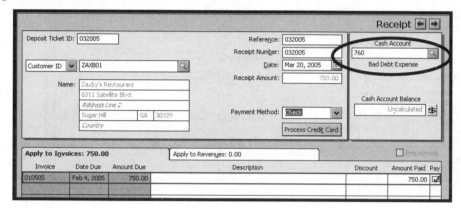

Figure 9. 3 Receipts form used to write off bad debt.

ALLOWANCE FOR UNCOLLECTIBLE ACCOUNTS

Under the direct write-off method, bad debts expense is seldom recorded in a period in which the revenue was recorded. No attempt is made to match bad debts expense to sales revenues in the income statement.

On the other hand, the allowance method of accounting for bad debts involves estimating uncollectible accounts at the end of each period. This method provides better matching on the income statement and ensures that receivables are stated at their cash (net) realizable value, which is the net amount expected to be received in cash. It excludes amounts that the company estimates it will not collect. Receivables are therefore reduced by estimated uncollectible receivables on the balance sheet through use of this method.

The allowance method is required for financial reporting purposes when bad debts are material in amount. The allowance for doubtful accounts is entered through a General Journal entry similar to the entry in Figure 9.4.

To illustrate the allowance method, assume Jordache Company has credit sales of $1,200,000. Of that amount, $200,000 remains uncollected at the end of year, December 31st. The credit manager estimates $12,000 of these sales will be uncollectible. The general journal entry made on December 31, 2005, is shown in Figure 9.4 below.

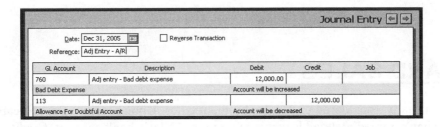

Figure 9. 4 Completed General Journal entry for Uncollectible Accounts

AGED RECEIVABLES REPORT

An aging schedule for accounts receivable is a listing of customer balances that are classified by the length of time they have been unpaid.

To obtain a sample aging report:

Step 1: Open on your student disk, Bellwether Garden Supply, Peachtree's tutorial company.

Step 2: Click on Reports, then click on Accounts Receivable

Step 3: Click on Aged Receivables on the reports list.

A portion of the aged receivables report is shown in Figure 9.5. Compare that with additional information provided in your text. Data may not be the same on your system. However, the basic format of the information should be similar.

		Bellwether Garden Supply				
		Aged Receivables				
		As of Mar 31, 2007				
Filter Criteria includes: Report order is by ID. Report is printed in Detail Format.						
Customer ID **Customer** **Contact** **Telephone 1**	**Invoice/CM #**	**0 - 30**	**31 - 60**	**61 - 90**	**Over 90 days**	**Amount Due**
ALIGOOD-01 Aligood Chiropractic Tony Aligood 770-555-0654	10332	129.97				129.97
ALIGOOD-01 **Aligood Chiropractic**		129.97				129.97
ARCENEAUX-01 Arceneaux Software Natasha Arceneaux 770-555-4660	10329 CCM4008 10317	59.98 -49.99 49.99				59.98 -49.99 49.99
ARCENEAUX-01 **Arceneaux Software**		59.98				59.98

Figure 9. 5 Portion of Aged Receivables Report from Bellwether Garden Supply.

CREDIT CARD SALES

Credit card sales are usually considered cash sales by the retailer. Upon receipt of credit card sales slips from the retailer, the bank immediately adds that amount to the seller's bank account. Credit card slips are recorded on the deposit much like the way in which checks are recorded. A fee ranging from 2 to 6 percent of the credit card sales is charged to the seller.

Before you can begin recording credit card transactions in Peachtree Complete Accounting, you must consider the following questions.

When are credit card payments deposited into the company's bank account? Are payments received when the bank receives the credit card transactions (within 24 hours)? Or, is payment received three or more days after submitting the charges?

When does the bank debit from your bank account the credit card processing fee? Is the processing fee deducted from each customer's credit card use? Or, does the credit card company charge one processing fee for the entire month?

SET UP PEACHTREE COMPLETE ACCOUNTING TO ACCEPT CREDIT CARD RECEIPTS

Before you can record a credit card receipt from a customer, you must first set up an expense account in the Chart of Accounts in which to charge the credit card processing fees. Again, make sure Jordache Co. is open on your Student Disk. To verify that account 765 is Credit Card Processing Expense:

Step 1: Click on "Maintain" from the main menu bar. Select Chart of Accounts. Peachtree displays the Maintain Chart of Accounts window.

Step 2: Use the drop down arrow to verify the existence of the 765 account and titling.

If you receive the entire credit card payment in one lump sum, then no other special accounts are required. However, if there is a delay between the time your customer makes the charge and when the credit card company reimburses you, you may want to set up unique accounts receivable accounts to track money owed by the credit card company. Still using Jordache Co. verify that account 122 is AMEX Receivable.

You also must set up the credit card company that deposits money in your bank account as a vendor, not a customer. This way you can record and track processing-fee expenses.

SET UP A CREDIT CARD VENDOR FOR CUSTOMER RECEIPTS

You must set up a vendor from whom you will receive monthly credit card reimbursements.

Step 1: From the Maintain menu, within the Jordache Co., select Vendors. Peachtree displays the Maintain Vendors window.

Step 2: Enter a vendor ID that represents the credit card (e.g., AMEX).

Step 3: Enter a vendor name that represents the bank or firm of your credit card (e.g., American Express or Wachovia Bank VISA).

Step 4: Enter any additional information, as needed on the General tab. Then, select the Purchase Defaults tab.

Step 5: Select account 765, the Credit Card Processing Expense account as the purchase account default.

Step 6: When finished entering vendor information, select Save, and close the window.

ENTER CUSTOMER CREDIT CARD RECEIPTS

When recording credit card receipts, always enter customer payments using "Receipts" from the Tasks menu. Apply the customer credit card receipts to open invoices or to revenue (prepayment). You cannot manage credit card receipts effectively when using the Amount Paid field in "Invoicing." You will also be unable to edit the invoice, if needed, later.

To keep the customer's ledger accurate and up-to-date, record the amount paid in Receipts as the "full" amount of the credit card charge, regardless of how the bank handles processing fees.

NOTES RECEIVABLE

Credit may also be granted in exchange for a promissory note, which is a written promise to pay a specified amount of money on demand or at a specific time. Promissory notes may be used when individuals or companies lend or borrow money; when the amount of the transaction and the credit period exceed normal limits or in settlement of accounts receivable.

On January 17, 2005, Mills Company purchased 1,000 towels on account. On February 28, 2005, it was agreed that the Accounts Receivable value of $7,500 would be placed on an interest bearing Notes Receivable by Jordache. This invoice is in your Student Data Set.

The Receipts form can be utilized to convert this Accounts Receivable to a Notes Receivable. This will allow you to apply the value to the invoice.

Open the Receipt form shown in Figure 9.6. Use the "Receipt" process from the Navigation Bar to make the entry changing the Cash Account to the Notes Receivable Account as shown. Change the Cash Account to 115, Notes Receivable. This form will allow you to apply the value of the note to outstanding invoices as shown in the lower section of the form.

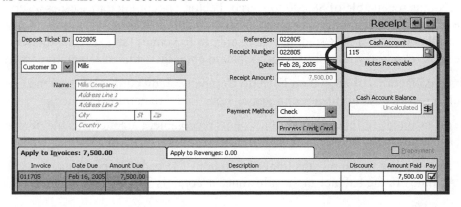

Figure 9. 6 Transferring an amount from Accounts Receivable to Notes Receivable.

Demonstration Problem, Falcetto Company, Chapter 9, Directory "falcomp Chap 9"

The following selected transactions relate to Falcetto Company during 2005. All accounts and customers have been established in your Student Data Set.

Mar 1   Sold 4,000 pots to Potter Company at $5 each, terms 2/10, n/30. Use 030105 as a reference.

Mar 11   Use the Receipts form to receive payment in full from Potter Company for balance due. Use 031105 as a reference.

Mar 12   Accepted Juno Company's $20,000, 6-month, 12% note for balance due. Use Receipts form and change the cash account to Notes Receivable. Use 031205 as a reference.

Mar 13   Sold 1,320 Credit Card Sales items for $10 each to Credit Card Customer. Utilize the Sales/Invoice form and Credit Card Customer for this event. Use 031305 as reference.

Mar 15   Made American Express credit sales of 670 items of Credit Card Sales items for $10 each totaling $6,700. A 5% service fee is charged by American Express. Use the Sales/Invoice form as shown: (Use 031505 as a reference.)

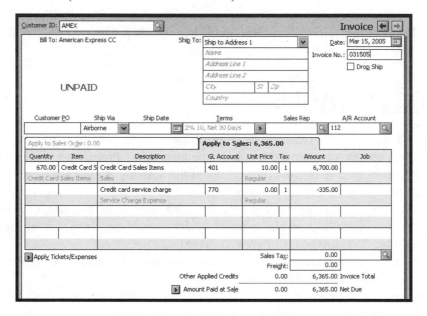

Mar 30   Received payment in full from American Express Company. Use 033005 as a reference.

Apr 11   Sold accounts receivable of $8,000 to Harcot Factor. Harcot Factor assesses a service charge of 2% of the amount of receivables sold. Within Receipts, use Apply to Invoices tab to record the $8,000 of A/R sold, use the Apply to Revenues tab to record the service charge as an expense within the GL account and enter the value as a negative value.

Apr 13   Received collections of $8,200 on Falcetto Company credit card sales. Use the General Journal to record adding finance charges of 1.5% to the remaining balance.

May 10   Wrote off as uncollectible $16,000 of accounts receivable. Falcetto uses the percentage of sales basis to estimate bad debts. Use Receipts to apply it to invoices.

Jun 30   Credit sales for the first 6 months total $2,000,000. The bad debt percentage is 1% of credit sales. At June 30, the balance in the allowance account is $3,500. Use a general journal entry.

Jul 16   One of the accounts receivable written off in May was from J. Simon, who pays the amount due, $4,000, in full. Use a single, compound journal entry to reinstate and receive the payment.

Instructions: (**Note:** Values and invoices have been entered as beginning balances.)

a. Familiarize yourself with the chart of accounts.
b. Journalize the events as instructed.
c. Use the range of March 1, 2005 through July 31, 2005, and print the following reports: Cash Receipts Journal, Sales Journal, and the General Ledger.

P9-6B, Derek Lu Company, Directory "derlucom"

Derek Lu Company closes its books monthly. On September 30th, selected ledger account balances are:

Notes Receivable	$29,000
Interest Receivable	210

Notes receivable include the following:

Date	Maker	Face	Term	Interest
August 16	Demaster Inc.	$8,000	60 days	12%
August 25	Almer Co.	$9,000	60 days	10%
September 30	Skinner Corp.	$12,000	6 months	9%

Interest is computed using a 360-day year. During October, the following transactions were completed. Peachtree Complete Accounting does not have a method of computing Notes Receivable. You should use the General Journal for your entries.

Oct   7   Made sales of $6,900 on Derek Lu credit cards.
      12   Made sales of $800 on MasterCard credit cards. The credit card service charge is 3%.
      15   Added $460 to Derek Lu customer balance for finance charges on unpaid balances.
      15   Received payment in full from Demaster Inc. on the amount due.
      24   Received notice that Almer note has been dishonored. (Assume that Almer is expected to pay in the future.)

Instructions:

a. Journalize the October transactions and the October 31st adjusting entry for accrued interest receivable.
b. Enter the balances at October 1st in the receivable accounts. Post the entries to all of the receivable accounts.
c. Show the balance sheet presentation of the receivable accounts as of October 31st.

CHAPTER 10

Plant Assets, Natural Resources, and Intangible Assets

OBJECTIVES
- Be able to set up a plant asset account
- Be able to set up an accumulated depreciation account

- Design and execute reoccurring transactions
- Be able to journalize depreciation and depreciation expense

SETTING UP A PLANT ASSET ACCOUNT

Plant assets are tangible resources that are used in the operations of a business and are not intended for sale to customers. In accounting, they are also called "Property, Plant, and Equipment"; "Plant and Equipment"; or "Fixed Assets". These assets are generally long-lived and are expected to provide services to the company for a number of years. With the exception of land, plant assets decline in service potential over their useful lives.

Plant assets often are split into four classes:

Land – the building site

Land Improvements – driveways, parking lots, fences, underground sprinkler systems, etc.

Buildings – stores, offices, factories, and warehouses

Equipment – checkout counters, cash registers, office furniture, factory machinery, and delivery equipment

In Peachtree, all property, plant, and equipment; plant and equipment; or fixed assets will be classified as "Fixed Assets" when the account is created as shown in Figure 10.1. On the balance sheet, they are classified as Property and Equipment.

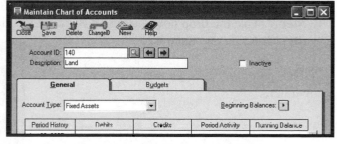

Figure 10. 1 Example of Fixed Asset in Maintain Chart of Accounts

154

Accumulated depreciation is a contra asset account to depreciable (fixed) assets. For example, depreciation will be charged against buildings, machinery, and equipment. The depreciable basis is the difference between an asset's cost and its estimated salvage value. Recording depreciation is a way to indicate that assets have declined in service potential during the period. Accumulated depreciation represents total depreciation taken to date on the assets.

An example from "Maintain Chart of Accounts" is shown in Figure 10.2.

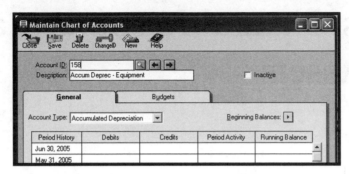

Figure 10. 2 Example of Accumulated Depreciation in Maintain Chart of Accounts

Peachtree does not provide any special way of entering transactions for the purchase of Fixed Assets or entering transactions for Accumulated Depreciation besides a General Journal entry, which was covered previously. Depreciable calculations must be done in a fixed asset manager or Excel and entered as a General Journal entry.

CREATING THE FIXED ASSET ACCOUNT(S)

Three accounts will be created in this exercise. The first account to be created is for the purchase of a warehouse, account 148, and accumulated depreciation for the warehouse, account 149.

Step 1: Open "Beyer Video" from within your Student Data Set. Be sure to use your most updated file.

Step 2: The account number for "Warehouse" is 148, the account type will be Fixed Assets.

Step 3: The account number for "Accum Deprec – Warehouse" is 149, the account type will be Accumulated Depreciation.

Step 4: Access Chart of Accounts through Maintain from the menu bar.

Step 5: Enter "148" in Account ID, the number of the account.

Step 6: Enter "Warehouse" in Description.

Step 7: Use the drop down arrow in Account type to find and select "Fixed Assets".

Step 8: Click on "Save".

The date entry is shown in Figure 10.3, shown here.

Figure 10. 3 Chart of accounts construction.

The construction of Account 149, Accumulated Depreciation – Warehouse parallels this construction. The differences are 1) the account title must be abbreviated to fit the window so try "Accum Deprec – Warehouse" which is adequate to identify the account. From the Account Type drop down selection, find and select "Accumulated Depreciation". Now build "Deprec Expense – Warehouse", number 619, type - expense.

MAKING THE ENTRY

Step 1: Make sure Beyer Video is open to the most up to date file. You will be making a compound General Journal entry on June 18, 2005 to purchase land for $150,000 and a warehouse on that land for $250,000.

Step 2: Using the General Journal, debit Land for $150,000 and Warehouse for $150,000, credit cash for $100,000, the down payment, and credit Notes Payable – Long-term for the balance of $300,000 for this acquisition. The journal entry is shown in figure 10.4, below.

Figure 10. 4 Compound General Journal entry to show purchase of land & warehouse.

Using the straight line method of depreciation, it has been determined that the useful life of the building will be 20 years and that the salvage value will be $15,000. Based on those figures, the monthly depreciation for the building will be $979.17

Cost of the Building – Salvage Value = Depreciable Value	250,000 – 15,000 = 235,000
Depreciable Value / 20 years = Yearly Depreciation	235,000 / 20 = 11,750
Yearly Depreciation / 12 months = Monthly Depreciation	11,750 / 12 = 979.17

RECURRING TRANSACTIONS FOR MONTHLY DEPRECIATION FOR THE WAREHOUSE

You learned how to make this basic entry in Chapter 3, Adjusting Entries. However, since this will be a recurring transaction, one that happens the same way, every time, Peachtree can automate that step for you.

Step 1: Make the general journal entry as you normally would to expense depreciation.

Step 2: Debit the Deprec Expense –Warehouse account no. 619 for $979.17.

Step 3: Credit the Accumulated Depreciation – Building Account No. 149 for $979.17. Do not save the journal entry yet. The entry is shown in Figure 10.5

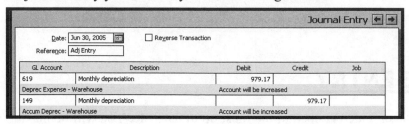

Figure 10. 5 Depreciation journal entry.

Step 4: Instead of saving the transaction as you did previously, click on "Recur" on the toolbar as shown in Figure 10.6 below

Figure 10. 6 Menu Bar for General Journal entry.

Step 5: You will be presented with the pull down menu as shown in Figure 10.7. Click "Monthly" and enter "18 as the number of accounting periods this transaction will occur. Peachtree will only recognize accounting periods – months through the end of the available periods.

Step 6: Click "OK" and on the last day of every month for the next 18 months, Peachtree will automatically make this entry for you.

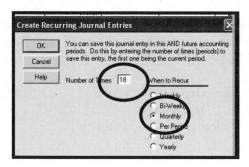

Figure 10. 7 Create Recurring Journal Entries window.

Run a copy of the Balance Sheet for the period January 1, 2005 through December 31, 2005, for Beyer Video. Look specifically at the assets section of the report, Figure 10.8. Notice the addition of the new accounts. Also, notice the Accumulated Depreciation account for the warehouse.

Beyer Video
Balance Sheet
December 31, 2006

ASSETS

Current Assets		
Cash	$ (100,000.00)	
Accounts Receivable	4,239.00	
Merchandise Inventory	32,483.00	
Total Current Assets		(63,278.00)
Property and Equipment		
Land	150,000.00	
Warehouse	250,000.00	
Accum Deprec - Warehouse	(17,625.06)	
Total Property and Equipment		382,374.94
Other Assets		
Total Other Assets		0.00
Total Assets	$	319,096.94

Figure 10. 8 Beyer Video's Asset Section of the Balance Sheet.

CHAPTER 11

Current Liabilities and Payroll Accounting

OBJECTIVES
- Discuss the objectives of internal control for payroll
- Describe and record employer payrolls taxes
- Compute and record the payroll for a pay period

PAYROLL OVERVIEW

The payroll system is totally automated in Peachtree Complete Accounting following the set up process for the company and each of your employees. Once you have set up the defaults and records you only have to select each employee using the payroll tasks. Peachtree Complete Accounting automatically computes the paycheck. Checks can be printed in batches or on an individual basis.

The payroll process in Peachtree is divided into four distinct levels:
- **Employee Defaults:** This is the area where you set up your company's defaults for your employees including general ledger accounts, pay levels, custom fields, and payroll fields.
- **Employee Information:** This is the area where you set up employee information such as name, address, social security number, tax filing status, and individual pay levels.
- **Payroll Journal Entries:** This is the area where you actually process payroll checks.
- **Payroll Reports:** This is the area that analyzes the data you enter including period and quarterly earnings, 941 and W-2 forms.

PAYROLL NAVIGATION AID

The Payroll Navigation Aid found at the bottom of the main Peachtree Window can be used to complete most of the required payroll tasks. It is shown in Figure 11.1 below.

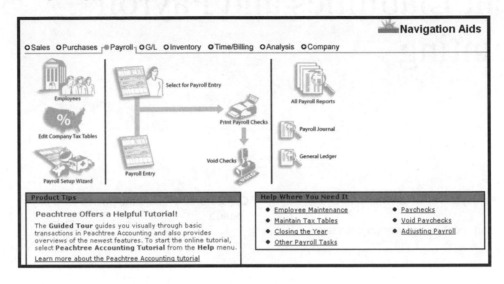

Figure 11. 1 Payroll Navigation Aid.

    Step 1: Open the Student Data Set for "Payroll Tax Example Company".

    Step 2: On the main menu bar, click "Maintain" to get the pull down menu.

    Step 3: On the pull down menu, click "Default Information" and then "Payroll Set Up Wizard". You will be presented with the screen as illustrated in Figure 11.2. Or click on "Payroll Setup Wizard" on the Navigation Bar.

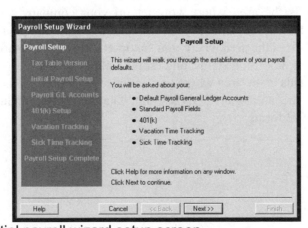

Figure 11. 2 Initial payroll wizard setup screen.

TAX TABLE INFORMATION

Peachtree Complete Accounting provides tax tables through a subscription service. These "standard" tables are used to calculate Federal, state and local payroll taxes and are known as "Global Tax Tables". A current tax table was included on the Peachtree CD provided with this book.

Many professional bookkeepers subscribe to the Peachtree Tax Service to receive annual global tax table updates. Peachtree software keeps track of all the latest changes and can save you time by providing this information for you.

Keep the default information provided on the screen as shown in Figure 11.3.

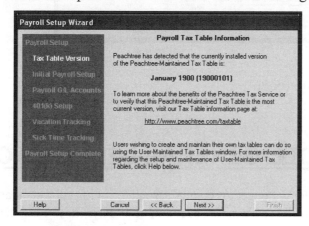

Figure 11. 3 **Default Tax Table Information.**

PAYROLL DEFAULTS

Step 1: Click "Next" at the bottom of the screen to get the initial payroll setup screen as shown in Figure 11.3.

Step 2: Select from the drop-down list the state abbreviation for the primary state in which your employees work. Use "GA" for Georgia. Leave locality blank for now. It would be used if the city where "Payroll Tax Example Company" was located levied a local withholding tax.

Step 3: Enter the unemployment percentage that the state requires your company to pay. Enter 2.7% (for example, enter 2-point-7 for 2.7%). This is used to create the calculation for SUI or State Unemployment insurance. Your company's accountant will provide this number to you.

Step 4: By default, the Tips and Meals fields (predominantly for restaurants) are memo fields. Their amounts are logged for reporting and tax calculations. Ensure that the "No" field is selected.

Step 5: Check your entries with Figure 11.4.

162

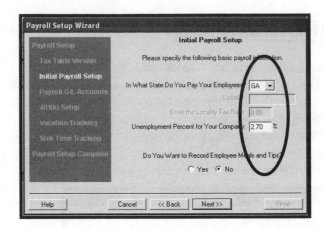

Figure 11. 4 Initial Payroll Setup (cont.)

DEFAULT PAYROLL GENERAL LEDGER ACCOUNTS

You now need to set up the General Ledger Accounts associated with your standard payroll fields. The "Wages Expense" account, "Payroll Tax Payable" account, and "Payroll Tax Expense" accounts must be established.

These are new accounts that must be created.

Step 1: Ensure that the chart of accounts includes account 725 for Wages Expense, account 270 for Payroll Tax Payable, an Other Current Liability, and account 629 for Payroll Tax Expense.

Step 2: Enter the account numbers in the spaces designated and compare your entries with those in Figure 11.5.

Step 3: Click on "Next" on the bottom of the screen to continue.

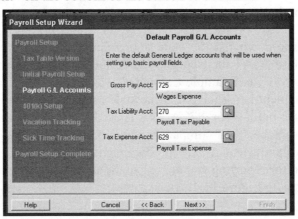

Figure 11. 5 General Ledger Accounts for Payroll

401(K) SETUP INFORMATION

The next step concerns 401(k) pre-tax deductions. A company's 401(k) plan allows a specified percentage of an employee's gross wage to be taken out prior to taxes and placed into a savings type plan set up by the company. The contributions and the savings plan proceeds are tax deferred by the US government.

There is not a 401(k) plan at Payroll Tax Example Company, click the "Next" button to continue.

VACATION AND SICK TIME TRACKING

Peachtree Complete Accounting can track vacation and sick time in your company. Vacation and sick time for employees can be set up two ways:

- Employees earn all their hours at one time, or
- Employees earn a specified number of hours each payroll period that accrues throughout the year.

When employees go on vacation or are sick, the used hours are recorded on their paychecks and are subtracted from their total hours allowed or earned. The remaining hours are continually tracked throughout the payroll year.

No entries are required on this screen or the next, click "Next" to the "Finish" screen and complete the process.

EMPLOYEE DEFAULT ENTRIES

Modifying the payroll setup to match your company's specific needs is the next task. The date found on the Employee Defaults window displays standard employee information that will be considered during payroll entry.

Step 1: On the "Main Menu" bar, select "Maintain", and then select Default information, then "Employees" to get the screen in Figure 11.6.

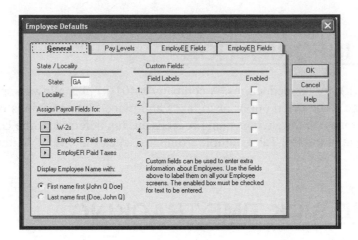

Figure 11. 6 Employee Defaults Screen

Employee Defaults is where constant information that serves as the basis for payroll processing is entered. Notice the last two tabs: EmployEE fields affecting your workers and EmployER fields for your company defaults.

Step 2: Select the "General" tab on the Employee Defaults window.

Step 3: Enter "GA" as your state and leave the locality code blank. These codes are already pre-set for you if the Payroll Setup Wizard was completed previously.

Step 4: The custom fields allow you to enter you own field labels to keep track of specific information. For example, you could enter "Birthday" as a field label and maintain the employee's birthday records. The information entered plays no part in the actual figuring of your payroll.

Step 5: Part of the payroll process includes setting up fields for W-2 Forms and paid taxes by the EmployEE and the EmployER. These fields are used to calculate and post employee deductions and allowances and employer taxes. Use the defaults already set up as shown in Figure 11.7.

The information used in the form on the right is also used for corresponding amounts on other forms.

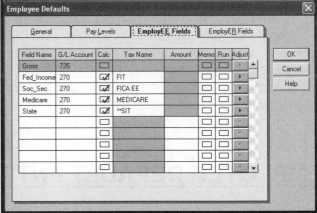

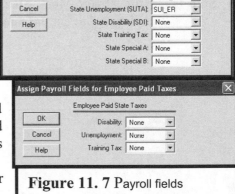

Figure 11. 7 Payroll fields

PAY LEVEL INFORMATION ENTRIES

The second tab of the Employee Defaults window is for levels of employee pay. You may enter both hourly and salary levels in this window. A maximum of 20 different pay levels and names can be entered.

Make or keep the entries as they are in Figure 11.8 below. Each of the payroll entries will be entered in the "generic" Payroll Expense Account (Account No. 510), which you set up earlier.

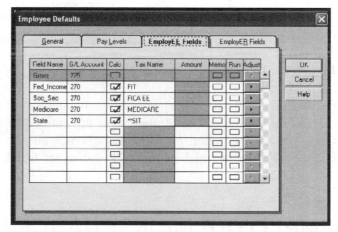

Figure 11. 8 Pay Level Information

EMPLOYEE FIELDS INFORMATION ENTRIES

The payroll fields listed below in Figure 11.9 serve three basic functions:

- Payroll deductions and allowances that subtract from the gross to compute the net pay.
- Memo amounts, such as Vacation and Sick hours, Tips and Meals are also tracked for reporting and tax calculations but not posted to the General Ledger.
- Tax Amounts, tracked for computing the employee's W-2 amounts.

Figure 11. 9 Employee Entry defaults.

These fields are used to hold amounts that should be accumulated and updated when your payroll gets posted. These fields can be changed if necessary, but for your example leave the defaults as they appear above. These are fields you set up earlier.

EMPLOYER INFORMATION FIELDS ENTRIES

Employer fields are the expenses for payroll which your company would be responsible for during payroll entry. These specific fields will not appear on an employee's paycheck. Two new accounts must be created for this form. Ensure that Payroll Tax Example Company has Account No. 255 titled State Unemployment Tax Payable and Account No. 630, State Unemployment Tax Expense. If not, create those accounts at this time.

State Unemployment Insurance for the State of Georgia, for this example, is shown in the EmployER Fields of Employee Defaults. If this field is not shown, it may be added by selecting the next available window in EmployER Fields under Employee Defaults. To change the liability account, click into the default selection and select the correct account from the drop-down menu, as shown in figure 11.10.

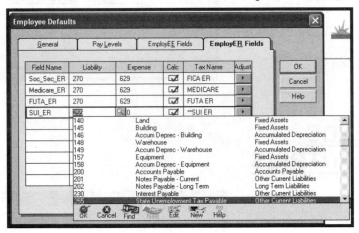

Figure 11. 10 Employer options

Both the liability and expense accounts can be independently set or changed.

Before employees and transactions are entered in the next section, keep in mind this special note: Once you start entering payroll transactions, you may not change the name of payroll field names or change the order in which payroll field names are listed.

EMPLOYEE MAINTENANCE INFORMATION ENTRIES

The information in the "Maintain Employees" window is displayed below as a completed form in Figure 11.11 and includes five working tabs on the form plus the header at the top of the form.

> **Step 1:** Under "Maintain" on the main menu bar, click on "Employees/Sales Representatives". You will be presented with the blank form where you will enter Employee Information.
>
> **Step 2:** Using the General Tab, enter the employee's ID, name and address information. The first employee's ID is #34, the employee's name is Valarie King, the address is 2555 Northwinds Parkway, Apt. 3, in Atlanta, GA 30341.
>
> **Step 3:** Enter the employee's social security number: 256-70-1116, skip type, but enter 770.555.4900 as the phone number.

Step 4: Enter the hire date: April 15, 1977 and the last pay raise date: April 15, 2000. the employee still works for Payroll Tax Example Company so leave the "Terminated" field blank. See the completed form, Figure 11.11.

Step 5: Complete the withholding information including the filing status for federal, state and local tax authorities. Use the Employee's W-4 form for this information. Any allowances and additional withholding amounts are entered here also. Valarie is single with one Federal and State exemption.

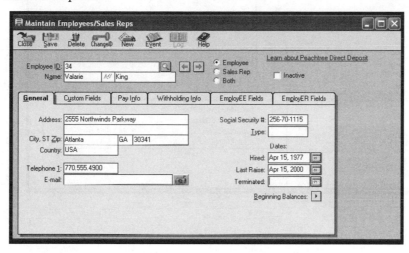

Figure 11. 11 Maintain Employees entry form.

If you had previous Payroll information you could, at this point, click on the "Beginning Balances" tab to fill all of the payroll information to date. Click on the arrow to see what is available, however, do not enter any information.

There are no custom fields at this point to worry about. EmployEE fields and EmployER fields were set up earlier and require no further attention. However, you still must enter the Pay Information for Valarie so that she correctly gets paid this pay period.

Click on the "Pay Info" tab. Valarie makes $17.50 regular pay and time and ½ for overtime. Complete the Pay Info fields for Valarie as shown in Figure 11.12. She is paid weekly and Frequency needs to be set to that periodicity. Use Save to record the data for Valarie.

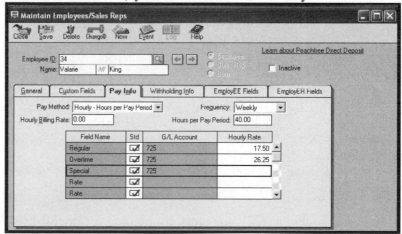

Figure 11. 12 Completed Payroll form.

You may use the "Payroll Navigation Aid" at the bottom of the Peachtree main window, Figure 11.13 whenever you wish to update employee or payroll information.

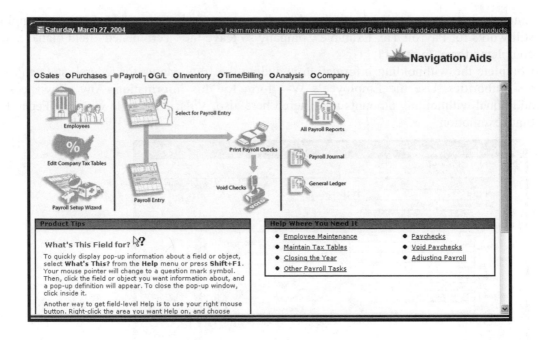

Figure 11.13 Payroll Navigation Aid

Step 1: Click on the Payroll Navigation Aid.
Step 2: Click on , in the left section labeled "Maintain", "Employees"
Step 3: Enter the following three employees from Table 11.1.

Table 11. 1 Employee Listing for Payroll Tax Example Company Payroll

ID	21	5	20
Name:	Mike Crofton	John Caine	Karen Cattz
Address	340 14th St., NE	15 W. Peachtree St.	21 5th Street., NW
City/ST/Zip	Atlanta, GA 30344	Atlanta, GA 30321	Marietta, GA 30321
SSN	256-90-5881	255-10-4467	010-14-7375
Phone	770.555.1943	770.555.7950.	404.555.9959
Date Hired	4/12/00	7/1/97	7/4/98
Last Raise	4/12/01		7/4/99
Filing Status	Married – 2 allowances	Married – 1 allowance	Single – 3 allowances
Pay Method	Salary	Hourly	Hourly
Frequency	Weekly	Weekly	Weekly
Hour/pay period	40	40	40
Regular Pay Rate	$575.00	$35.00	$25.00
Overtime Pay	None	Time and a half	Double time.

You can double check your work by running a "Payroll List" from the Reports menu on the main menu bar.

PAYROLL TAXES & TAX TABLES

Tax tables in Peachtree are used with employee and employer payroll field. Changing and editing payroll tax tables is beyond the scope of this workbook. Most likely, you would not want to change these anyway and depend on a tax service provided by Peachtree. In figuring payroll in the next section you will use the tax tables and percentages as of January 2005. These example percentages are not current and are always subject to change based on current Federal, State, and Local ordinances.

CREATING THE PAYROLL AND ISSUING PAYCHECKS

Once your payroll is set up in Peachtree, there is little work left to do. When it comes time to pay your employees you:
- Enter or select the employee ID of the person(s) you wish to pay.
- Specify the pay period.
- Enter any special amounts.
- Verify the information
- Save, Post and Print the Paychecks

All entries made in Payroll are posted to the General Ledger and the Employee File. Once a valid employee ID has been entered, the rest of information is filled in automatically. You entered enough information in the Maintain Employees record previously to determine what a "normal" paycheck would be. If that data is correct (verification process) you save the paycheck and proceed to next employee.

Here's how it is done:

Step 1: Click on the "Payroll Navigation Aid" and select "Select for Payroll Entry". If needed, refer to Figure 11.14.

Step 2: You will be presented with the "Select Employees – Filter Selection" dialog window as shown in Figure 11.15.

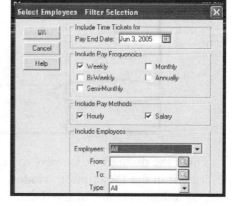

Figure 11. 15 Select Employees - Filter Selection window.

Step 3: The pay end date is June 3, 2005. Include all weekly pay frequencies. Checks will be issued on June 10, 2005.

Step 4: You have two types of pay, either hourly or salary. Select both to include this pay period.

Step 5: Include all employees to be paid.

Step 6: Check your work with Figure 11.15 above, correct any errors and Click "OK" to continue.

Step 7: The "Select Employees to Pay" window appears. Make sure the employees you wish to pay have check marks by them. Your deductions should have been figured for you.

Step 8: Double check your payroll, if satisfied, print the paychecks and close the dialog window.

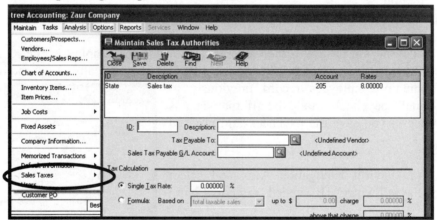

Figure 11. 16 Select Employees To Pay window.

SALES TAXES

Sales taxes are set up through the path Maintain > Sales Taxes as shown in this screen print:

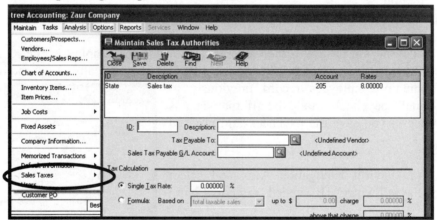

Once the dialog box is open you can identify the tax you desire such as "County" in the ID window, describe it in the Description window, identify the payee in the Tax Payable To window, and identify the general ledger account in the Sales Tax Payable G/L Account window. In the Single Tax Rate window enter the tax rate, such as 7.75 and Peachtree will read it as 7.75%. Peachtree can handle multiple tax structure, such as a city, county, and state tax structure, if you are burdened with this tax structure. The Sales Tax category has been set up and is available for use within most of the data sets. Once the fields are entered, use the "Save" icon on the top to save the sales tax information.

Now that the sales taxes have been set up, to "tax" a sale, click into the Sales Tax window at the bottom of the Sales/Invoicing window, as shown here, to select the tax rate from the pop up dialog box. Simply double click on the desired tax structure and invoice will be taxed accordingly. You can also click on the appropriate tax structure

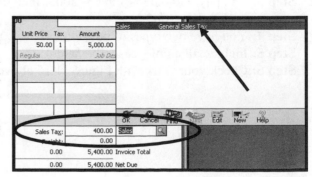

line and then click on the "OK" icon on the lower left corner of the pop up dialog box.

When making sales for cash, the sales tax information is at the bottom of the form as shown here:

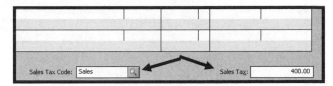

Demonstration Problem, Indiana Jones Company, Directory "indjonco"

Indiana Jones Company had the following selected transactions. Assume the Peachtree Complete Accounting Payroll system was not used and all entries are General Journal entries. Open the Indiana Jones Company on your Student Data Set. Since the tax tables of Peachtree do not accurately portray these values for payroll, use the general journal to record these events.

Feb	1	Signs a $50,000, 6-month, 9%- interest bearing note payable to Citibank and receives $50,000 in cash.
	10	Cash register sales total $43,200, which includes an 8% sales tax.
	28	The payroll for the month consists of Sales Salaries $32,000 and Office Salaries $18,000. All wages are subject to 8% FICA taxes. A total of $8,900 federal income taxes are withheld. The salaries are paid on March 1.
Feb	28	The following adjustment data are developed:

1. Interest expense of $375 has been incurred on the note.
2. Employer payroll taxes include 8% FICA taxes, a 5.4% state unemployment tax and a 0.8% federal unemployment tax.
3. Some sales were made under warranty. Of the units sold under warranty, 350 are expected to become defective. Repair costs are estimated to be $40 per unit.

Instructions:
a. Familiarize yourself with the problem's chart of accounts within the Peachtree Complete Accounting Student Data Set.
b. Journalize the February transactions.
c. Journalize the adjusting entries at February 28th.
d. Print the general journal for February 2005.

Solution to Demonstration Problem

General Journal for February 2005:

Indiana Jones Company
General Journal
For the Period From Feb 1, 2005 to Feb 28, 2005

Filter Criteria includes: Report order is by Date. Report is printed with Accounts having Zero Amounts and with Truncated Transaction Descriptions and in Detail Format.

Date	Account ID	Reference	Trans Description	Debit Amt	Credit Amt
2/1/05	101	Trans #1	Attained cash through N/P, 6-mo, 9	50,000.00	
	200		Attained cash through N/P, 6-mo, 9		50,000.00
2/10/05	101	Trans #2	Sales with 8% sales tax collected	43,200.00	
	401		Sales with 8% sales tax collected		40,000.00
	205		Sales with 8% sales tax collected		3,200.00
2/28/05	718	Adj Entry #1	Interest expense - $50,000 X 9% X (	375.00	
	230		Interest expense - $50,000 X 9% X (		375.00
2/28/05	627	Adj Entry #2	Payroll tax expense Feb 05	7,100.00	
	220		FICA payable - Feb 05 - ER		4,000.00
	250		Fed Unemploy payable - Feb 05 - E		400.00
	255		State Unemploy payable - Feb 05 -		2,700.00
2/28/05	750	Adj Entry #3	Warranty liability due to Feb 05 sale	14,000.00	
	235		Warranty liability due to Feb 05 sale		14,000.00
2/28/05	627	Trans #3	Sales salaries for Feb 05	32,000.00	
	727		Office salaries for Feb 05	18,000.00	
	220		FICA payable on salaries for Feb 05		4,000.00
	225		FIT payable on salaries for Feb 05 -		8,900.00
	212		Salaries payable for Feb 05		37,100.00
		Total		164,675.00	164,675.00

P11-1B, Zaur Company, Directory "zaucompa"

On January 1, 2005, the ledger of Zaur Company, found on your Student Data Set, contains the following liability accounts:

Accounts Payable	$52,000
Sales Taxes Payable	7,700
Unearned Service Revenue	16,000

There is a "Credit Customer" established and sales tax of 8%. During January, the following selected transactions occurred:

Jan 5　Use the Receipts form and Receipt number 010505 to sell 800 units of "Jan 5 Sales Item" at $20 each, for cash totaling $17,280, which includes 8% sales taxes. Ensure that the form is taxed.

12　Provided services for customers who had made advance payments of $10,000. The receipts were recorded on Jan 01, 2005, with reference 010105PP. Use the Receipts form and Apply to Invoices with reference 011205 to apply the value to the prepayment. Ensure that the Cash account is reset to Unearned Service Revenue.

14　Use the Write Checks form to pay Franchise Tax Board sales taxes collected in December 2004 ($7,700), use check #101 and ensure that Expense Account is set to Sales Taxes Payable.

20　Use the Sales/Invoicing to sell 600 units of "Jan 20 Sales Item" at $50 each on credit, plus 8% sales tax. Ensure that the form is taxed. This new product is subject to a 1-year warranty.

21　Use the Receipts form to record borrowing $18,000 from UCLA Bank on a 3-month, 9%, $18,000 note. Ensure that the account is set to Notes Payable.

25　Use the Receipts form to sell 575 units of Jan 25 Sales Item at $20 each for cash totaling $12,420, which includes 8% sales taxes. Ensure that the form is taxed.

Instructions:
a. Open the file and familiarize yourself with the chart of accounts.
b. Record the January transactions as indicated.
c. Use the General Journal to journalize the adjusting entries at January 31st for:
   1. The outstanding notes payable, and
   2. Estimated warranty liability, assuming warranty costs are expected to equal 7% of sales of the new product.
d. Print the General Journal, the General Ledger for the month of January 2005, and the Balance Sheet at January 31, 2005.

P11-4B, Nordlund Company, Directory "norcompa"

The following payroll liability accounts are included in the ledger of Nordlund Company on January 1, 2005.

FICA Tax Payable	$ 760.00
Federal Income Tax Payable	1,204.60
State Income Tax Payable	108.95
Federal Unemployment Tax Payable	288.95
State Unemployment Tax Payable	1,954.40
Union Dues Payable	870.00
U.S. Savings Bonds Payable	360.00

In January, the following transactions occurred:

Jan 10 Sent check for $870 to union treasurer for union dues.
     12 Deposited check for $1,964.60 in Federal Reserve bank for FICA tax payable and federal income tax payable obligations.
     15 Purchased U.S. Savings Bonds for employees by writing check for $360
     17 Paid State Income Taxes Payable withheld from employees
     31 Completed monthly payroll register, which shows Office Salaries Expense $21,600, Store Wages Expense $28,400, FICA Tax (Payable) withheld $4,000, Federal Income Tax Payable $1,958, State Income Tax Payable $414, Union Dues Payable $400, United Fund Contributions Payable $1,888 and net Wages Payable $41,340.
     31 Prepared payroll checks for the net pay and distributed checks to employees.

At January 31st, the company also makes the following accrued adjustments pertaining to employee compensation.
   1. Employer payroll taxes: FICA taxes 8%, federal unemployment taxes 0.8%, and state unemployment taxes 5.4%
   2. Vacation pay: 6% of gross earnings.

Instructions:
a. Familiarize yourself with the Chart of Accounts for Nordlund Company found within your Student Data Set.
b. Use the General Journal to journalize the January transactions.
c. Use the General Journal to journalize the adjustments pertaining to employee compensation at January 31.
d. Print the General Journal.

CHAPTER 12

Accounting Principles

There are not issues or problems to be addressed in relation to chapter 12.

CHAPTER 13

Accounting for Partnerships

OBJECTIVES
- Be able to set up a partnership accounting method
- Be able to Determining partnership retained earnings

- Identify and determine beginning capital in a newly formed partnership
- Prepare the entries for partnership withdrawals.

PARTNERSHIP FORM OF ORGANIZATION

There are basic rules for partnerships set forth by The Uniform Partnership Act. These rules outline the formation and operation of partnerships and are recognized in most states. This act defines a partnership as an association of two or more persons to carry on as co-owners of a business for profit. Partnerships are common in retail establishments and in small manufacturing companies

Accountants, lawyers, and doctors find it desirable to form partnerships with other professionals in their field. Partnerships are easy to form in Peachtree Complete Accounting.

SETTING UP A PARTNERSHIP IN PEACHTREE

Step 1: Create a new company called "Paul England & Partners." Make sure to highlight "Partnership" in the "Business Type" box as shown in Figure 13.1. This company has not been set up on your Student Data Set.

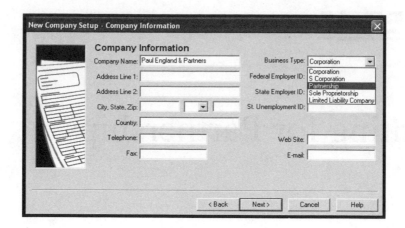

Figure 13. 1 Business Type section of New Company Information.

As you build Paul England & Partners, other information will be

1) Select "Build your own company on the Chart of Accounts dialog box,
2) Select "Accrual Accounting" on the Accounting Method dialog box,
3) Select "Real Time" in the Posting Method dialog box,
4) Select "12 Monthly Accounting Periods" in the Accounting Periods dialog box,
5) Select the month of January and the year of 2005 in the appropriate windows on the Monthly Accounting Periods dialog box,
6) Click Next and then Finish to complete the process.

Step 2: Set up the "Chart of Accounts" for Paul England as shown in Figure 13.2. Note specifically how the equity accounts are set up. Each partner has an account for his capital account, each partner has a drawing account, and there is a retained earnings account – a requirement of Peachtree Complete Accounting. Paul England & Partners is a service company.

Paul England & Partners
Chart of Accounts
As of Jan 31, 2005
Filter Criteria includes: Report order is by ID. Report is printed with Accounts having Zero Amounts and in Detail Format.

Account ID	Account Description	Active?	Account Type
101	Cash	Yes	Cash
112	Accounts Receivable	Yes	Accounts Receivable
201	Accounts Payable	Yes	Accounts Payable
301	Paul England, Capital	Yes	Equity-doesn't close
302	Paul England, Drawing	Yes	Equity-gets closed
303	Charles Door, Capital	Yes	Equity-doesn't close
304	Charles Door, Drawing	Yes	Equity-gets closed
305	Gene Song, Capital	Yes	Equity-doesn't close
306	Gene Song, Drawing	Yes	Equity-gets closed
310	Retained Earnings	Yes	Equity-Retained Earnings
407	Service Revenue	Yes	Income

Figure 13. 2 Chart of Accounts for Paul England & Partners

Step 3: Each of the partners contributes various amounts of cash to the company. They could have contributed equipment, fixed assets, or anything else of value. Use the Receipts form to record the cash contributions of each partner on January 2, 2005, as listed below.

Paul England	$75,000
Charles Door	$50,000
Gene Song	$25,000

Use Receipt and Reference numbers generated by the date in a format of 010205 as required. Enter each partner's GL account number and enter text identifying the individual line event. Check your Receipts form with Figure 13.3, shown below. Make adjustments as necessary and save the form.

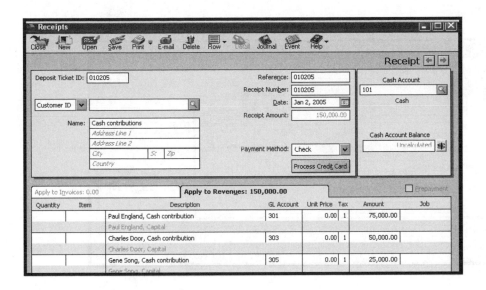

Figure 13. 3 Receipts form for Partner's contribution.

Step 4: On January 5, 2005, the partners earn $34,000 in service revenues. Use the Receipts form to record the receipt of cash paid by the client. All invoice and reference numbers should be the date in format of 010505. The Receipt form is shown in Figure 13.4. Note that when "Cash customer" or any other text is entered directly into the "Name" window, a customer ID is not required. Ensure that the GL Account is set to Service Revenues and appropriate text is entered.

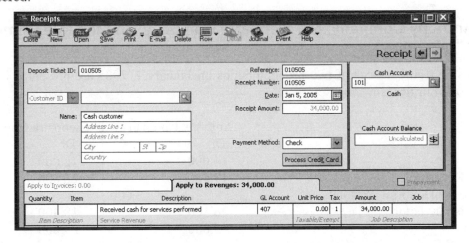

Figure 13. 4 Receipts form for services rendered for cash on January 5, 2005.

Step 5: View the "Balance Sheet" report to see how your entries affected the overall financial position of the company. The cash has increased from $150,000 to $184,000, and Net Income is now shown as $34,000 since there has been no cost of services provided recorded.

Step 6: On January 15, 2005, Mr. Door would like to withdraw $10,000 from the business. Use the Write a Check form and place "Mr. Charles Door" in the Name window. Ensure that you set the Expense Account number to Mr. Door's drawing account. The form is shown in Figure 13.5.

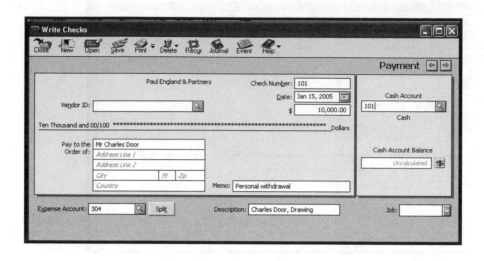

Figure 13. 5 Write Check form Mr. Door's withdrawal of funds.

Review the Balance Sheet report for the period. At this point the partnership has $174,000 in cash, and Charles Door is still showing that his contribution or retained value to date is $50,000 while he is showing that he has withdrawn $10,000 for the period. The drawing accounts are utilized to "capture" or "detail" drawings within a fiscal period and are closed at the end of each period.

P13-1B, Anthony Company, the Cleopatra Company, and the Nile Company, Directory "nilcompa"

The post closing trial balances of two proprietorships on January 1, 2005 are presented below. The Nile Company is on your Student Data Set.

	Anthony Company		Cleopatra Company	
	Dr.	Cr.	Dr.	Cr.
Cash	14,000		12,000	
Accounts Receivable	17,500		26,000	
Allowance for Doubtful Accounts		3,000		4,400
Merchandise Inventory	26,500		18,400	
Equipment	45,000		29,000	
Accumulated Depreciation – Equipment		24,000		11,000
Notes Payable		20,000		15,000
Accounts Payable		20,000		31,000
Anthony, Capital		36,000		
Cleopatra, Capital				24,000
	103,000	103,000	85,400	85,400

Anthony and Cleopatra decide to form a partnership, the Nile Company, with the following agreed upon valuations for noncash assets:

	Anthony Company	Cleopatra Company
Accounts Receivable	17,500	26,000
Allowance for Doubtful Accounts	4,500	4,000
Merchandise Inventory	30,000	20,000
Equipment	23,000	18,000

All cash will be transferred to the partnership and the partnership will assume all the liabilities of the two proprietorships. Further, it is agreed that Anthony will invest an additional $5,000 in cash, and Cleopatra will invest an additional $19,000 in cash.

Instructions:
  a. Open the Nile Company from within your Student Data Set.
  b. Familiarize yourself with the chart of accounts.
  c. Utilize the General Journal to record the consolidation of the Anthony and the Cleopatra companies into the Nile Company.
  d. Use the General Journal to journalize the additional cash investment by each partner.
  e. Print the General Journal for the month ended January 31, 2005, and the Balance sheet January 31, 2005.

P13-3B, Road Show Company, Directories "roadshoco (a)", and "roashoco (b)"

The partners in Road Show Company decide to liquidate the firm. The balance is shown below and is also available on your Student Data Set.

Road Show Company
Balance Sheet
May 31, 2005

Assets		Liabilities and Owners' Equity	
Cash	27,500	Notes Payable	13,500
Accounts Receivable	25,000	Accounts Payable	27,000
Allowance for Doubtful		Wages Payable	
Accounts	(1,000)		3,800
Merchandise Inventory	34,500	B. Crosby, Capital	33,000
Equipment	21,000	B. Hope, Capital	21,000
Accumulated Depreciation	(5,500)	D. Lamour, Capital	3,200
	$101,500		$101,500

The partners share income and loss ratio is 5:3:2. During the process of liquidation, the following transactions were completed in the following sequence.

  1. A total of $50,000 was received from converting noncash assets into cash.
  2. Liabilities were paid off in full.
  3. D. Lamour paid his capital deficiency.
  4. Cash was paid to the partners with credit balances.

Instructions:

a. There are two "Road Show Companies within your Student Data Set. Road Show (a) has D. Lamour paying his capital deficiency. Road Show (b) is provided for instruction (c), D. Lamour is unable to pay his deficiency.

b. Open the Road Show Company (a) data set found on your Student Data Set and familiarize yourself with the chart of accounts.

c. Utilize the General Journal to record the required journal entries as if D. Lamour is paying his capital deficiency.

d. Print the General Journal for the month of May 2005.

e. Open the Road Show Company (b) data set found on your Student Data Set and familiarize yourself with the chart of accounts.

f. Utilize the General Journal to record the required journal entries as if D. Lamour is unable to pay his capital deficiency.

g. Print the General Journal for the month of May 2005.

CHAPTER 14

Corporations: Organization and Capital Stock Transactions

OBJECTIVES

- Describe the corporate form of a business organization
- Describe the effect of sales on a corporate balance sheet

- Create a new corporation in Peachtree Accounting
- Determine the entries for Treasury Stock

THE CORPORATE FORM OF ORGANIZATION

A corporation is defined as "… an artificial being, invisible, intangible and existing only in contemplation of law". The definition as stated in 1819 by then Chief Justice John Marshall has laid the foundation for the prevailing legal interpretation that a corporation is an entity separate and distinct from its owners.

The initial step in forming a corporation is to file an application with the Secretary of State in the state in which incorporation is desired. The application will contain:

- The corporate name
- The purpose of the proposed corporation
- The amounts, kinds, and number of shares of capital stock to be authorized
- The names of the incorporators
- The shares of stock to which each has subscribed

When chartered, the corporation may begin selling ownership rights in the form of shares of stock. When a corporation has only one class of stock that stock is identified as common stock. Each share of common stock gives the stockholder certain ownership rights. The authorization of capital stock does not result in a formal accounting entry and has no immediate effect on either corporate assets or stockholders' equity.

In a corporation, as compared to a sole proprietorship, owners' equity is now identified as "Stockholders' Equity," "Shareholders' Equity," or "Corporate Capital." Two sections of capital are now presented on the balance sheet, Paid in Capital (contributed) and Retained Earnings (earned capital from income). The distinction between paid-in capital and retained earnings is important from both a legal and accounting point of view. Legally, dividends can be declared out of retained earnings. Many states forbid paying dividends out of paid-in capital. From an analysis standpoint, continued existence and growth of a corporation is based on earnings. Paid-in capital is the total amount of cash and other assets paid in to the corporation by stockholders in exchange for capital stock.

RETAINED EARNINGS

Throughout the text and Student Data Sets Peachtree has required a Retained Earnings account. This is where the results of the equation Revenues less Expenses ends up in the closing process. The definition of retained earnings is net income that is retained in a corporation. Peachtree records net income in the Retained Earnings account as earnings occur automatically.

THE NEW CORPORATION

Setting up the new corporation.

Step 1: Open the "Hydro Slide" found within your Student Data Set and familiarize yourself with the chart of accounts.

Step 2: Verify that Hydro Slide is a corporation through Maintain – Company Information.

Step 3: On January 1, 2005, Hydro Slide issues 1,000 shares of $1 par value common stock at par for cash. Use the Receipts form to record the issuance of the stock. Ensure that appropriate text is used as a description. The Receipts form is shown in Figure 14.1

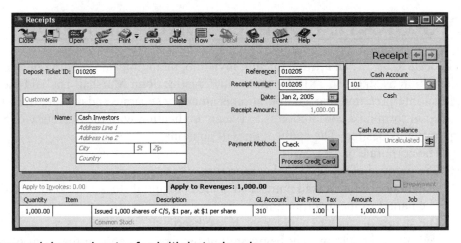

Figure 14.1 General Journal entry for initial stock sale.

TREASURY STOCK

Treasury stock is a Contra Equity account that represents a corporation's own stock that has been issued, fully paid for by a stockholder, and reacquired by the corporation. Treasury stock, a different classification than an investment in another company through a stock purchase is never an asset of the corporation. Treasury Stock – Common Stock is an equity account that does not close.

Step 1: On January 15, 2005, Hydro Slide purchases back from shareholders 250 shares of its common stock for $1 per share. Utilize the Treasury Stock – Common Stock, account 315, to record this event.

Step 2: Utilize the Write Checks form and check number 101 to purchase the Treasury Stock. Ensure that the Expense Account is set to Treasury Stock – Common Stock, number 315. The transaction is shown in Figure 14.2.

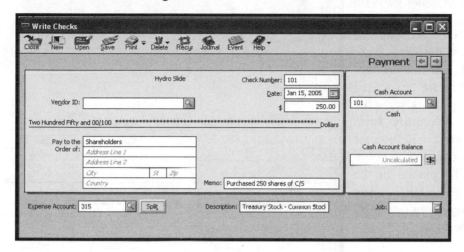

Figure 14 2 Journal entry to record purchase of Treasury Stock.

RECORDING OF SALES

Hydro Slide provides services to Rapid River Amusement Park and invoices the park for $2,850 on January 20, 2005. Use the Sales/Invoice form to record the event. The Service Revenue account is number 407. Rapid River Amusement Park is set up as a customer. Use the date in a format of 012005 as all invoice and reference numbers. The Sales/Invoicing form is shown in Figure 14.3.

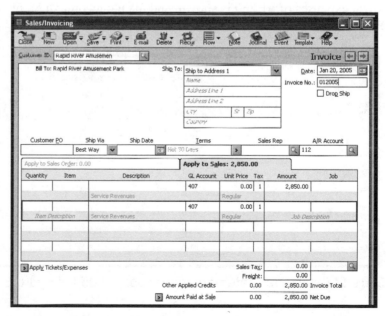

Figure 14 3 Sales/Invoicing form to record providing services on account.

RECORDING OF EXPENSES

On January 20, 2005, Hydro Slide purchased $1,250 in repair parts on account from Happy Rides Parts to fix the Rapid River Amusement Park ride. Because the parts were used for the park and not brought into inventory, they are "expensed upon purchasing". Use the Purchase/Receive Inventory form to record this event. The Repair Parts Expense account is number 775 and should be placed in the GL Account window. The Purchases/Receive Inventory form is shown in Figure 14.4.

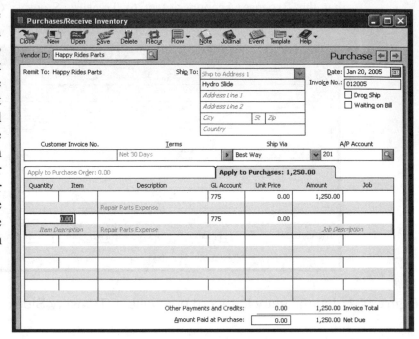

Figure 14 4 Purchases/Receive Inventory form for the purchasing of repair parts to an expense account.

View the Income Statement for the month of January 2005. The only service revenue of $2,850 is shown, expenses of $1,250 is shown, and the net income of $1,600 is shown. This is shown in figure 14.5, below.

	Current Month		Year to Date	
			Hydro Slide Income Statement For the One Month Ending January 31, 2005	
Revenues				
Service Revenues	$ 2,850.00	100.00	$ 2,850.00	100.00
Total Revenues	2,850.00	100.00	2,850.00	100.00
Cost of Sales				
Total Cost of Sales	0.00	0.00	0.00	0.00
Gross Profit	2,850.00	100.00	2,850.00	100.00
Expenses				
Repair Parts Expense	1,250.00	43.86	1,250.00	43.86
Total Expenses	1,250.00	43.86	1,250.00	43.86
Net Income	$ 1,600.00	56.14	$ 1,600.00	56.14

Figure 14 5 Income Statement for January 2005 for Hydro Slide.

View the Statement of Retained Earnings for the month of January 2005. Since this is a "start up", there is no beginning balance. The net income for the period is shown and the ending balance of Retained Earnings is shown. This is shown in figure 14.6.

```
                              Hydro Slide
                        Statement of Retained Earnings
                     For the One Month Ending January 31, 2005


Beginning Retained Earnings          $         0.00
Adjustments To Date                            0.00
Net Income                                 1,600.00
                                          _____
Subtotal                                   1,600.00


                                          _____
Ending Retained Earnings             $     1,600.00
                                          =========
```

Figure 14.6 Statement of Retained Earnings for January 2005 for Hydro Slide.

View the Balance Sheet, figure 14.7, as of January 31, 2005, and you will see the current assets of cash and accounts receivable. Accounts payable, the purchased parts are under current liabilities. The Capital or "Equity" section shows the issued stock of 1,000 shares ($1,000 / $1 par value per share), the treasury stock, and period net income of $1,600, as shown on the income statement and the statement of retained earnings. This presentation indicates the period has not been closed.

```
                              Hydro Slide
                             Balance Sheet
                            January 31, 2005

                                ASSETS

Current Assets
Cash                          $       750.00
Accounts Receivable                 2,850.00

Total Current Assets                               3,600.00

Property and Equipment

Total Property and Equipment                           0.00

Other Assets

Total Other Assets                                     0.00

Total Assets                                   $   3,600.00


                         LIABILITIES AND CAPITAL

Current Liabilities
Accounts Payable              $     1,250.00

Total Current Liabilities                          1,250.00

Long-Term Liabilities

Total Long-Term Liabilities                            0.00

Total Liabilities                                  1,250.00

Capital
Common Stock                        1,000.00
Treasury Stock - Common Stock        (250.00)
Net Income                          1,600.00

Total Capital                                      2,350.00

Total Liabilities & Capital                    $   3,600.00
```

Figure 14.7 Balance Sheet with Net Income.

When the period has been closed, this "net income" value will be converted to retained earnings in the closing process. The closing process, accessed through Tasks > System > Year End Wizard. This process will walk you through the year end closing system. This selection can not be reversed. Do not accomplish this on a Student Data Set company unless specifically being instructed to. And, you are NOT being instructed to do it here! Once this process is complete, the Capital or "Equity" section of the balance sheet will be adjusted to include retained earnings. The year end wizard was accomplished on Hydro Slide in figure 14.8, below. Notice the change from "Net income" to "Retained earnings" of $1,600.

```
                                         Hydro Slide
                                        Balance Sheet
                                       January 31, 2006

                                    LIABILITIES AND CAPITAL

Current Liabilities
  Accounts Payable               $          1,250.00

  Total Current Liabilities                               1,250.00

Long-Term Liabilities                       _____

  Total Long-Term Liabilities                                 0.00

  Total Liabilities                                       1,250.00

Capital
  Common Stock                              1,000.00
  Treasury Stock - Common Stock             (250.00)
  Retained Earnings                         1,600.00
  Net Income                                    0.00

  Total Capital                                           2,350.00

  Total Liabilities & Capital          $                  3,600.00
```

Figure 14.8 Balance Sheet with Retained Earnings.

Retained Earnings, by definition, is net income not disbursed through dividends or reduced by losses from this or prior periods. The $1,600 of net income was earned the period being reported. Notice the date of this balance sheet and the "0.00" value of Net Income since the year end wizard was utilized.

THE CLOSING PROCESS

The Closing Process within Peachtree Complete Accounting is almost automatic. It is a series of steps which:

a. Identify the open Fiscal and Payroll years,
b. The choice to close both Fiscal and Payroll years,
c. Which year end reports to print,
d. The election to backup your data,
e. Where to backup your data,
f. What new fiscal year do you want to open,
g. Begin the year end closing process – Important, once beyond this point, you are committed and can not return,
h. And, a report of completion.

You can run this process on a company you do not need again and can easily replace. Do not perform year-end closings on Student Data Sets since you will not be able to access prior periods and make adjustments to your work.

Demonstration Problem, Rolman Corporation, Directory "rolcorpo",

The Rolman Corporation is authorized to issue 1,000,000 shares of $5 par value common stock. In its first year, the company has the following stock transactions:

> **Note:** The dates have been modified to keep all activities within one month for your convenience within Peachtree Complete Accounting. The Reference Number is the textbook date.

Jan 1   Issued 400,000 shares of stock at $8 per share. Reference 011005

Jan 10 Issued 100,000 shares of stock for land. The land had an asking price of $900,000. The stock is currently selling on a national exchange at $8.25 per share. Reference Number 070105.

Jan 20 Purchased 10,000 shares of common stock for the treasury (Treasury Stock) at $9 per share. Reference Number 090105

Jan 31 Sold 4,000 shares of the treasury stock at $10 per share. Reference Number 120105.

Instructions:

a. Open the Rolman Corporation file on your Student Data Set and familiarize yourself with the chart of accounts.

b. Use the General Journal to journalize the transactions on the dates indicated.

c. Print the General Journal for the month of January 2005 and the Balance Sheet as of January 31, 2005.

d. The journal entry to recognize the $200,000 in retained earnings has been made for you.

Solution to the Demonstration Problem

The General Journal for Rolman Corporation for the month of January 2005.

Rolman Corporation
General Journal
For the Period From Jan 1, 2005 to Jan 31, 2005

Filter Criteria includes: Report order is by Date. Report is printed with Accounts having Zero Amounts and with Truncated Transaction Descriptions and in Detail Format.

Date	Account ID	Reference	Trans Description	Debit Amt	Credit Amt
1/1/05	101	011005	Issued 400,000 sh of C/S, $5 par at	3,200,000.00	
	310		Issued 400,000 sh of C/S, $5 par at		2,000,000.00
	311		Issued 400,000 sh of C/S, $5 par at		1,200,000.00
1/10/05	140	070105	Issued 100,000 sh of C/S for land at	825,000.00	
	310		Issued 100,000 sh of C/S for land at		500,000.00
	311		Issued 100,000 sh of C/S for land at		325,000.00
1/20/05	315	090105	Purchased 10,000 sh T/S at $9 / sh	90,000.00	
	101		Purchased 10,000 sh T/S at $9 / sh		90,000.00
1/31/05	101		Entry for R/E	200,000.00	
	310		Entry for R/E		200,000.00
1/31/05	101	120105	Sold 4,000 sh of T/S at $10 / sh, pur	40,000.00	
	315		Sold 4,000 sh of T/S at $10 / sh, pur		36,000.00
	316		Sold 4,000 sh of T/S at $10 / sh, pur		4,000.00
		Total		4,355,000.00	4,355,000.00

The Capital section of Rolman Corporation's Balance Sheet as of January 31, 2005.

```
                            Rolman Corporation
                              Balance Sheet
                             January 31, 2005

                          LIABILITIES AND CAPITAL

Current Liabilities              _____

  Total Current Liabilities                        0.00

Long-Term Liabilities            _____

  Total Long-Term Liabilities                      0.00

  Total Liabilities                                0.00

Capital
  Common Stock            $     2,700,000.00
  Paid-in Cap/Excess of Par-C/S  1,525,000.00
  Treasury Stock - C/S            (54,000.00)
  Paid-in Cap/Excess of Par T/S    4,000.00

  Total Capital                             4,175,000.00

  Total Liabilities & Capital   $          4,175,000.00
```

P14-1B, Keeler Corporation, Directory "keecorpo"

Keeler Corporation was organized on January 1, 2005. It is authorized to issue 10,000 shares of 8%, $100 par value preferred stock, and 500,000 shares of no-par common stock with a stated value of $3 per share. The following stock transactions were completed during the first year.

Jan 10	Issued 80,000 shares of common stock for cash at $4 per share
Mar 1	Issued 5,000 shares of preferred stock for cash at $105 per share
Apr 1	Issued 24,000 shares of Common stock for land. The asking price of the land was $90,000. The fair market value of the was $85,000
May 1	Issued 80,000 shares of common stock for cash at $4.50 per share.
Aug 1	Issued 10,000 shares of common stock to attorneys in payment of their bill of $40,000 for services rendered in helping the company organize.
Sept 1	Issued 10,000 shares of common stock for cash at $5 per share
Nov 1	Issued 1,000 shares of preferred stock for cash at $109 per share

Instructions:
a. Open the Keeler Corporation file on your Student Data Set and familiarize yourself with the chart of accounts.
b. Use the General Journal to journalize the transactions.
c. Print the General Journal for the year 2005 and the Balance Sheet as of December 31, 2005.

P14-4B, Sasser Corporation, Directory "sascorpo"

Sasser Corporation is authorized to issue 20,000 shares of $50 par value, 10% convertible preferred stock and 125,000 shares of $5 par value common stock. On January 1, 2005, the ledger contained the following stockholders' equity balances:

Preferred Stock (10,000 shares)	$500,000
Paid In Capital in Excess of Par Value – Preferred	75,000
Common Stock (70,000 shares)	350,000
Paid In Capital in Excess of Par Value – Common	700,000
Retained Earnings	300,000

During 2005, the following transactions occurred:

Feb 1	Issued 2,000 shares of preferred stock for land having a fair market value of $125,000.
Mar 1	Issued 1,000 shares of preferred stock for cash at $65 per share
July 7	Issued 16,000 shares of common stock for cash at $7 per share.
Sept 1	Issued 400 shares of preferred stock for a patent. The asking price of the patent was $30,000. Market values were preferred stock $65 and patent indeterminable.
Dec 1	Issued 8,000 shares of common stock for $7.50 per share.
Dec 31	Net income for the year was $260,000. No dividends were declared. (Use a general journal entry debiting cash and crediting sales.

Instructions:

a. Open Sasser Corporation found within the Student Data Sets and familiarize yourself with the chart of accounts.
b. Verify the beginning balances.
c. Use the General Journal to journalize the transactions.
d. Print the General Journal for the year 2005 and the Balance Sheet as of December 31, 2005.

CHAPTER 15

Corporations: Dividends, Retained Earnings and Income Reporting

OBJECTIVES

- Describe the form and content of a corporate income statement.
- . Prepare the entries for cash dividends.

- Identify the items that are reported in a retained earnings statement.
- Prepare and analyze a comprehensive stockholders' equity section of the balance sheet

DIVIDENDS

While there are several types of dividends available to a corporation, this text will focus on Cash Dividends. A Cash Dividend is a cash distribution of retained earnings to shareholders on a per share basis. All shareholders within the same class – common stock or preferred stock – will get the same amount per share. But all shareholders may not hold the same number of shares so some shareholders will receive more while others receive less. Some shareholders may also hold two or more classes of stock. Dividends are usually expressed in percentage of par – 2% of par which would be $2 per share if par or stated value is $100 per share or as a value such as $2 per share – par value is not a factor in the amount per share paid. If there is preferred stock or cumulative preferred stock, dividends payable to these classes must be paid before common stock receives dividends.

For a corporation to pay a cash dividend it must have:
- Retained Earnings
- Adequate Cash
- A Board of Directors' authorization

PEACHTREE ENTRIES FOR CASH DIVIDENDS

Three dates are important in connection with dividends: the declaration date, the record date, and the payment date. There is normally about a month between the dates. Accounting entries are required for the declaration date and the payment date.

On the declaration date, the board of directors formally announces or declares (authorizes) the cash dividend. The announcement is made to the shareholders. And, at that point, the obligation is binding and cannot be rescinded. The corporation has now entered into a liability for the declared dividends.

Makers Inc., within your Student Data Set, declares a cash dividend of 2% on its 2%, $100 par preferred stock and $0.25 per share on its common stock on February 1, 2005. At that time there are 50,000 shares of preferred stock and 650,000 shares of common stock outstanding. The date of record is February 14, 2005 and the date of payment is February 28, 2005.

Step 1: Open "Makers Inc. found within your Student Data Set and familiarize yourself with the chart of accounts.

Step 2: Create a General Journal entry debiting the Dividends - P/S account for (50,000 shares X $100 par X 2%) $100,000 and crediting Dividends Payable - P/S for the same amount. Complete the common stock dividends by debiting Dividends - C/S for (650,000 shares X $0.25) $162,500 and crediting Dividends Payable – C/S. While it is acceptable to place all dividends payable into a single account – Dividends Payable, the use of preferred and common stock accounts may make tracking cumulative dividends issues easier. The

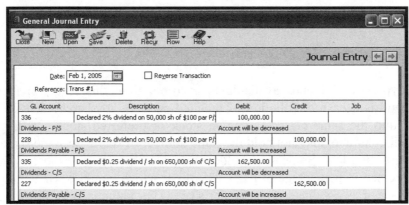

completed entry is shown in Figure 15.1.

Figure 15. 1 General Journal entry to declare dividends.

Notice that Peachtree states that both Dividends – P/S, 336, and Dividends – C/S, 335 will be decreased by the entry. This is because these accounts are "Equity - gets closed" and equity accounts normally increase with credits and decrease with debits This advisory that the account will be decreased is not an issue and is brought to your attention to avoid confusion if you use the presentation of Peachtree as an aid in your work. Dividends Payable is a current liability because it will be paid within the current period.

The next step is the Record Date, which identifies the stockholders who will receive the dividend. The stockholder must be owner of record on the Record Date to receive the dividend. No accounting entry is required for the date of record.

On the Payment Date, February 28, 2005, dividend checks are mailed to the stockholders and the payment of the dividend is recorded. Use the Write Checks form to write two checks, one to the preferred shareholders and one to the common stock shareholders for the appropriate amounts. The preferred shareholders check, number 101 is shown in Figure 15.2.

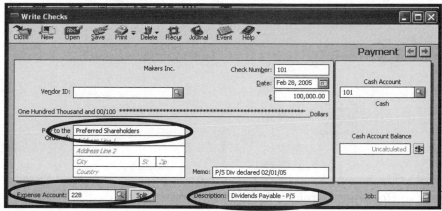

Figure 15. 2 Write Check form to pay preferred dividends.

Remember to write check 102 to the common shareholders for the appropriate amount.

Look at the income statement to ensure that none of the dividends activities have appeared as an issue in the determination of net income. View a Statement of Retained Earnings for February 28, 2005, and see how your entries affected retained earnings. A print is shown in Figure 15.3.

Makers Inc.		
Statement of Retained Earnings		
For the Two Months Ending February 28, 2005		
Beginning Retained Earnings	$	1,000,000.00
Adjustments To Date		0.00
Subtotal		1,000,000.00
Dividends - C/S		(162,500.00)
Dividends P/S		(100,000.00)
Ending Retained Earnings	$	737,500.00

Figure 15. 3 Statement of Retained Earnings for Makers Inc.

View the balance sheet, figure 15.4, for Makers as of February 28, 2005 and notice how the dividends activity have affected shareholders equity. The dividends accounts will be closed, as instructed through the chart of accounts set up – Equity-Gets closed, and the Year End Wizard. When the wizard is run, closing the fiscal year of 2005, the capital section of the balance sheet will show the consolidation as depicted in figure 15.5. Do not run the Year End Wizard as this will close this portion and preclude any further actions within this timeframe.

```
                        Makers Inc.
                       Balance Sheet
                     February 28, 2005

                   LIABILITIES AND CAPITAL

Current Liabilities
  Total Current Liabilities                        0.00

Long-Term Liabilities
  Total Long-Term Liabilities                      0.00

  Total Liabilities                                0.00

Capital
  Preferred Stock          $     5,000,000.00
  Common Stock                   6,500,000.00
  Dividends - C/S                 (162,500.00)
  Dividends - P/S                 (100,000.00)
  Retained Earnings              1,000,000.00

  Total Capital                                12,237,500.00

  Total Liabilities & Capital        $        12,237,500.00
```

Figure 15. 4 Statement of Retained Earnings for Makers Inc.

```
                     Makers Inc. - Closed
                        Balance Sheet
                      January 31, 2006

                   LIABILITIES AND CAPITAL

Current Liabilities
  Total Current Liabilities                        0.00

Long-Term Liabilities
  Total Long-Term Liabilities                      0.00

  Total Liabilities                                0.00

Capital
  Preferred Stock          $     5,000,000.00
  Common Stock                   6,500,000.00
  Retained Earnings                737,500.00

  Total Capital                                12,237,500.00

  Total Liabilities & Capital        $        12,237,500.00
```

Figure 15. 5 Balance Sheet for Makers Inc. after Year End Wizard is accomplished for fiscal year 2005.

CORPORATE INCOME STATEMENTS IN PEACHTREE

In Peachtree Complete Accounting, income statements for corporations are the same as the statements for proprietorships, including the way income tax and income tax expense is handled. Income Tax Expense is listed as a normal expense item.

P15-1B, Argentina Corporation, Directory "argcorpo"

On January 1, 2005, Argentina Corporation had the following stockholders' equity accounts:

Common Stock ($20 par value, 75,000 shares issued and outstanding)	$1,500,000
Paid In Capital in Excess of Par Value	200,000
Retained Earnings	600,000

During the year, the following transactions occurred:

Feb 1	Declared a $1 cash dividend per share to stockholders of record on February 15, payable March 1.
Mar 1	Paid the dividend declared in February
Apr 1	Announced a 2-for-1 stock split. Prior to the split, the market price per share was $36.
July 1	Declared a 10% stock dividend to stockholders of record on July 15, distributable July 31. On July 1, the market price of the stock was $13 per share.
July 31	Issued the shares for the stock dividend.
Dec 1	Declared a $0.50 per share dividend to stockholders of record on December 15, payable January 5, 2006.
Dec 31	Determined that net income for the year was $350,000. Record this as a debit to Cash and a credit to Sales since no sales events are given in the text.)

Instructions:

a. Open the Argentina Corporation file on your Student Data Set and familiarize yourself with the chart of accounts.

b. Use the General Journal to journalize the transactions.

c. Print the General Journal and the Statement of Retained Earnings for the year 2005. Print the Balance Sheet as of December 31, 2005.

P15-2B, Hassan Company, Directory "hascompa"

The stockholders' equity accounts of Hassan Company at January 1, 2005 are as follows:

Preferred Stock, 6%, $50 par	$600,000
Common Stock, $5 par	500,000
Paid-In Capital in Excess of Par Value - Preferred Stock	200,000
Paid-In Capital in Excess of Par Value - Common Stock	300,000
Retained Earnings	800,000

There are no dividends in arrears on preferred stock. During 2005, the company had the following transactions and events.

July	1	Declared a $.50 cash dividend on common stock.
Aug	1	Discovered $25,000 understatement of 2004 depreciation. Ignore income taxes.
Sept	1	Paid the cash dividend declared on July 1
Dec	1	Declared 10% stock dividend on common stock when the market value of the stock was $18 per share.
Dec	15	Declared a 6% cash dividend on preferred stock payable January 15, 2006.
	31	Determined that net income for the year was $385,000. (Record this as a debit to Cash and a credit to Sales since no sales events are given in the text.)
	31	Recognized a $200,000 restriction of retained earnings for plant expansion. (Record this as a debit to Retained Earnings and a credit to Restricted Retained Earnings.)

Instructions:

a. Open Hassan Company found within your Student Data Set and familiarize yourself with the chart of accounts and verify the beginning balances.

b. Use the General Journal to journalize the transactions and events.

c. Print the General Journal, the Incomes Statement, and the Statement of Retained Earnings for the year 2005. Print the Balance Sheet as of December 31, 2005.

CHAPTER 16

Long-Term Liabilities

OBJECTIVES

- Prepare entries for issuance of bonds and interest expense
- Describe and prepare entries for a bond sinking fund.

- Prepare the entries when bonds are redeemed
- Describe the accounting for long-term notes payable

BOND BASICS

To obtain large amounts of long-term capital, corporate management usually must decide whether to issue common stock (equity financing) or issue bonds (debt financing). Bonds are a form of interest bearing notes payable. They are usually sold in denominations of $1,000. Bond interest paid is a deduction for taxes while dividends paid on stock are not. A disadvantage of bonds is that interest payments are required in accordance with the terms of the bond issue – annually, semiannually, or quarterly. If these payments are not made the bond is in default. Recurring or periodic stock dividends are not a formal requirement and need not be declared. The default of bond interest payments will most likely incur legal action, a loss of faith and reputation of the issuing company, and decline in the issuer's credit rating and therefore an increase in their risk, resulting in higher interest requirements in the future.

Terms related to bonds are:

Face value – the amount of principal that the issuer must pay upon redemption. This is frequently $1,000 but can be any value determined by the issuer.

Contractual interest rate, also known as stated or nominal interest rate – the annual rate of interest printed or stated on the bond itself. The value is part of the factor determining the present value of the issue and the actual interest payment being made.

Effective interest rate, also known as market interest – the actual interest rate on the open market for similar financial instruments in risk and time. This value is part of the factor that will determine the present value of the issue and the period interest expense.

Life – the life of a bond issue is usually stated in whole years – 5 years, 10 years, etc. This is stated on the bond itself and in the issue documents.

Periods of the bond – this is the number of times the bond will pay interest during its life. If the bond is a 10-year bond paying interest semiannually the periods of the bond is (10 years X 2 interest payments per year) 20 periods.

Period interest rate – the face interest is stated as an annual percentage rate although the interest may be paid more frequently. If interest payments are made semiannually, the annual interest rate must be divided by the number of interest payments being made annually. In this example, if the contractual interest rate is 10% and the bonds pay semiannual interest the period interest rate is (10% / 2 interest payments per year) 5%. Period interest rate must be calculated for contractual and effective interest.

Double check – there is a simple check process for period interest – Years of the issue X Contractual rate must equal Periods of the bond X Period interest rate. In the example if the bond is a 10-year, 10% bond paying semiannual interest, 10 years X 10% must equal 20 periods X 5%. This should be done with contractual and effective interest values.

In authorizing a bond issue, the corporation's board of directors stipulates the number of bonds to be issued, the denomination of the bonds, the total face value, and the contractual interest rate. The contractual interest rate is the rate used to determine the amount of cash interest the borrower (the company) pays to the investor. This is often referred to as the stated rate. Although the contractual rate is stated as an annual rate, it can be paid as stated in the issue – annually, semiannually, quarterly or monthly. Semiannually is the most common.

ISSUING BONDS

Bonds may be issued at face value, below face value (a discount) or above face value (a premium). This is determined by the relationship of contractual interest rate to effective or market interest rate. If the contractual interest rate is 10% and the market interest rate for this risk level and duration of bonds is 11%, these bonds will sell at a discount. This "discount" adjusts the total value of the issue and the interest payments to effective or market interest. If the contractual interest rate is 10% and the market interest rate for this risk level and duration of bonds is 9%, these bonds will sell at a premium. This "premium" adjusts the total value of the issue and the interest payments to effective or market interest. Discounts and premiums are not "bad" or "good", they are mathematical adjustments to the issue to effective or current market interest rates. If the bond contractual interest rate is the same as effective interest, the bond will sell "at face" value. Computing the present value of a bond issue is addressed completely in text.

There are three versions of Weohu Incorporated within your Student Data Set. "Weohu – Discount" for bond issuances at a discount, "Weohu – Face" for bond issuances at face value, and "Weohu – Premium" for bond issuances at a premium. This will allow you to accomplish all three events in the same chart of accounts and retain your work without interference.

Earlier the board of directors decided to issue bonds on January 1, 2005. The issue will be for 1,000 bonds with a face value of $1,000, the contractual or face interest rate is 10%, the life of the bonds are 10 years and the bonds pay semiannual interest payments on July 1 for the period January 1 through June 30, and on December 31 for July 1 through December 31.

Step 1: Open the Weohu Inc – Discount within your Student Data Set and familiarize yourself with the chart of accounts.

Step 2: Utilizing the tables within the textbook, the capability of Microsoft Excel, or a calculator with time value of money (TVM) capability, compute the present value of the issue if the issue is accomplished at 11% effective interest rate and the bond discount or premium, if any.

Step 3: Utilize the Receipts form to journalize the issuance of the bonds on January 1, 2005. Use the reference and deposit number of 010105D. The entry is shown in figure 16.1. Of note is the fact that the discount amount should be entered as a negative value so that cash received is the result of $1,000,000 less the discount of $59,751.98. You can verify this by checking the general ledger. Note: Use Bond Purchasers in the name or Pay to the order of windows on all entries.

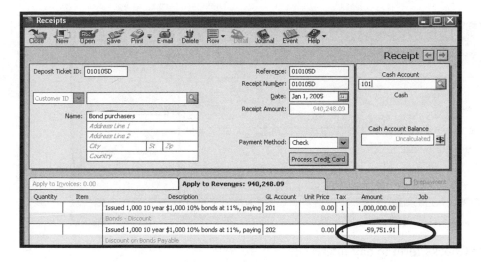

Figure 16. 1 Receipts form for the issuance of bonds at a discount.

On June 30th, the cnd of a fiscal quarter, Weohu must recognize the cost or expense of having the funds available to them since the issuance of the bonds. They will recognize thc expense with a journal entry on June 30th and pay the obligation by printing a check on July 1st, in accordance with the issuance statement.

Step 1: For simplicity, utilize "Straight-line amortization" of the discount – the discount value of $59,751.91 divided by the number of periods of the bond – 20 to determine the period discount amortization is $2,987.60.

Step 2: Determine the interest to be paid in cash - $1,000 bonds X 1,000 bonds X 10% X (6/12) = $50,000.

Step 3: Utilize the General Journal entry form to journalize the recognition of this cost and obligation to pay it at a later date – July 1st, in accordance with the issue statement. Remember that is the discount was a debit, the amortization will be a credit value. The journal entry is shown in figure 16.2.

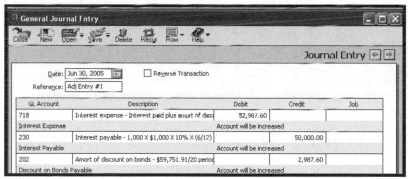

Figure 16. 2 General Journal entry to recognize interest obligation and amortization of discount.

Step 4: Use the Write Checks form to write check 101 on July 1, 2005 to pay the Bond Purchasers the amount due. This form is shown in figure 16.3.

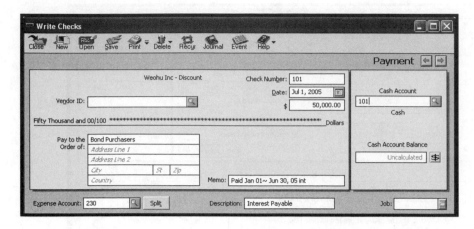

Figure 16. 3 Write Checks form to pay interest on July 1, 2005.

Step 5: Utilize the Write Checks form to calculate and pay interest on December 31, 2005. The form is shown in figure 16.4 and utilizes the "Split" function of Expense Accounts. Notice that the cash value of the check is entered into the appropriate window, the interest expense is placed into the "Split" line, and the debit, a negative value, is entered into the split line also. A debit of $52,987.60 equals a credit of $50,000 cash paid plus amortization of the discount of $2,987.60. This is shown in figure 16.4.

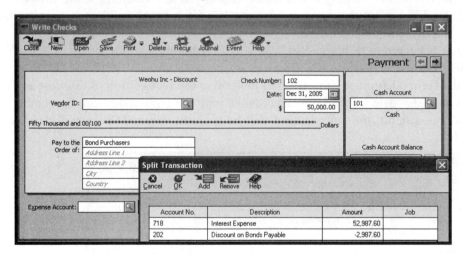

Figure 16. 4 Write Checks form to pay interest on July 1, 2005.

Utilize Weohu – Face to record the issuance of the bonds at 10% market interest rate and the paying of the two interest periods. Print the general ledger for the year 2005 for Weohu – Face. The journal entry to record the issuance of the bonds and the first interest payment are as follows:

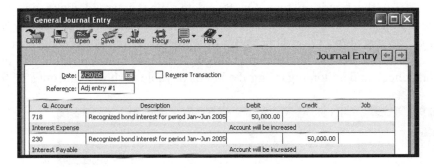

Figure 16. 5 Issuance of bonds at face value

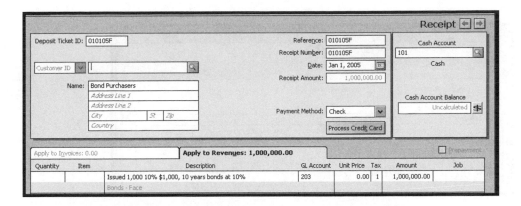

Figure 16. 6 Journal entry for the first period's interest.

Utilize Weohu – Premium to record the issuance of the bonds at 9% market interest rate and the paying of the two interest periods. Print the general ledger for the year 2005 for Weohu – Premium. The journal entry to record the issuance of the bonds and the first interest payment are as follows.

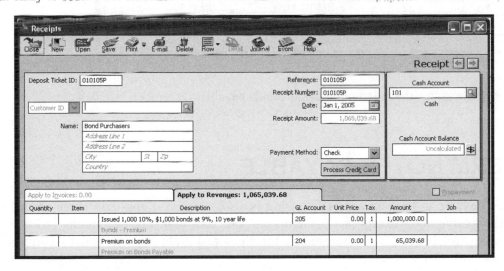

Figure 16. 7 Issuance of bonds at a premium.

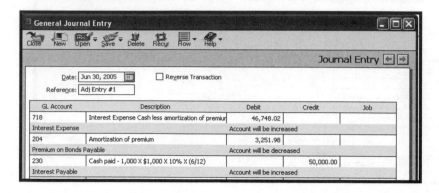

Figure 16. 8 Journal entry for the first period's interest.

On December 31, 2014, the bonds mature. On this date, Weohu would make one journal entry utilizing the Write Checks form to pay period interest from July 1, 2014, through December 31, 2014 and the final amortization of the discount or premium. With this process, complete Weohu utilizes the Write Checks form again to redeem the bonds. This check is simple – debit to bonds payable and credit to cash for $1,000,000. This last check and action regarding the bonds payable is shown in figure 16.9.

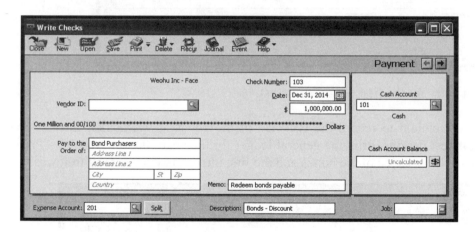

Figure 16. 9 Write Check for the redemption of the bonds payable, December 31, 2014.

LONG-TERM NOTES PAYABLE

The use of Notes Payable in long-term debt financing is also common. Long-term notes are similar to short-term interest bearing notes except that the terms will exceed a year. The accounting procedures are similar to accounting for bonds, creating accounts for the actual Note Payable and its corresponding interest payable and interest expense.

CHAPTER 17

Investments

OBJECTIVES

- Discuss why corporations invest in debt securities.
- Explain the accounting for stock investments
- Indicate how debt and stock investments are valued and reported on the financial statements.

- . Describe the use of consolidated financial statements.
- Explain the accounting for debt investments
- Distinguish between short term and long term investments.

WHY CORPORATIONS INVEST

There are three reasons why corporations purchase investments in either debt or securities:

1. A corporation may have excess cash that it does not need for the immediate purchase of operating assets or for general operations.
2. Some companies purchase investments to generate investment income. For example, although banks make most of their earnings by lending money, they also generate earnings by investing in debt and equity securities.
3. Strategic reasons are the third basis for investing. A company may purchase an interest in another firm in a related industry in which it wishes to establish a presence.

ACCOUNTING FOR DEBT INVESTMENTS

Three types of entries are required for debt investing such as government or corporate bonds:

1. The acquisition
2. The interest revenue
3. The sale

At acquisition, the cost principle applies. The cost will include all expenditures necessary to acquire these investments. For example, the price paid and commissions would be included in the cost. Kuhl Corporation acquires 50 Doan, Inc. 12%, 10-year, $1,000 bonds on January 1, 2005, for $54,000, including brokerage fees of $1,000.

Step 1: Open the file "Kuhl Corporation" from within your Student Data Set.

Step 2: Use the Write Checks form, as shown, to record the investment in Doan bonds. Use check 101 and insure that Debt Investments, account 165 is set in the Expense Account window as shown in Figure 17.1.

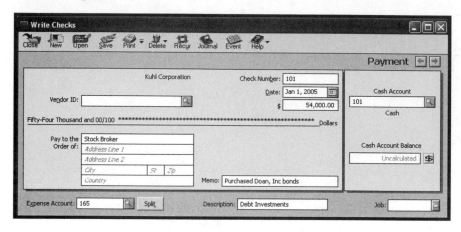

Figure 17. 1 Acquisition of Bonds

The bonds pay interest of $3,000 ($50,000 X 12% X (6/12) semiannually on July 1 and January 1.

Use the Receipts form to record the receipt of the interest on July 1, 2005. Ensure that the GL account is set to Interest Revenue, 410. Use the date format of 070105 as any deposit, reference, and receipt number. This entry is shown in Figure 17.2.

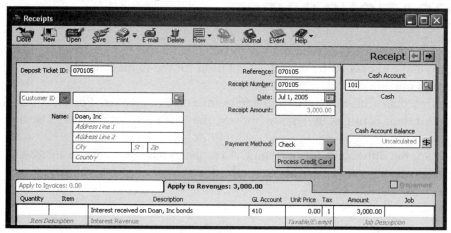

Figure 17. 2 Receipt of interest on bonds.

If Kuhl's fiscal year ends on December 31, an accrual of the interest of $3,000 earned since July 1 must be recorded. It is an adjusting entry as shown in Figure 17.3. Use the General Journal form to make the adjusting entry as shown in figure 17.3.

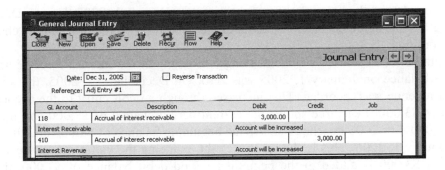

Figure 17. 3 Adjusting entry for accrued interest revenue on bonds.

Interest revenue is reported on the income statement while interest receivable is reported on the balance sheet. When the interest is received on January 1, 2006, figure 17.4, the entry is:

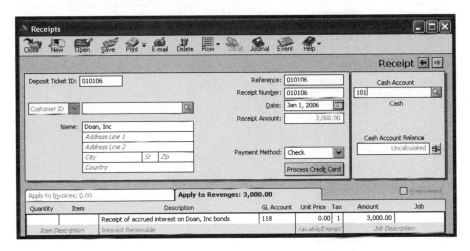

Figure 17. 4 Receipt of accrued interest.

When the bonds are sold, it is necessary to debit cash, credit the Debt Investment account for the cost of the bonds, and recognize any gain or loss on the sale.

For example, Kuhl Corporation receives net proceeds of $58,000 on the sale of the Doan bonds, which they sell on January 1, 2006. Since the securities cost $54,000, a gain of $4,000 will be realized. The interest earned does not come into play here; it has already been received and recorded.

Use the Receipts form and the "Split" function to receive the $58,000, remove the cost value of the Doan, Inc bonds and realize the gain. This form is shown in Figure 17.6.

Figure 17. 5 Sale of Doan Bonds

View the income statements and the balance sheets for the ranges January 1, 2005 through December 31, 2005, and January 1, 2005 through December 31, 2006, to see the effects on income and the change in assets caused by these recordings.

Appreciate the presentation of Peachtree's General Ledger. Looking at the Interest Receive account, shown in figure 17.6, the balance on January 1, 2005 was zero. On December 31, 2005, the adjusting entry for accrued interest revenue was recorded. This increased through a debit entry to the account, the value within the account to $3,000. Peachtree shows the current period change of $3,000 and the fiscal year ending balance of $3,000. For 2006 Peachtree shows the beginning balance of $3,000 and the receipt of interest payment on January 1, 2006. This is shown as a credit, reducing the value within the account. When this period credit of $3,000 is added to the beginning period debit balance of $3,000, the next period, February 1, 2006, beginning balance is zero. Peachtree does not show zeros to provide a neater presentation.

Kuhl Corporation
General Ledger
For the Period From Jan 1, 2005 to Dec 31, 2006

Filter Criteria includes: Report order is by ID. Report is printed with Truncated Transaction Descriptions and in Detail Format.

Account ID Account Description	Date	Reference	Jrnl	Trans Description	Debit Amt	Credit Amt	Balance
Interest Receivable	2/1/05			Beginning Balanc			
	3/1/05			Beginning Balanc			
	4/1/05			Beginning Balanc			
	5/1/05			Beginning Balanc			
	6/1/05			Beginning Balanc			
	7/1/05			Beginning Balanc			
	8/1/05			Beginning Balanc			
	9/1/05			Beginning Balanc			
	10/1/05			Beginning Balanc			
	11/1/05			Beginning Balanc			
	12/1/05			Beginning Balanc			
	12/31/0	Adj Entry #1	GEN	Accrual of interest	3,000.00		
				Current Period Ch	3,000.00		3,000.00
	12/31/0			Fiscal Year End B			3,000.00
	1/1/06			Beginning Balanc			3,000.00
	1/1/06	010106	CRJ	Doan, Inc - Receip		3,000.00	
				Current Period Ch		3,000.00	-3,000.00
	2/1/06			Beginning Balanc			
	3/1/06			Beginning Balanc			
	4/1/06			Beginning Balanc			
	5/1/06			Beginning Balanc			
	6/1/06			Beginning Balanc			
	7/1/06			Beginning Balanc			
	8/1/06			Beginning Balanc			
	9/1/06			Beginning Balanc			
	10/1/06			Beginning Balanc			
	11/1/06			Beginning Balanc			
	12/1/06			Beginning Balanc			
	12/31/0			**Ending Balance**			

Figure 17. 6 General Ledger Interest Receivable account for Kuhl Corporation.

P17-2B, Match Company, Directory "matcompa"

In January 2005, the management of Match Company concludes that it has sufficient cash to permit some short-term investments in debt and stock securities. During the year, the following transactions occurred:

Feb 1   Purchased 600 shares of Loder common stock for $31,800, plus brokerage fees of $600.

Mar 1   Purchased 800 shares Greer common stock for $20,000, plus brokerage fees of $400.

Apr 1   Purchased 50 $1,000, 8% Roy bonds for $50,000, plus $1,000 brokerage fees. Interest is payable semiannually on April 1 and October 1.

Jul 1   Received a cash dividend of $0.60 per share on the Loder common stock.

Aug 1   Sold 200 shares of Loder common stock at $57 per share less brokerage fees of $200.

Sept 1   Received a $1 per share cash dividend on the Greer common stock.

Oct 1   Received the semiannual interest on the Roy bonds.

Oct 1   Sold the Roy bonds for $49,000 less $1,000 brokerage fees.

At December 31, the fair value of the Loder common stock was $55 per share. The fair value of the Greer common stock was $23 per share.

Instructions:

a. Open the Match Company from within your Student Data Set and familiarize yourself with the chart of accounts.
b. Using the General Journal, journalize the provided transactions.
c. Using the General Journal, journalize the adjusting entry for the fair value at the end of the year.
d. Print the general journal, general ledger, and the income statement for the period January 1, 2005 through December 31, 2005.
e. Print the balance sheet for December 31, 2005.
f. Identity the income statement accounts and statement classification of each account.

CHAPTER 18

The Statement of Cash Flow

OBJECTIVES

- Indicate the primary purpose of the statement of cash flow
- Analyze a cash flow statement.

- Generate a statement of cash flow using Peachtree Complete Accounting.

THE PURPOSE OF A CASH FLOW STATEMENT

The three basic financial statements presented thus far provide very little information concerning a company's cash flow. An analyst would like to know more about the cash receipts and cash payments of the firm. For example, balance sheets generated by Peachtree show the increases (or decreases) in property, plant, and equipment during the year, but they do not show how the additions were paid for or financed.

The income statement shows revenues and expenses under the accrual accounting concepts but the statement does not show the amount of cash that was generated by operating activities. The statement of retained earnings shows net income added to beginning balances and dividends declared deducted from that amount but not the statement does not show the cash dividends that were paid during the year. The balance sheet shows the values of many accounts such as cash, accounts receivable, accounts payable and inventory but only the cash accounts usually directly relate to actual cash dollars.

The primary purpose of the statement of cash flow is to provide information about cash receipts and cash payments during a fiscal period. A secondary objective is to provide information about operating, investing, and financing activities. Reporting the causes of changes in cash helps managers, investors, creditors, and other interested parties understand what is happening to a company's most liquid resource – cash.

Open the Peachtree Complete Accounting sample company for Bellwether Garden Supply. Under Reports, select Financial Reports and then <Standard> Cash Flows. The period the report opens to should be for the first three months ending March 31, 2007. If this is not the case, reset the date range through the Options icon on the report. A segment of this report is provided as Figure 18.1. This Statement of Cash Flows is an indirect statement since it starts with Net Income. Familiarize yourself with the report. It contains the three critical areas – Operations, Investments, and Finance. To ensure that information is conveyed or presented, the default is to show accounts or processes that would influence the report even if their current value is zero.

Bellwether Garden Supply Statement of Cash Flow For the three Months Ended March 31, 2007		
	Current Month	Year to Date
Cash Flows from operating activities		
Net Income	$ (1,332.89)	$ (3,052.23)
Adjustments to reconcile net income to net cash provided by operating activities		
Accum. Depreciation-Furniture	841.60	2,524.80
Accum. Depreciation-Equipment	770.10	2,530.50
Accum. Depreciation-Vehicles	2,875.78	8,627.34
Accum. Depreciation-Other	129.14	387.42
Accum. Depreciation-Leasehold	0.00	0.00
Accum. Depreciation-Buildings	792.74	2,378.22
Accum. Depreciation-Bldg Imp	113.26	339.74
Accounts Receivable	(7,162.12)	(9,913.28)
Contracts Receivable	0.00	0.00
Other Receivables	0.00	(3,672.24)
Allowance for Doubtful Account	0.00	0.00
Inventory	2,337.52	5,555.19
Prepaid Expenses	0.00	0.00
Employee Advances	0.00	0.00
Notes Receivable-Current	0.00	0.00
Other Current Assets	0.00	0.00
Accounts Payable	3,938.63	6,279.41
Accrued Expenses	0.00	0.00
Sales Tax Payable	950.25	1,869.68
Wages Payable	0.00	0.00
401 K Deductions Payable	654.95	654.95
Health Insurance Payable	(530.64)	(530.64)
Federal Payroll Taxes Payable	13,088.92	13,088.92
FUTA Tax Payable	0.00	0.00
State Payroll Taxes Payable	1,911.17	1,911.17
SUTA Tax Payable	0.00	0.00
Local Payroll Taxes Payable	0.00	0.00
Income Taxes Payable	0.00	0.00

Figure 18. 7 Statement of Cash Flows for Bellwether Garden Supply for the three months ending March 31, 2007.

The period of the Statement of Cash Flows can be changed through the Options icon on the report screen. The report details the cash flows of Operations in the first section, the details of Investing in the second section, and the details of Finance in the third section. In the final and fourth section the tie to cash is accomplished. This details the cash generated or consumed for the period, the beginning balance of cash and the ending balance of cash. This complies with the GAAP and SEC presentation requirements.

As a general statement, the printing and presentation of financials is normally the Income Statement then the Statement of Retained Earnings. This is because Net Income, the final line of the Income Statement, is an element of the Statement of Retained Earnings. The Statement of Retained Earnings is followed by the Balance Sheet since the ending capital values generated by the Statement of Retained Earnings are elements of the Balance Sheet. Lastly the Statement of Cash Flows is generated. This is because of the "string" of the first three reports and the requirement for Net Income as a starting point of the (Indirect) Statement of Cash Flows as presented by Peachtree Complete Accounting.

Chapters 19 ~ 27

There are no additional issues that need to be addressed to continue your use of Peachtree Complete Accounting as a tool in both the academic and professional environment. There are no other academic challenges within the textbook for Peachtree Complete Accounting.

APPENDIX A

Identifying Your Work

Peachtree Complete Accounting is designed to operate in a "real world" environment. With that being so, the only identifying tools built into Peachtree are the company names. That does not help your professor in identifying the work you turn in to them since there could be 40 "Softbyte, Inc." income statements received by the professor.

There are ways to identify your work. We'll look at the most popular. It will be up to your professor to decide as how they would like you to identify your work.

LABELING YOUR DISK

All disks (and disk drives) used in a Microsoft Windows® environment can be labeled. In other words, they can specifically be identified.

First, to check the label on a disk:

Step 1: Click on "Windows Explorer." The icon is shown below in Figure A.1. The Windows Explorer icon can usually be found on your desktop.

Figure A.1: The Windows Explorer Icon

Step 2: Scroll up until your screen looks similar to the one partially shown in Figure A.2. Your screen may be a little different because of how everyone sets their computer up different.

Step 3: Click on "3 ½ Floppy A." The right side of the screen will indicate the title of the files that are in that directory or folder.

NOTE: You will get an error message if there is not a disk in the "A" drive.

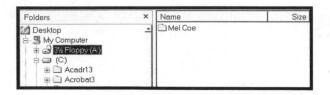

Figure A.2: Windows Explorer showing folders in the "A" drive.

Step 1:   Right click your mouse button to get a pull down menu.

Step 2:   Click "Properties" to get a screen similar to that in Figure A.3.

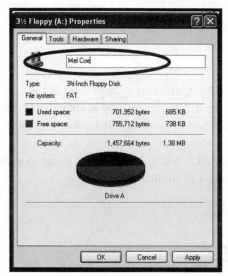

Figure A.3: The Properties Box of Diskette "A"

The label text box, shown in Figure A.3 above, shows how the current disk is labeled. For example, the author's name is used. Anything could be used as a label as long as it fits within Microsoft labeling guidelines. The system will send back an error message if the label chosen is "illegal".

Since the current label shown "Mel Coe" is highlighted you may change it (or whatever is in the text box) to reflect either your name or student number or what ever your professor would like for you to use to identify the disk.

Step 3:   Click "OK" when you are finished changing the label.

You may follow the steps above again to see the label for identification.

AN IDENTIFYING A FOLDER

As a professor, I prefer this identification method – Identify the folder with the student's name. This is preferable because I can see the name as soon as the disk is put in my computer.
Open MS/Explorer as before:

Step 1:   Again, click "Windows Explorer". The icon is shown below in Figure A.4 and can usually be found on your desktop.

Figure A.4: The Windows Explorer Icon

Step 2:   Again, scroll up until your screen looks similar to the one partially shown in Figure A.5. Your screen should be a little different because of how everyone sets his or her computer up different.

Step 3:   Click on "3 ½ Floppy A" The right side of the screen will indicate the title of the files that are in that directory or folder. NOTE: You will get an error message if there is not a disk in the "A" drive.

Figure A.5: Directory/Folder structure.

Step 4: Create a new folder by clicking on "File" at the top of window.

Step 5: Click on "New".

Step 6: On the "Pull down menu" click on "Folder". You will be presented with the "New Folder" label shown in Figure A.6, which can be changed.

Step 7: In the highlighted area type in the Name or ID asked for by your professor.

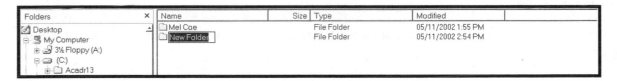

Figure A.6: The "New Folder" shown in the directory structure.

IDENTIFYING YOUR WORK DIRECTLY ON A PEACHTREE REPORT

You may identify your work by putting your name on the reports turned in to your professor.

Step 1: Open the Peachtree company from which you want to individualize a report.
Step 2: Click on "Reports" to get the Reports Selection pull down menu.
Step 3: Select "Financial Statements". In our example, we will use the Income Statement from Softbyte, Inc., our demonstration company from the first chapter.
Step 4: Click on the "<Standard>Income Statement". An example is shown below in Figure A.7.

> **NOTE:** Your figures in this statement *may not agree* with the ones shown in the example. That is OK – the format of the statement is what is important in this example. In fact, any <Standard> statement from any company would work.

Softbyte Computer Software
Income Statement
For the One Month Ending January 31, 2005

	Current Month		Year to Date	
Revenues				
Service Revenue	$ 4,700.00	100.00	$ 4,700.00	100.00
Total Revenues	4,700.00	100.00	4,700.00	100.00
Cost of Sales				
Total Cost of Sales	0.00	0.00	0.00	0.00
Gross Profit	4,700.00	100.00	4,700.00	100.00
Expenses				
Advertising Expense	250.00	5.32	250.00	5.32
Salaries Expense	900.00	19.15	900.00	19.15
Rent Expense	600.00	12.77	600.00	12.77
Utilities Expense	200.00	4.26	200.00	4.26
Total Expenses	1,950.00	41.49	1,950.00	41.49
Net Income	$ 2,750.00	58.51	$ 2,750.00	58.51

Figure A.7: An example of a <Standard> financial statement.

Several Financial Statements under the "Reports" menu are designated <Standard> as the prefix of the title of the report. In Peachtree accounting, the format of those <Standard> reports cannot be changed. However, you may use those reports, make changes and save them as another report as in the example we are about to perform.

Click on the "Design" icon on the statement's toolbar to get a window similar to the one below in Figure A.8.

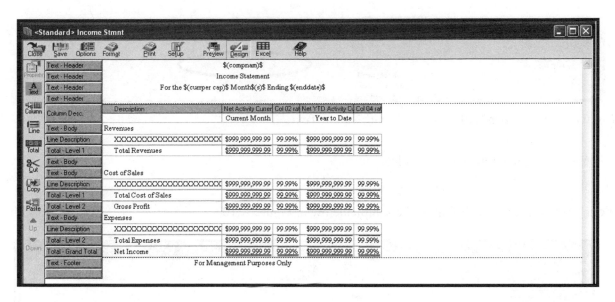

Figure A.8: The design screen for the <Standard> Income Statement.

Placing Your Name In The Upper Right Hand Corner Of The Report

Step 1: To place your name in the upper right hand corner of the report, click "Text" on the menu bar that goes down the left margin of the window

Step 2: Click on the top line of "Text - Header". You should be presented with a window that looks like Figure A.9.

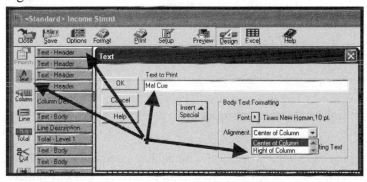

Figure A.9: Header Text information input box.

Step 3: Fill in the required information such as your name or other identification your professor requires.

Step 4: Make sure the alignment is set where your professor requests. In our example, it is set for the "Right of Column".

Step 5: Make sure the first "Text-Header" box is highlighted. It is on the parallel with the company header which looks like figure A.10, following.

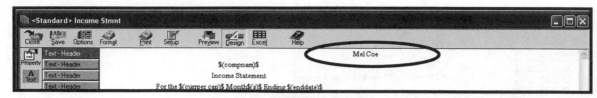

Figure A.10: Header With Inserted Identification Text

Step 6: Click OK when complete.

Your work should look similar to the sample below in Figure A.10.

Figure A.10: Sample design financial statement reflecting student's name.

Before continuing you must save your work. Remember that a <Standard> financial statement cannot be changed. You first must change the name of the statement to reflect your customization.

Step 7: Click on "Save" in the design menu bar. You will be presented with the window shown below in Figure A.11.

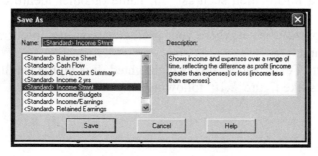

Figure A.11: The Save window where you change the name of the customized report.

Step 8:   It is recommended that you change the name by including the prefix "ID" in front of <Standard> as shown in the "Name" textbox above.

Step 9:   Write a description of the changes you made in the description box.

Step 10: Click "Save" to complete the process.

The printed Income Statement that would be turned in to a professor is shown in Figure A.12.

	Current Month		Year to Date	
Revenues				
Service Revenue	$ 4,700.00	100.00	$ 4,700.00	100.00
Total Revenues	4,700.00	100.00	4,700.00	100.00
Cost of Sales				
Total Cost of Sales	0.00	0.00	0.00	0.00
Gross Profit	4,700.00	100.00	4,700.00	100.00
Expenses				
Advertising Expense	250.00	5.32	250.00	5.32
Salaries Expense	900.00	19.15	900.00	19.15
Rent Expense	600.00	12.77	600.00	12.77
Utilities Expense	200.00	4.26	200.00	4.26
Total Expenses	1,950.00	41.49	1,950.00	41.49
Net Income	$ 2,750.00	58.51	$ 2,750.00	58.51

Softbyte Computer Software
Income Statement
For the One Month Ending January 31, 2005

Mel Coe

Figure A.12: The printed income statement reflecting the changes adding the student's name to the upper right hand corner of the statement.

APPENDIX B

Using The General Journal

OBJECTIVES

- Be able to understand how to generate and read the basic financial statements in Peachtree Accounting
- Be able to enter transactions into Peachtree's general journal system

- Be able to check for errors in entries made into the general journal

- Be able to edit a general journal entry

PEACHTREE VS. THE GENERAL LEDGER PACKAGE

Entering data into Peachtree's General Journal system is comparable to the General Ledger Software provided by John Wiley and Sons as a supplement to accounting textbooks. Peachtree Complete Accounting however, is a total accounting software package that is much more robust than the General Ledger Software. Peachtree Accounting Complete is a commercial software application used by many businesses as their sole accounting software package.

In this workbook, many of the sections or modules of the Peachtree software correlates with the Weygandt text. The subject matter is explained in the workbook and Demonstration Problems and "translated problems" from the text, ones that are marked with the Peachtree logo are introduced. When we discuss "translated problems", remember that the problems appearing in the textbook were created and written for a manual entry accounting system and *not* for an automated or integrated system. Each problem in the workbook has been edited somewhat from the Weygandt text for ease in making entries in an automated system. That is why the wording and the deliverables are different.

In any case, the various Peachtree modules *do not* have to be used along with the text in the classroom. The instructor may elect to use only the General Journal entry system (without special ledgers and journals) and arrive at the basic financial statements.

This appendix walks you through the use of the General Journal entry system employed by Peachtree Complete Accounting using the ten provided examples.

GENERAL JOURNAL TRANSACTIONS

Transaction (1) Investment by Owner. Ray Neal decides to open a computer programming service. On January 1, 2005, he invests $15,000 cash in the business, which he names Softbyte Computer Software. This transaction results in an equal increase in assets and owner's equity. The asset cash increases by $15,000 and the owner's equity, R. Neal, Capital increases by the same amount. Using Peachtree Complete Accounting, step through this initial entry.

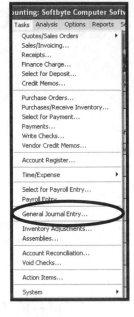

Step 1: Using the menu bar from the main Peachtree window, click on Tasks.

Step 2: On the pull down menu, as shown in Figure B.1, click on General Journal Entries.

Figure B. 1 Pull down menu from "Tasks" on menu bar.

Step 3: Make sure that your window looks like that shown in Figure B.2.

Figure B. 2 Blank screen for General Journal entry.

Step 4: As a reference, type in "Trans 1" in the blank Reference Box, just under the date of January 1, 2005.

Step 5: Click on the magnifying glass that appears next to the Account No. column to get a pull down menu that lists the available accounts for Softbyte, the Chart of Accounts, as shown in Figure B.3.

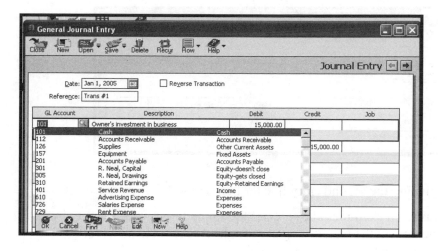

Figure B. 3 Chart of Accounts

Step 6: Double click on Account Number 101 (Cash). In the description column type in "Initial Investment". And, in the Debit column, type in "1-5-0-0-0-decimal point-0-0" (Don't type in the minus signs – they represent the separation between the numerals.)

> Be careful in Peachtree Accounting how you enter numbers requiring decimal points. The "system" may *automatically* insert a decimal point two places to the left of the last numeral entered number. For example, if you entered "1-5-0-0", Peachtree may recognize it as $15.00 not $1,500.00, a capital mistake. Make sure your screen looks like Figure B.4.

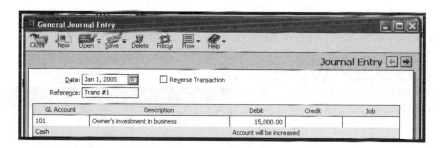

Figure B. 4 First entry line for the first transaction.

Step 7: Press the enter key (or tab key) three times to get your insertion point to the next line, as shown in Figure B.5.

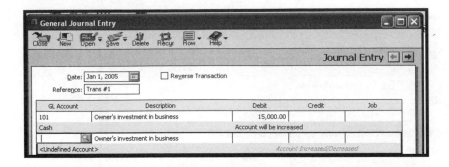

Figure B. 5 Beginning the second entry line for transaction 1.

Using the illustrated examples above, enter the amount for owner's equity by:

Step 8: Clicking on the magnifying glass in the Account No. column.

Step 9: Double clicking the account number 301

Step 10: In the Credit column, entering the amount, $15,000.00 – the dollar sign is not necessary, but the decimal point should be entered manually. Your entry should look like Figure B.6.

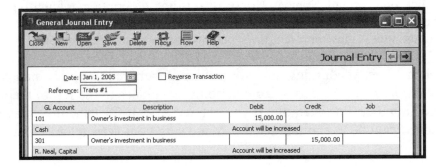

Figure B. 6 Entry for owner's investment of cash in the business.

Before you continue

Look at the window in Figure B.7. Notice the amounts at the bottom of the window, in the gray area outside the entry area. They indicate whether or not your entry is in balance. In Figure B.7, $15,000 appears under the Debit column <u>and</u> under the Credit column. The figure next to "Out of Balance" is zero. Therefore, your entry is in balance.

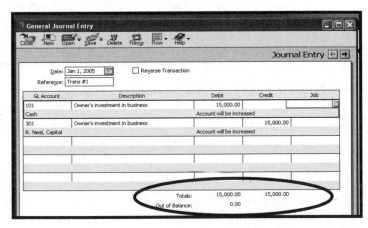

Figure B. 7 In balance journal entries.

If we had mistakenly entered both amounts in the Debit column, as shown in Figure B.8, or both amounts in the credit column, we would be "Out of Balance".

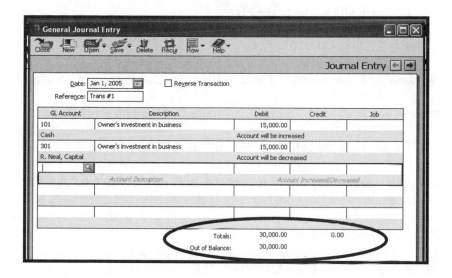

Figure B. 8 Entry error as shown by out of balance tally.

Always double-check your entries before continuing. Just because the system indicates you are "In Balance" does not necessarily mean your transaction is correct. It just means what you have entered is "In Balance". However, as shown in Figure B.9, the system will not let you continue if you are "Out of Balance" and will return an error message.

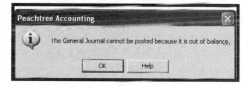

Figure B. 9 The system will not let you continue if you are "Out of Balance" on your entry.

POSTING THE TRANSACTION

Step 3:   To post the transaction (enter it into the system) click on the "Post" icon (see Figure B.10) in the tool bar section toward the top of the window.

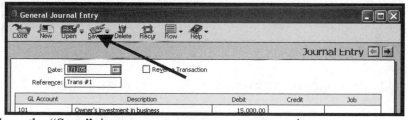

Figure B. 10 Click on the "Save" icon to post or enter your transaction.

Step 4: The General Journal window clears all that has been previously entered and is now ready for the second transaction. Notice that the General Journal window's Transaction Number has now automatically advanced to "Trans 2".

You are now ready for the next transaction.

Transaction (2). Purchase of Equipment for Cash. Softbyte purchases computer equipment for $7,000 cash.

Using the process you learned in Transaction 1 make this General Journal entry.

Step 1: Type in "Trans 2" in the reference box, if it is different. Leave the date as it is, January 1, 2005.

Step 2: Click on the magnifying glass to get the pull down menu of the Chart of Accounts. Highlight "Equipment" and double click (you may also press the <ENTER> key).

Step 3: Press the <TAB> key to move your insertion point over to the Description column and type in "Paid cash for equipment".

Step 4: Press the <TAB> key to move your insertion point to the next column, the Debit column and enter, in error the amount $8,000.00. This amount is in error because in the second part of this exercise you will learn how to edit a General Journal entry, after it has been posted. Remember you do not have to enter the "$," but you should enter the decimal point.

Step 5: Press the <ENTER> key three times so that your insertion point is in the Account No. column of the next line. Click on the magnifying glass to get the pull down menu of the Chart of Accounts. Highlight "Cash" and double click (you may also press the <ENTER> key).

Step 6: Press the <TAB> key to move your insertion point over to the Description column and type in "Paid cash for equipment". (The system may have already generated this for you.)

Step 7: Press the <TAB> key twice to move your insertion point to the credit column and enter the amount, *purposely in error* $8,000.00. We enter this amount in error for our books to balance. This will be edited in the next part of this exercise. Again, remember you do not have to enter the "$," but you should enter the decimal point.

Step 8: Make sure your screen looks like Figure B.11 before continuing. If there are no errors (besides the intentional ones you typed in) go ahead and post your transaction. Notice that even though we know there is an error, the system will let you post because technically your books are in balance.

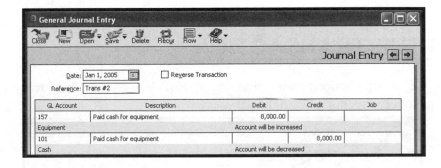

Figure B. 11 General Journal entry shown in error.

EDITING A GENERAL JOURNAL ENTRYEDITING A GENERAL JOURNAL ENTRY

Editing a General Journal entry is just as simple as making the original entry.

Step 1: Make sure you have a blank General Journal screen. If not, create one by clicking on Tasks, then General Journal Entries.

Step 2: On the Toolbar menu, illustrated in Figure B.12, click on the "OPEN" icon.

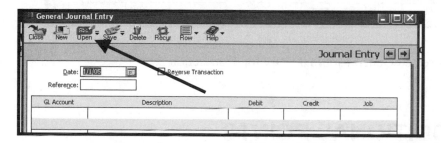

Figure B. 12 General Journal tool bar.

Step 3: You will be presented with a Select General Journal Entry menu listing all of the General Journal entries you have entered in this accounting period. Do not worry about accounting periods at this time. Figure B.13 below shows only two entries for demonstration purposes. The first transaction, for $15,000 is the first entry you made and the second one, for $8,000 is the one with the error, which you are going to correct. Click on the second entry.

Figure B. 13 Select General Journal entry menu.

Step 4: You will be returned to the General Journal entry screen like the one you had when you made the earlier entry. Your screen should look like Figure B.14.

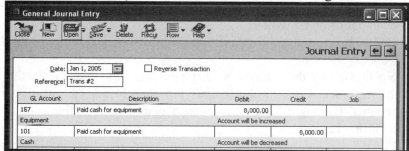

Figure B. 14 General Journal entry screen showing second transaction in error.

Step 5: Any field on the screen can be changed and saved. However, we are only interested in changing the amounts, $8,000 to $7,000. Place the insertion point in the first amount field, the debit value, highlight the $8,000, and change it to $7,000.

Step 6: Do the same with the second amount, the credit value. Your screen should match the one shown in Figure B.15.

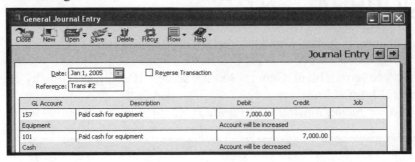

Figure B. 15 Corrected General Journal Entry for Transaction 2.

SOME ADDITIONAL POINTS

Notice that written below the amount you entered in the "Debit" column in Figure B.15, the system has told you that the Equipment account is going to be *increased* by the amount you entered. A "Debit" entry will always increase an asset account.

Also, notice that written below the amount you entered in the "Credit" column in Figure B.15, the system has told you that the Cash account is going to be *decreased* by the amount you entered. A "Credit" entry will always decrease an Asset account.

Step 7: Click on "Save" on the General Journal Entry toolbar. Peachtree will ensure that you want to record the changes before it saves or records the journal entry.

Transaction (3). Purchase of Supplies on Credit. Softbyte purchases computer paper and other supplies expected to last several months for $1,600.00 from Acme Supply Company.

Using the process you learned in transaction 1 make this General Journal entry on your own.

Step 1: Type in "Trans 3" in the reference box, if it is different. Leave the date as it is, January 1, 2005.

Step 2: Click on the magnifying glass to get the pull down menu of the Chart of Accounts. Highlight "126 - Supplies" and double click (you may also press the <ENTER> key).

Step 3: Press the <TAB> key to move your insertion point over to the Description column and type in "Purchased supplies on account".

Step 4: Press the <TAB> key to move your insertion point to the next column, the Debit column and enter $1,600.

Step 5: Press the <ENTER> key three times so that your insertion point is in the Account No. column of the next line. Click on the magnifying glass to get the pull-down menu of the Chart of Accounts. Highlight "201 - Accounts Payable" and double click (you may also press the <ENTER> key).

Step 6: Press the <TAB> key to move your insertion point over to the Description column "Purchased supplies on account" should have automatically been generated for you; if not go ahead and enter it.

Step 7: Press the <TAB> key twice to move your insertion point to the credit column and enter the amount $1,600.

Step 8: Make sure your screen looks like Figure B.16 and correct any errors before continuing.

Before you save your entry, again double-check what you have entered.

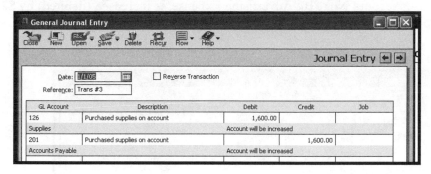

Figure B.16 Journal entry for a credit (on account) purchase.

Step 9: Click on the "Save" icon on the toolbar to post your transaction into the General Journal.

Transaction (4). Services Rendered for Cash. Softbyte receives $1,200 cash from customers for programming services it has provided. This transaction represents the company's principal revenue producing activity. Remember that revenue will increase owner's equity. However, revenue does have its own separate account under "Equity".

Make the General Journal entry:

Step 1: The account no. 101, Cash, should be increased by $1,200 (a debit entry).

Step 2: The account no. 401, Service Revenue, should be increased by $1,200 (a credit entry).

Step 3: Before posting, make sure your entry matches the one below in Figure B.17.

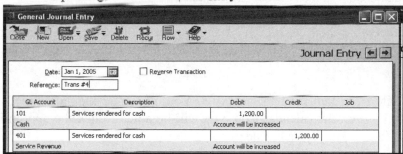

Figure B. 17 General Journal entry for Service Revenue.

Step 4: If there are no errors, "Save" the entry.

Transaction (5). Purchase of Advertising on Credit. Transaction #5, on January 2, 2005, Softbyte receives a bill for $250 from the *Daily News* for advertising. Softbyte decides to postpone payment of the bill until a later date. This transaction results in an increase in liabilities and an increase in expenses which is a decrease in equity.

Step 1: The expense Account No. 610, Advertising Expense, is increased (debited) by $250.
Step 2: The Accounts Payable Account, No. 201, is also increased (credited) by $250.

The entry is shown in Figure B.18.

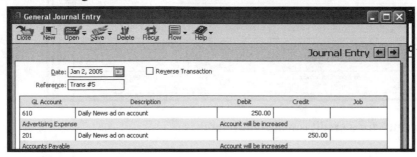

Figure B. 18 Advertising Expense to be paid later.

Step 3: If your entries are correct, save the General Journal entry.

Transaction (6). Services Rendered for Cash and Credit. Softbyte provides $3,500 of programming services for customers. On January 7, 2005, Cash, $1,500 is received from customers and the balance of $2,000 is billed on account. This transaction results in an equal increase in assets and owner's equity.
Three specific accounts are affected:
- Cash is increased by $1,500
- Accounts Receivable is increased by $2,000
- The revenue account is increased by $3,500.

Cash and Accounts Receivable, both assets, will be increased (debited). Cash increases by $1,500 whereas Accounts Receivable increases by $2,000. The third entry will increase the revenue account by $3,500.

Step 1: Change the date from January 1 to January 7. You may enter the date directly in the date box or by clicking on the calendar icon, you will be able to click the appropriate date for entry directly from a pull-down calendar.
Step 2: Change the transaction number under the date to "Trans 6".
Step 3: Using the magnifying glass, find the account number (#101) for Cash and press <ENTER>. In the Description column type in "Received cash from customers for services rendered" and enter the amount, $1,500 in the Debit column.
Step 4: Using the magnifying glass, find the account number (#112) for Accounts Receivable and press <ENTER>. In the Description column type in "Services On Account" and enter the amount, $2,000, in the Debit column.
Step 5: And again, using the magnifying glass, find the account number (#401) for Service Revenue and press <ENTER>. In the Description column type in "Service revenues". Tab over to the Credit column and enter the amount, $1,500.
Step 6: Notice that all three entries will increase the appropriate accounts and that glancing at the bottom of the window, you should be in balance at $3,500.

Step 7: Your entry should match Figure B.20. Make any necessary changes before posting your entry.

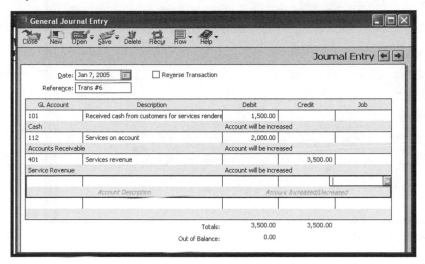

Figure B. 19 General Journal Entry showing date change and account entries.

Transaction (7) Payment of Expenses. Expenses paid in cash on January 15 include the Store Rent $600; Salaries of employees $900; and Utilities $200. These payments will result in an equal decrease in assets (cash) and owner's equity (the individual expense items).

Step 1: Change the date to January 15, 2005.

Step 2: Change the transaction number to "Trans 7".

Step 3: Identify Rent Expense, account, number 729, highlight it and press <ENTER> (or click) to place it the account number column. Type in "Paid store rent" in the description column and $600 in the debit column.

Step 4: On the next line, identify Salaries Expense, account number 726, making sure it appears in the account number column on the second line. Type in "Paid salaries of employees" on the description line and type in $900 in the debit column. (We will worry about payroll tax in a later chapter.)

Step 5: On the third line, identify Utilities Expense, account 732, make sure it appears in the account number column on the third line. In the description column, enter "Paid utilities expense". In the debit column, type in $200.

Step 6: Cash will be decreased by the total amount of the above expenses, $1,700. By now you should know that the account number for Cash is 101. You may type that in directly or search for it using the magnifying glass. Type in a description of each of the expenses paid in the description column along with the corresponding debit amount – the amount paid on the expense. The total credit amount (we are decreasing an asset) is $1,700 that is credited to cash.

Step 7: Check to see that your entries are in balance before posting. Your entry should match the one in Figure B.21.

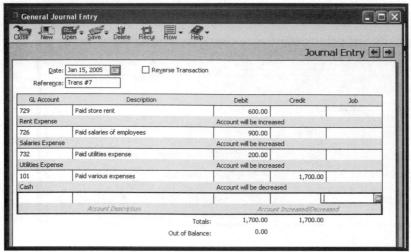

Figure B. 20 Paid cash for monthly expenses.

Transaction (8). Payment of Accounts Payable. Softbyte pays its *Daily News* advertising bill of $250 in cash. The bill had been previously recorded in Transaction 5 as an increase in Accounts Payable and an increase in expenses (a decrease in owner's equity). This payment "on account" will decrease the asset cash (a credit) and will also decrease the liability accounts payable (a debit) – both by $250.

Step 1: Keep the date, January 15, 2005 as is, but change the transaction number to "Trans 8".
Step 2: Entering the debit amount first, the account number is 201 for Accounts Payable.
Step 3: Type in "Paid Daily News for ads on account" in the description column. And, type in $250 in the debit column to complete the first line.
Step 4: Account number 101 is the number for the cash account which goes in the first column of the second line.
Step 5: "Paid Daily News for ads on account." This should have been automatically generated by the system. If so, press the <TAB> key twice to move to the credit column and enter $250.
Step 6: Check to make sure your entry is in balance and matches Figure B.22.

Figure B. 21 Paid Daily News account due.

Transaction (9). Receipt of Cash on Account. The sum of $600 in cash is received from those customers who have previously been billed for services in Transaction 6. This transaction does not change any of the totals in assets, but it will change the composition of those accounts. Cash is increased by $600 and Accounts Receivable is decreased by $600.

Step 1: If you went directly to Transaction 9 from Transaction 8, you will notice that the reference has automatically changed to "Trans 9". If that change did not occur, enter "Trans 9" in the reference box. Leave the date at January 15.

Step 2: Enter account number 101 for the Cash account. In addition, in the Description column type in "Received cash from customers on account". In the Debit column, enter $600.

Step 3: On the second line, enter account number 112 for the Accounts Receivable account. "Received cash from customers on account" should have been automatically entered by the system. However, you need to enter $600 in the Credit column so that your entry will balance.

Step 4: Check your entry with the one in Figure B.23 before posting. Make any necessary changes.

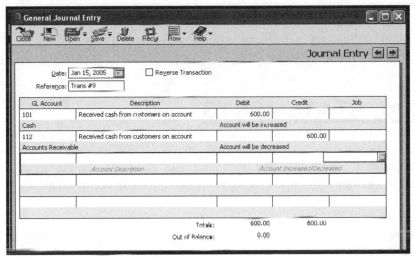

Figure B. 22 Received cash from customers on account.

Transaction (10). Withdrawal of Cash By Owner. On January 31, Ray Neal withdraws $1,300 in cash from the business for his personal use. This transaction results in an equal decrease in assets (Cash) and Owner's Equity (Drawing).

Step 1: Change the date to January 31. Also, make sure that Transaction 10 is in the reference window.

Step 2: Account number 305 is the R. Neal, Drawings account that will be debited. Enter "305" as the account number. In the Description column, type in "Ray Neal, drawing" and in the Debit column (a decrease to capital) enter $1,300.

Step 3: Because Neal wants cash for his withdrawal, the asset Cash must be decreased (a credit). Enter account number 101 for the Cash account. "Ray Neal, drawing" will most likely have been defaulted in the Description column; if not, make the appropriate entry. And, in the Credit column, enter $1,300.

Step 4: Check your entry with Figure B.24 and make any corrections before posting your entry.

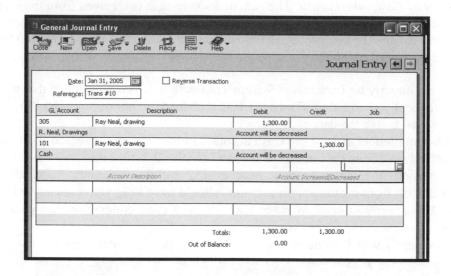

Figure B. 23 Owner withdraws cash from the business for personal use.

FINANCIAL STATEMENTS

After all of the transactions have been identified, analyzed, and entered into the Peachtree System, the, four financial statements can be prepared from your data. In fact, when you made your first entry each of the statements were automatically updated, and kept up to date as you went along.

Those statements are:
- An income statement presents the revenues and expenses and resulting net income or net loss for a specific period of time.
- An owner's equity statement (also known as the change in capital or equity) summarizes the changes in owner's equity for a specific period of time.
- A balance sheet reports the assets, liabilities, and owner's equity at a specific date.
- A statement of cash flow is a summary of information about the cash inflows (receipts) and outflows (payments) for a specific period of time.

Each Peachtree financial statement provides management, owners, and other interested parties with relevant financial data. The statements are interrelated. For example, Net income of $2,750 shown on the income statement is added to the beginning balance of owner's capital (equity) in the owner's equity statement. Owner's capital of $16,450 at the end of the reporting period shown in the owner's equity statement is reported on the balance sheet. Cash of $8,050 on the balance sheet is reported on the statement of cash flows.

Every set of financial statements is accompanied by explanatory notes and supporting schedules that are an integral part of the statements.

The reports used throughout this workbook are provided already preset for each of your assignments. The Peachtree assignments in the textbook have a "Peach" icon in the margin.

Other than adding your name, as shown in the appendices, the customizing of the appearance and information appearing on the reports is outside the scope of this text.

In addition to the four statements mentioned previously, several other reports also deserve attention. They are included, under the General Ledger heading:

- The Chart of Accounts which is a listing of all of the accounts for the company. This will change as controlled by the company which is open.
- The General Journal is a chronological listing of the journal entries.
- The General Ledger which is a listing of the accounts and is a grouping of all of the influences on each specific account.

GENERATING THE INCOME STATEMENT

Step 1: On the main menu bar, Figure B.24, click on "Reports" to get the pull down menu shown here:

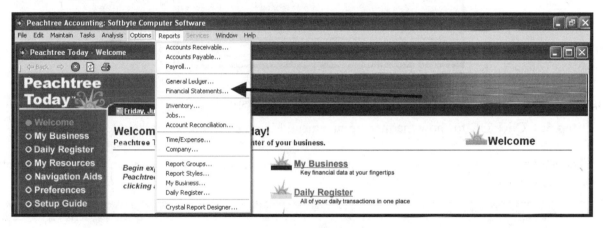

Figure B. 24 Main Menu Bar and Reports Drop-Down Menu.

Step 2: Click on Financial Statements to get the "Select A Report" menu of shown in Figure B.27.

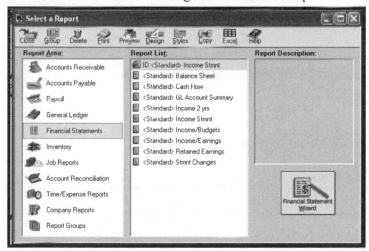

Figure B. 25 Select a Financial Report

Step 3: Double click on <Standard> Income Stmnt (Statement).

Step 4: The Dialog Box, shown in Figure B.26, gives several option choices including the choice of financial periods, the margins for the printer, whether or not we want to show accounts that have a zero balance, whether or not we want page numbers, and so on. To print the report you click on the "Print" icon once the report is open and viewed. The printer is selected through the "Setup" icon.

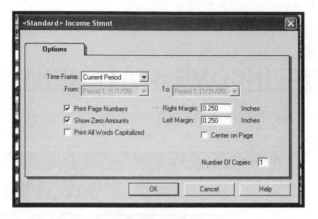

Figure B. 26 Dialog box to prepare Income Statement for display

Step 5: Click OK to show the income statement, Figure B.27, on your computer screen.

The <Standard> Income Statement is a complete income statement already set up by the Peachtree system during the original company set up.

	Current Month			Year to Date	
Softbyte Computer Software					
Income Statement					
For the One Month Ending January 31, 2005					
Revenues					
Service Revenue	$ 4,700.00	100.00	$	4,700.00	100.00
Total Revenues	4,700.00	100.00		4,700.00	100.00
Cost of Sales					
Total Cost of Sales	0.00	0.00		0.00	0.00
Gross Profit	4,700.00	100.00		4,700.00	100.00
Expenses					
Advertising Expense	250.00	5.32		250.00	5.32
Salaries Expense	900.00	19.15		900.00	19.15
Rent Expense	600.00	12.77		600.00	12.77
Utilities Expense	200.00	4.26		200.00	4.26
Total Expenses	1,950.00	41.49		1,950.00	41.49
Net Income	$ 2,750.00	58.51	$	2,750.00	58.51

Figure B. 27 Full Screen display of the Income Statement for Softbyte.

The revenues and expenses are reported for a specific period of time, the month ending on January 31, 2005. The statement was generated from all of the data you entered since the beginning of the chapter. Make sure your data matches what is shown in Figure B.27. Go back and edit changes if your figures do not match.

On the income statement the revenues are listed first, followed by expenses. Finally, net income (or net loss) is determined. Although practice sometimes varies in the "real world", the expenses in our example have been generated based on account number. In some cases, expenses appear in order of financial magnitude.

Investment and withdrawal transactions between the owner and the business are not included in the measurement of net income. Remember, R. Neal's withdrawal of cash from Softbyte was not regarded as an expense of the business.

GENERATING THE STATEMENT OF OWNER'S EQUITY

In Peachtree Accounting, changes in Owner's Equity are presented in the Retained Earnings report and Statement of Changes in Financial Position. This data, again, was obtained from the entries you made in the earlier transactions.

When learning accounting principles, Retained Earnings, is usually covered as a part of corporate accounting and not while learning about sole proprietorships. We will look at Retained Earnings more in depth in our section on corporate accounting. However, the Peachtree Complete Accounting system, when setting up the original company, requires the creation of a Retained Earnings account in the set up procedure.

By definition, retained earnings are the net income retained in a corporation. Net income is recorded and added to Retained Earnings by a closing entry in which Income Summary is debited and Retained Earnings is credited. Closing entries are covered elsewhere in the textbook. R. Neal's Capital account would contain all of the paid-in contributions by the sole proprietor (R. Neal).

To generate the Retained Earnings Statement:

Step 1: On the main menu bar, click on "Reports" to get the pull down menu.
Step 2: Click on Financial Statements to get the "Select A Report" menu of shown in Figure B.28.

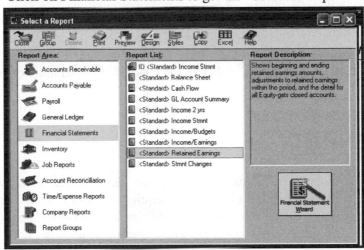

Figure B. 28 Select A Report Menu

Step 3: Double click on <Standard> Retained Earnings.

Step 4: Again, a Dialog Box such as that for the income statement appears which gives you several choices including fiscal period. Make your selections and click on OK to advance and see the Statement of Retained Earnings. As with the Income Statement, page setup, printer selection, and printing is done through the "Setup" and "Print" icons on the report's menu bar.

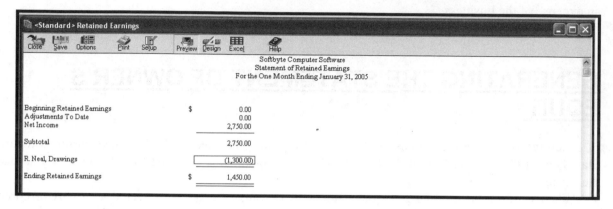

Figure B. 29   Statement of Retained Earnings

Step 5: Click OK to show the Retained Earnings statement, Figure B.29, on your computer screen.

The beginning Retained Earnings balance is shown on the first line of the statement. The balance is zero since this is a start up company with no previous earned income. Next month, the amount should equal (for the beginning balance) the ending balance, $16,450 as of January 31, 2005.

The next line shows the amount of money invested, paid-in by Neal not earned through revenue, this accounting period. Recall that Ray Neal invested $15,000 in his business. The net income, obtained from the Income Statement produced earlier shows a net income of $2,700. This figure was acquired by subtracting all of this period's expenses from all of the period's revenue. The results: Net Income, which will eventually be "rolled into" Retained Earnings.

The amount Ray Neal took out or withdrew from the company is shown next as a subtraction from equity. And, the final figure is the ending Retained Earnings balance, $16,450 that will be shown on the balance sheet and become the beginning balance for the next accounting period.

The statement of changes in financial condition is obtained in a similar manner and not covered here.

THE BALANCE SHEET

The balance sheet is also prepared from all of the data you previously entered. The assets will appear at the top of the balance sheet, followed by liabilities, then owner's equity. Recall from the beginning of the chapter that assets must equal the total of the liabilities plus (in addition to) the owner's equity. Peachtree Complete Accounting will make sure this balances for you. The system will let you know if it does not balance.

The balance sheet is obtained in a similar manner as the Income Statement and Retained Earnings Statement were obtained.

Step 1: On the main menu bar click on Reports to get the pull-down menu.
Step 2: Click on Financial Statements to get the "Select A Report" menu.
Step 3: Double click on <Standard> Balance Sheet.
Step 4: Again, the Dialog Box gives us several choices discussed earlier.
Step 5: Click OK to show the Softbyte Balance Sheet, Figure B.30, on your computer screen. It is shown below in full screen.

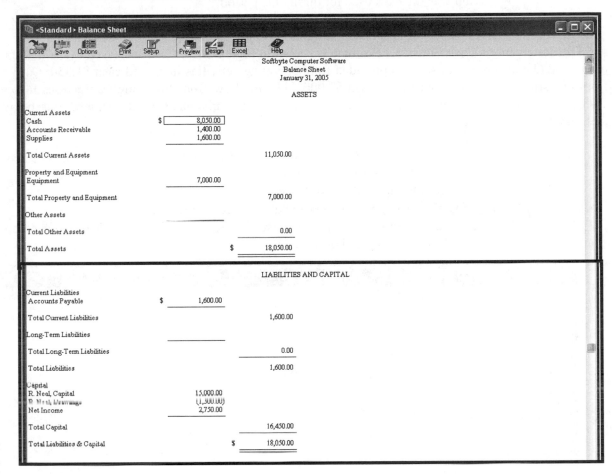

Figure B. 30 Full screen balance sheet for Softbyte.

GENERATING THE STATEMENT OF CASH FLOW

The statement of cash flows reports:

1. The cash effects of a company's operations during a period
2. Its investing transactions
3. Its financing transactions
4. The net increase or decrease in cash during the period
5. The cash amount at the end of the period

Reporting the sources, uses, and net increase or decrease in cash is useful because investors, creditors, and others want to know what is happening to a company's most liquid resource. Thus the Statement of Cash Flows provides answers to the following simple but important questions:

- Where did the cash come from during the period?
- What was the cash used for during the period?
- What was the change in the cash balance during the period?

The Statement of Cash Flows for Softbyte is shown in Figure B.34. Cash increased by $8,050 during the period (January). Net Cash flow provided from operating activities increased cash $1,350. Cash flow from investing transactions decreased cash $7,000 and cash flow from financing transactions increased cash $13,700. Do not be concerned at this point with how these amounts were determined, but, be aware that they are based on your earlier entries.

Step 1: On the main menu bar click on "Reports" to get the pull down menu. Click on Financial Statements to get the "Select A Report" menu.

Step 2: Double click on <Predefined> Cash Flow.

Step 3: Again, the Dialog Box gives you several choices as addressed earlier.

Step 4: Click OK to show the Cash Flows statement for Softbyte, Figure B.31, on your computer screen. It is shown full screen below.

Figure B. 31 Statement of Cash Flows

APPENDIX C

Problems and Directory Reference

Usage:	Company Name:	Directory:
Chapter 6	Average Sales Company	"avesalco"
Chapter 5	Beyer Video	"beyvideo"
Chapter 7	Cedzo Co.	"cedco"
Chapter 6	FIFO Sales Company	"fifosalco"
Chapter 8	High Cotton Farms	"higcotfa"
Chapter 14	Hydro Slide	"hydslide"
Chapter 9	Jordache Co.	"jorco"
Chapter 17	Kuhl Corporation	"kuhcorpa"
Chapter 6	LIFO Sales Company	"lifosalco"
Chapter 15	Makers Inc.	"makinc"
Chapter 11	Payroll Tax Example Company	"paytaxex"
Chapter 1	Softbyte Computer Software	"sofcompso"
Chapter 16	Weohu Inc - Discount	"weohinco Disc"
Chapter 16	Weohu Inc - Face	"weohinco Face"
Chapter 16	Weohu Inc - Premium	"weohinco Prem"
Demonstration Problem	Campus Laundromat	"camlaund"
Demonstration Problem	Falcetto Company, Chapter 5	"falcomp Chap 5"
Demonstration Problem	Falcetto Company, Chapter 9	"falcomp Chap 9"
Demonstration Problem	Green Thumb Lawn Care Company	"grethula"
Demonstration Problem	Indiana Jones Company	"indjonco"
Demonstration Problem	Joan Robinson, Attorney at Law	"joarobat"
Demonstration Problem	K. Poorten Company	"kpoocomp"

244

Demonstration Problem	Rolman Corporation	"rolcorpo"
Demonstration Problem	The Celine Dion Company	"theceldi"
Demonstration Problem	Watson Answering Service	"watansse"
P2-1B	Frontier Park	"fropark"
P2-5B	Lake Theater	"laktheat"
P3-2B	Spring River Resort	"sprrivre"
P3-5B	Beck Equipment Repair	"becequre"
P4-2B	Mr. Watson Company	"mrwatcom"
P4-5B	Young's Carpet Cleaners	"youcarcl"
P5-2B	Shmi Distributing Company	"shmdisco"
P5-4B	Ackbar's Tennis Shop	"acktensh"
P6-1A	Kananaskis Country Limited	"kancouli"
P7-1B	Iqbal Company	"iqbcompa"
P7-3B	Odeon Company	"odecompa"
P7-5B	Scott Co.	"scoco"
P8-2B	Sammy Sosa Company	"samsosco"
P8-5B	Cell Ten Company	"celten"
P9-6B	Derek Lu Company	"derlucom"
P11-1B	Zaur Company	"zaucompa"
P11-4B	Nordlund Company	"norcompa"
P13-1B	Anthony Company the Cleopatra Company and the Nile Company	"nilcompa"
P13-3B (a)	Road Show Company (a)	"roadshoco (a)"
P13-3B (b)	Road Show Company (b)	"roadshoco (b)"
P14-1B	Keeler Corporation	"keecorpo"
P14-4B	Sasser Corporation	"sascorpo"
P15-1B	Argentina Corporation	"argcorpo"
P15-2B	Hassan Company	"hascompa"
P17-2B	Match Company	"matcompa"

NOTES

NOTES

PEACHTREE COMPLETE ACCOUNTING--EDUCATIONAL VERSION

Thank you for trying Peachtree Complete Accounting! This is a fully functional version of Peachtree Accounting. It includes a limited-use license intended for educational purposes only and does not require user registration.

To purchase Peachtree Accounting software for your business, visit a local software reseller or contact Peachtree Software, Inc. For information on additional products and services that Peachtree Software provides, call 1-800-336-1420 (within the US), +1-770-724-4000 (outside the US), or visit our Web site at www.peachtree.com.

PEACHTREE SOFTWARE LICENSE AGREEMENT FOR EDUCATIONAL USE
The following states the license agreement that governs your use of this product. You acknowledge and accept this agreement by proceeding with the installation of this computer software from disks or CD-ROM.

LICENSE
PLEASE READ CAREFULLY THIS LICENSE AGREEMENT BEFORE CLICKING YES BELOW. PROCEEDING WITH THE INSTALLATION OF THIS COMPUTER SOFTWARE INDICATES YOUR ACCEPTANCE OF THE TERMS OF THIS LICENSE. IF YOU DO NOT AGREE WITH THESE TERMS, YOU SHOULD CANCEL THE INSTALLATION PROCESS AND RETURN THE PACKAGE AND ITS CONTENTS.

Peachtree Software, Inc. ("Peachtree"), provides the computer software program(s) and documentation (printed manuals, guides, bulletins, and/or online Help) contained in the package as well as any modifications, updates, revisions, or enhancements received by you from Peachtree or its dealers (the "Program"). Peachtree licenses its use under the terms below:

a. You are granted a nontransferable license to use the Program under the terms stated in this Agreement for educational use only. Title and ownership of the Program and of the copyright in the Program remain with Peachtree.

b. You may not make copies, translations, or modifications of or to the Program, except you may copy the Program into a machine-readable or printed form for backup purposes in support of your use of the Program. You must reproduce the copyright notice on any copy of the Program or portion of the Program merged into another program. All copies of the Program and any portion of the Program merged into or used in conjunction with another program are and will continue to be the property of Peachtree and subject to the terms and conditions of this Agreement.

c. You may not assign, sell, distribute, lease, rent, sublicense, or transfer the Program or this license or disclose the Program to any other person. You may not Web-enable the Program or sell, distribute, lease, rent, sublicense, or otherwise offer access to or use of, the Program via the Internet or via any other network available to or accessible by third parties. You may not reverse-engineer, disassemble, or decompile the Program or otherwise attempt to discover the source code or structural framework of the Program.

d. This license terminates if you fail to comply with any provision in this Agreement. You agree upon termination to destroy the Program, together with all copies, modifications, and merged portions in any form, including any copy in your computer memory or on a hard disk.

LIMITED WARRANTY
Peachtree warrants that the Program substantially conforms to the specifications contained in Peachtree's packaging and promotional materials for a period of sixty (60) days from delivery as evidenced by your receipt, provided that the Program is used on the computer operating system for which it was designed. Peachtree further warrants that the media on which the Program is furnished will be free from defects in material or workmanship for a period of sixty (60) days from delivery. All warranties stated in this Agreement apply only when the Program is used within the United States of America and its territories. Peachtree's sole obligation and liability for breach of the foregoing warranties shall be to replace or correct

the Program so that it substantially conforms to the specifications or to replace the defective media, as the case may be.

Any modification of the Program by anyone other than Peachtree voids the foregoing warranty. NO OTHER WARRANTIES ARE EXPRESSED AND NONE SHALL BE IMPLIED. PEACHTREE DOES NOT WARRANT THAT THIS SOFTWARE IS FREE OF BUGS, VIRUSES, IMPERFECTIONS, ERRORS, OR OMISSIONS. PEACHTREE SPECIFICALLY DISCLAIMS AND EXCLUDES ANY IMPLIED WARRANTIES OF MERCHANTABILITY AND FITNESS FOR A PARTICULAR PURPOSE. SOME STATES DO NOT ALLOW THE EXCLUSION OF IMPLIED WARRANTIES, SO THE FOREGOING MAY NOT APPLY TO YOU.

Support
Peachtree Software, Inc. does not provide technical support for education versions of the Program. For assistance, you must refer to your institution or instructor. To receive technical support from Peachtree Software, you must purchase a single-workstation or multiple-workstation license of the Program.

Tax Updates
Peachtree Software, Inc. does not provide tax updates for education versions of the Program. Changes in state, federal, or local tax laws may render this software, or previous versions, obsolete. To continue to operate successfully, you must purchase a single-workstation or multiple-workstation license of the Program. Also, it may be necessary for you to purchase an update. In addition to these fees, Peachtree may require you to purchase an upgrade to a current version of the Program as tax laws change. Peachtree does not update versions of the Program that are not shipping at the time of a change in tax laws.

Links to External Sites
Peachtree provides links in Peachtree Today to other Web sites on the Internet that are owned and operated by third party vendors and other third parties not under the control of Peachtree. These links are provided for your convenience only and are not intended as a warranty of any type regarding the other Web sites or the information or services offered on such Web sites. Under no circumstances shall Peachtree, or its subsidiaries or affiliates, be responsible or liable in any way for the availability of, services or products offered, or the content located on or through any such external Web site.

RECOMMENDED ENVIRONMENT
This Program has been designed to work optimally in the environment documented within the system requirements. Any defects, inconsistencies, or issues arising out of operating outside the parameters set forth therein may require the licensee to pay additional maintenance/upgrade costs to Peachtree to support and/or rectify.

LIMITATION OF LIABILITY
IN NO EVENT SHALL PEACHTREE'S LIABILITY TO YOU FOR DAMAGES HEREUNDER FOR ANY CAUSE WHATSOEVER EXCEED THE AMOUNT PAID BY YOU FOR USE OF THE PROGRAM. IN NO EVENT WILL PEACHTREE BE LIABLE FOR ANY LOST PROFITS OR OTHER INCIDENTAL OR CONSEQUENTIAL DAMAGES ARISING OUT OF THE USE OR INABILITY TO USE THE PROGRAM EVEN IF PEACHTREE HAS BEEN ADVISED OF THE POSSIBILITY OF SUCH DAMAGES.

U.S. Government Restricted Rights
The Program is provided to the Government with RESTRICTED RIGHTS. Use, duplication, or disclosure by the Government is subject to restrictions set forth in subdivision (c) (1) of The Rights in Technical Data and Computer Software clause at 252.227-7013. Contractor/Manufacturer is Peachtree Software, Inc., 1505 Pavilion Place, Norcross, GA 30093.

This Agreement is governed by the laws of the state of Georgia. In the event that any provision of this Agreement is found invalid or unenforceable pursuant to judicial decree, the remainder of this Agreement shall be valid and enforceable according to its terms. ONE-WRITE PLUS, PEACHTREE, and PEACHTREE SOFTWARE are registered trademarks of Peachtree Software, Inc.